W9-ATD-696

142405

DANIEL
&
REVELATION:
RIDDLES OR REALITIES?

DANIEL
&
REVELATION:
RIDDLES OR REALITIES?

A. BERKLEY MICHELSON

THOMAS NELSON PUBLISHERS
Nashville • Camden • New York

Copyright © 1984 by A. Berkeley Mickelsen

All rights reserved. Written permission must be secured from the publisher to use or repro-
duce any part of this book, except for brief quotations in critical reviews or articles.

Published in Nashville, Tennessee, by Thomas Nelson, Inc., Publishers and distributed in
Canada by Lawson Falle, Ltd., Cambridge Ontario.

Library of Congress Cataloging in Publication Data

Mickelsen, A. Berkeley.
  Daniel and Revelation.

  Includes bibliographical references.
  1. Bible. O.T. Daniel—Criticism, interpretation,
etc. 2. Bible. N.T. Revelation—Criticism,
interpretation, etc. I. Title.
BS1555.2.M53 1984   224'.506   84-19022
ISBN 0-8407-5359-4

Printed in the United States of America

Contents

Contents

Contents

Dedication

To my wife, Alvera,
for what she is and
for what she does:

She is...
an unfailing source of new ideas;
always attentive to the needs of others;
alertly dedicated to effective communication;
an ideal marriage partner because she contributes
   more than her share of growth in all areas of
   a loving relationship;
resolutely faithful to the Gospel of God's Redeeming love.

Preface

During my years as a teacher of seminary students, I have observed two contrasting responses to the study of Daniel and Revelation. Some fine students have a deep interest in these two books and want to know more about them. They spend much time studying Daniel and Revelation and reading other books about them. But other excellent students avoid these two books because of the dogmatism of some strange interpreters and bizarre approaches. Even when these students see the beauty of the various literary forms and acknowledge the profoundness of brief sections, they remain withdrawn. The difficulties so dominate their minds that they cannot persevere to discover the powerful and practical truths that God has for us in these writings.

Daniel and Revelation *are* worth the effort of serious study because their message centers in God, sin, and redemption (present and final). The purpose of *this* book is to acquaint lay people with the meaning of Daniel and Revelation as both address six basic questions, which enable serious readers to discover how much in these books pertain to each theme:

1. Who is the God of the Bible and what is He like?
2. How has the God of the Bible communicated with His creatures?
3. What is moral evil? How does it operate? How does God react to it?
4. How is human government related to moral good and moral evil?
5. Who are the people of God and what are they to do?

6. What will be the outcome of human history?

These questions are important to us, and the answers we need (and which Daniel and Revelation give) are not polished or technically astute. They are simple, down-to-earth principles that determine how we live, how we act, and how we die.

When we resolve to study seriously Daniel and Revelation, we need some controls to help us find what is really in them. Inadequate controls have helped to bring these books into disrepute in many people's minds. Because few understand the nature of apocalyptic literature, some writers with novel and original approaches believe they have made fresh discoveries that have been missed by everyone except them.

To correct such distortions, it is essential to control one's study of these books by looking first at what the writings in Daniel meant for God's people in Daniel's day and from that day until the time of Christ. We also must see what Revelation meant for God's people in the first century A.D., especially for the seven churches of Asia Minor to whom it was originally written. Only after we have done this can we ask, "What do these books mean for God's people living in our day?"

Each generation of people is unique. Of course, each generation also has much in common with earlier ones. It is what we have in common that makes God's truths given to earlier generations have significance for us. Nevertheless, neither our experiences nor the events of our times are carbon copies of earlier days. Neither are they composites of earlier ones. It is true that if we only look at the similarities between our time and earlier times, it can seem as if nothing has really changed. But if we take into account the differences, the uniqueness of our own situation quickly becomes apparent.

Some interpreters, unfortunately, project into the future events predicted in the Bible about past tyrants and fulfilled by those tyrants. These interpreters may announce to their readers or listeners that they are sure of those events, but Scripture warns us that the events in connection with the second coming of Christ will not be identical to earlier crises (Acts 1:7). Our situation is unique, and so will the situation of the generation present when Christ returns be unique. Every generation—including ours—must consider that His return will take place in its lifetime.

Preface

This book does not pretend to pull back the curtains of history to give readers a preview of what may soon occur. However, by tracing the strategies of moral evil and of people in revolt against God we can become alert so that, when Christ returns and we see the final outbreak of this revolt, we will not be deceived. In the meantime, the detailed events of the future are known only to God.

I thank my wife, Alvera, for her tireless efforts in editing and re-editing these materials. She worked hard to make the pictorial language of apocalyptic literature understandable to lay persons.

I thank Bethel College and Seminary for the lively academic environment where I teach. The Board of Regents granted me a sabbatical in 1979 when I taught the books of Daniel and Revelation in two Baptist seminaries in Sweden. The Orebromissionens Teologiska Seminariet in Orebro and Betel Seminariet in Bromma (a suburb of Stockholm) provided me with marvelous hospitality and stimulating dialogue. Administrators, faculty members, denominational leaders, and students—all my Swedish friends—contributed to my growth both intellectually and spiritually.

Thanks be to the triune God to whom belong the blessing and the honor and the glory and the power forever and forever (Rev. 5:13).

—A. Berkeley Mickelsen

Chapter 1

Solid Teachings
In Strange Forms

When the books of Daniel and Revelation are mentioned to the average Christian, he or she commonly reacts one of two ways: (1) "I don't understand them and can get little or nothing out of them," or (2) "Those books give a blueprint of the future, if we can just find the right code to unlock their secrets." The first group passes over Daniel and Revelation with a shrug. The second group looks for the formula that promises to "break the code."

Daniel and Revelation demand the same basic principles of sound interpretation that are applied to other books in the Bible. We must read and reread, study and restudy them. We must try to see how the author expected the earliest readers to understand the message. We must see how this same message relates to us today although our historical and cultural situation differs greatly from that of the first readers. God speaks to both audiences through His servants, and we dare not twist that message into something other than He intended.

I. Vital Questions and Vital Answers

We can learn the true nature of Daniel and Revelation if we ask the right questions and examine carefully all the material that provides the answers.

A. Areas in Which These Questions and Answers Concentrate

In Daniel and Revelation we learn who God is, why He has communicated with people, and some of what God has communicated. Since sin (moral evil) casts a cloud over all human existence, in Daniel and Revelation we learn what moral evil is, some of God's responses to it, and how human government can function either as God's agent or as the agent of moral evil. Redemption is revealed to be a change from sinful living to upright living, belonging to God's redeemed people who share God's life and live the way He wants them to live. Thus Daniel and Revelation make clear who God's people are, what they should be doing, and the part God and His people will play in the climax of history.

B. Why These Questions Were Important for the First Readers of Daniel and Revelation

The first readers of Daniel and Revelation had a vital interest in the matters discussed in the books; theirs was no academic consideration. Their lives in this world and the next depended on how they responded to God, to people, to governmental authority, and to God's revelation concerning the end of history.

Surrounded by idolatry, they had to know how different their God was from the idols around them. In both books the people of God faced not only similar crises but also similar lifestyles and the corrupting influence of various forms of idolatry. The false gods were not alive, but the satanic and demonic powers that encouraged idolatry moved people to create idols. Although God had created these people, they did not acknowledge Him. Instead, they acknowledged the gods who were works of their own hands.

The true God of Daniel and Revelation is always contrasted with the idols about whom such grandiose claims were made. The description of God in Revelation is richer and deeper than that in Daniel, although the picture in Daniel is also profound. The first readers faced a constantly enlarging picture of God, just as we do. In light of what Revelation tells us about the being of God, the first-century Jewish rejection of Jesus Christ was truly tragic. At the time of the coming of Christ, the Jewish people had finally fled from idolatry. The pictures they had of God, however, left no room for enlargement. How sad that many Jewish people turned away from the Messiah, the one who could give them a larger and greater understanding of God.

The living God, the Maker of heaven and earth, must communicate with people if He is to be more than an object of human speculation. The God of Daniel and of Revelation communicated in various ways with His own people and with those not in fellowship with Him.

All people have been confronted with moral evil, whether they admit it or not. When Daniel and the writer of Revelation probed into the nature of moral evil, they delineated moral evil as a powerful reality. In the times of the first readers of Daniel and of Revelation, individuals who underestimated the power of moral evil were victims rather than victors; but those who saw what moral evil was, and sought God's strength for the right kind of endurance, emerged victorious.

The people of Israel in Daniel's time and the Christians to whom the Book of Revelation was first addressed all lived under varying degrees of despotism. Yet sometimes these governments were helpful to the people of God. For example, at the end of Daniel's life, Cyrus the Great (550-529 B.C.) made his famous decree that permitted Jewish exiles to return to their own land (Dan. 9:25a; Isa. 44:24-45:6, 13; Ezra 1:1-12).

But on other occasions, believers lost their lives as tyrannical dictators sought to extinguish genuine faith in the God of Abraham, Isaac, and Jacob and the Father of Jesus Christ. Two of these dictators were Antiochus IV Epiphanes (who ruled Syria from 175 to 164 B.C.) and Nero (who ruled the Roman Empire from A.D. 54 to 68). Daniel describes Antiochus in his visions (8:11-14, 22-26; 9:27a; 11:21-39, with some statements in 11:40-45) as a formidable opponent of God's people. He sought to convert them to a Greek way of life and force them to give up their worship. However, heroic and faithful Jews defeated the forces of Antiochus IV.

Nero ruled the Roman Empire for about fifteen years. Although he was a poor administrator, he seemed to rule effectively during his first years. But later he emptied the treasury and sought ways to replenish it. When fire destroyed a large part of Rome in A.D. 64, many persons suspected that Nero started it to clear a place for a new palace he wanted. Looking for scapegoats, Nero blamed the Christians for the fire and ordered many of them tortured and killed. When the Book of Revelation speaks of the Christians who had already been martyred (6:9-11), the original readers knew quite well the sufferings John had in mind.

Both Daniel and Revelation say much about government, its true function and its source of power. These books show what happens when government becomes the instrument of evil and the tool of Satan, when moral evil seeks to move into the political realm. Both books hint at how God will take final action in this political realm. The first readers needed this teaching because they were being pressured to adopt an ungodly lifestyle and knew they would be persecuted if they did not conform to it.

Daniel and Revelation show the unity of the people of God throughout history. In Daniel, as in most of the Old Testament, the people of God are described as the children of Israel who were scattered among various nations. Daniel was concerned about his people in Babylon and Medo-Persia not only in his generation but also in the "latter days," or the time of the end. The "latter days" cover a long period—from Maccabean times (166-135 B.C.) to the time of the resurrection of the dead (Dan. 12:1-2).

Why was Daniel so concerned with the people of God? He spent his whole life as a high-ranking diplomat in two of the great world empires—the Babylonian Empire and the Medo-Persian Empire. He had firsthand knowledge of their policies and actions toward subject peoples. It was only natural for him to ask God about the prospects for his own people. Daniel knew of God's promises and wondered how and when these promises would be realized. The first readers of Daniel needed to know that they were God's people and what they must do as His people.

Revelation describes the people of God as those who keep the commandments of God and have faith in Jesus (14:12-13). The people of God included both Jews and Gentiles who acknowledged Jesus as the redeeming Messiah. According to John, a Jew who did not acknowledge Jesus as the Messiah did not really have the right to the term "Jew." John also spoke harshly about the Jews in local synagogues who persecuted local churches. (For the experiences of the churches of Judea, we need only read 1 Thess. 2:14-16.) John's statement about Jews "who say that they are Jews but are not, but are a synagogue of Satan" (Rev. 2:9; cf. 3:9) means that the synagogue became an instrument of Satan when it opposed the messiahship of Jesus. Hence, John viewed the people of God as one people that encompassed all those who attached themselves to Jesus as the redeeming Messiah.

But John was not anti-Semitic, for he was himself a Jew. In his picture of the New Jerusalem, he pictures this city as having twelve gates on which the names of the twelve tribes of the sons of Israel are written (Rev. 21:12-13). The city also has twelve foundations on which are the names of the twelve apostles of the Lamb (Rev. 21:14). From New Testament times to the end of history, believers (whether Jews or Gentiles) are a kingdom and priests to God (Rev. 5:10; cf. 1:6). They have become heirs of God's promise found in Exod. 19:5-6 (cf. Titus 2:14; 1 Pet. 2:5, 9; Rev. 1:6; 5:10; 20:6). Whether they were Jews or Gentiles, believers were unique because of what they had become through the atoning death of Jesus Christ (Rev. 1:5b-6).

The first readers were aware that Daniel and Revelation express a philosophy of history quite different from a secular outlook. One prominent Greek view interpreted history in a series of cycles, returning again and again to similar situations and experiences. Daniel and Revelation both teach that history is moving to a climax controlled and guided by God. The basics in their view of history were: God; humankind; God's people; moral evil in the angelic, satanic, and demonic realms; moral evil in the human realm; and God's action in history, which includes salvation and judgment.

Because of their premises about a living God who acts and about the devastating effects of moral evil in the world, Daniel and Revelation do not have a simplistic view about the end of history. The two books suggest no magical means of eliminating moral evil. What they do say about the end of history is satisfying because their message is a true word from God, and they show how difficult it is to root out moral evil and establish final harmony. The first readers needed these helpful pictures, however incomplete, of God's perfect intention. These sketches brought a certainty that God has a plan, and readers learned enough about His plan to have confidence in Him.

C. Why These Questions Are Important for Us Today

We have already noted that in the past many people were polytheists (believers in many gods) and idolatry was rampant. There were also large groups of people who believed in one God but differed dramatically in *how* they believed.

In our day there are genuine concern and interest in the crucial question: "How do we understand God?" Daniel and Revelation can help us to describe the unique nature of God and His reality because God is central in both books. Through them we can see that God is not just an idea in the mind of an individual; He is the reality that makes it possible for a person to have all other ideas, experiences, and perceptions.

Another question commonly raised is, "What kind of book is the Bible?" The Bible is God's Word in human language and culture, co-authored by God and His servants, with God in control. Consequently, the Bible has a human side and a divine side.

Daniel and Revelation illustrate some of the various events, experiences, and means by which God communicated with, through, and to His people. From believers in both the Old and New Testaments, God selected certain ones to speak for Him. These individuals found it an exhausting experience, and Daniel and Revelation give us on-the-spot chronicles of how some of them were affected when God revealed great truths to them. Careful study will help us understand how God and His dedicated servants worked together to convey the truths that God wanted us to know.

The reality of moral evil cannot be denied. War, domestic crime, and a generalized inhumanity all show that moral evil is dominant. Few people are still naive enough to think that more education will remedy the situation because educated people who embrace moral evil often do more harm than the uneducated. Certain questions persist: "Why is moral evil so powerful? Why, when something is known to be wrong, does moral evil still seem so attractive? If God has all power, why does He not banish moral evil?"

Both Daniel and Revelation say much about these issues. When one individual damages another, we see moral evil at work. But moral evil often entwines itself in the action of a group, nation, or world power, and when it does, we see terrible physical and spiritual destruction. Daniel and Revelation address people who know firsthand the oppressive and seductive power of moral evil. Rich in pictures, these books will not allow us to forget that moral evil is a deadly enemy.

The role of government is a profound issue on both its practical and theoretical sides. As a result of recent tragic wars and the repeated discovery of the wrong use of power by a variety of individuals in authority, citizens of the United States have been forced to ask: "What is the role of government? Where does any government get its power?" Since political power has such possibilities for both good and evil and affects almost every aspect of life, the discussion of such power cannot be dismissed as "worldly" or "irrelevant." How should we respond to governments when they are not properly fulfilling their God-given role?

Daniel and Revelation highlight the important roles that government plays in human affairs. Both books are concerned with a divine alternative to political power in the hands of fallible, finite, and sometimes foolish people. After carefully studying the pictures of government in Daniel and Revelation, we will see why constant vigilance is absolutely essential for God's people, no matter where they live.

Today most people are impressed with the number of different Christian groups. Their names, as subtitles for Christ's people, reflect the effects of controversies and emphases in some past period. So it is very important to discover who the people of God are and what their roles are. Since the nation Israel in the Old Testament and the true Israel (Jews and Gentiles who acknowledge Jesus as the Messiah) in the New Testament are designated as God's people, a careful study of Daniel and Revelation shows that the contrasts between the two do not change the picture of God's people in terms of their function and destiny. We will see what an important part the one people of God play in His plan and how they are involved with God in bringing about total harmony in His universe.

Daniel and Revelation paint graphically what God's people are to be doing now and in the future. Our present and future jobs should fill us with amazement and wonder. Christ will indeed build His church and the gates of hell will not prevail against it (Matt. 16:18). Glory is to be given to God in the church and in Christ Jesus for all human generations (Eph. 3:21). The Book of Revelation was first for the seven churches of Asia Minor and then for "the churches" (i.e., all other groups of Christian believers [Rev. 22:16]). To be sure, if these pictures become a part of us, we will live in an entirely different manner. We will purify ourselves, make ourselves clean, and be refined (Dan. 12:10) in the light of our revealed destiny.

Many people are consumed by a desire to pierce the veil between the living and the dead and to know the future. Traditionally, the Christian church has rejected the claims of individuals who insist they can converse with the dead, and it has resisted fortunetellers who promise to unfold what will happen in the future. However, for much of the twentieth century many evangelical Christians have become enamored with knowing the future by studying Dan-

7

iel and Revelation, plus parts of Ezekiel, Zechariah, the Gospels, and the Pauline Epistles. Some people have developed complicated schemes, supposedly based on these books in the Bible, that detail specific events occurring from now until the end of history. Although they quote many texts and avow certain perceptions derived from these texts, one must ask honestly: "Is the Bible being manipulated? What is the basis for each and every conclusion? What is each text or passage really saying in its own context?" Sometimes well-meaning people make the language of the Bible serve a purpose quite foreign to the concepts of the original human writer, who was God's servant.

Therefore, to know what Daniel and Revelation actually say about the future and the close of history, we must hear what they said to the first readers in their situations. When we know that, we can begin to understand what they tell us about God and the close of history. *We must recognize that these two books are God-centered first;* events are always secondary to the immensity of God and His plan. Any modern approach that centers on events and places God in a secondary role—His coming on the scene at just the right time—has made a subtle switch in the emphasis of Daniel and Revelation. Any program of events must not usurp the Programmer (God) who will freely accomplish His will. What Daniel and Revelation say is *sufficient* for God's people until Christ comes and tells us more. We must recognize our limitations as well as our small amount of genuine information concerning the end of history. God has willed that we do not know very much, and we must not pretend that we do.

II. The Answers Available to Us

No one disputes the importance of getting genuine answers to questions about: (1) the being of God, (2) whether or not God communicates to His people, (3) moral evil and its widespread influence, (4) the function and malfunction of human government, (5) the distinctive calling and role of the people of God, and (6) how much we really know about the end of history. But a basic question lies behind these issues: "Just what kind of an answer ought one to expect from the material available in Daniel and Revelation or, for that matter, from the rest of the Bible?"

Pessimists in our day maintain that we can get no answers to these questions. Some skeptics believe that the only valid answers are found in controlled scientific research—work in scientific laboratories, case studies, or statistics that can be put into a computer. Although data is available on the six biblical topics we are addressing, these experiences were not controlled and repeatable in the modern scientific sense. If answers must come from repeatable observations in similar experiences, then no "provable" answers can be given to questions that involve ultimate destiny. When people say, "We have not found any answers to these questions," they are giving their own testimony about what they have failed to discover for themselves. When a person says, "There *are* no answers," that person is presenting a philosophical view that affirms that all people are locked into a meaningless world. Such skepticism must be rejected.

In contrast there is a dogmatism that says that complete, absolute knowledge is revealed in the Bible. This view insists that the Scriptures cover certain subjects with such thoroughness that no further questions need to be raised. However, Paul declared that we know in part and we prophesy in part (1 Cor. 13:12). Only when Christ returns and there is face-to-face fellowship with Him will the era of incomplete knowledge come to an end. Daniel and Revelation provide for us not only valuable information but also truths to observe, keep, and practice (Rev. 1:3; 22:7). Though much remains hidden from us, what we learn about these six major areas in Daniel and Revelation will make us alert and eager to live for God.

III. *Proper Interpretation: Meaning Then and Now*

If answers are available to questions in these six areas, then how we interpret the material becomes crucial. If our method of interpretation provides us with the "answers" that we knew in advance, we would find there is something very wrong in the life lived as a result of such interpretations.

A. *Hermeneutical Procedures Behind This Book*

In interpreting a biblical passage students should ask: "(1) What did this passage mean for the first hearers or readers? (2) What does this passage mean for us today if the meaning, in part or in entirety, should be applied today?" For example, "what was John

9

saying to those seven churches of Asia Minor to which the Book of Revelation was addressed? If the passage means something for our times, how should we state these truths today?"

There are two kinds of teachings in the Bible: (1) highest norms or standards, and (2) temporary regulations for particular times and places. For instance, all of the regulations in the Old and New Testaments pertaining to animal sacrifices were for a particular people and time. How can we speak so confidently? We must turn to the highest norm. Read Heb. 9:11—10:10; the passage concludes: "He [Christ] abolishes the first [animal sacrifices] in order to establish the second [God's will]. And by that will we have been sanctified through the offering of the body of Jesus Christ once for all" (Heb. 10:9-10).

We rejoice that Judas Maccabeus re-established temple worship in December 164 B.C. The Maccabeans (from the nickname Maccabeus, meaning "the hammer") involved four priests—a father and three of his sons. These men and their followers resisted and defeated the Syrians in their attempt to destroy the Jewish worship and faith. Judas Maccabeus cleansed and then reopened the temple that had been closed for three years. The annual Jewish feast of Hanukkah celebrates the victory of Judas Maccabeus over the Syrians. This Jewish festival coincides with the Christian celebration of Christmas. Our glad response to the Maccabean revolt does not change the fact that animal sacrifices were part of God's regulations for Jewish people only and are declared by the writer of Hebrews to be made unnecessary by the atoning death of Christ.

Daniel, as well as the writer of Hebrews, affirms the highest norms: "To thee O Lord belongs righteousness...To the Lord our God belong mercy and forgiveness" (Dan. 9:7, 9). Throughout the Old and New Testaments, the God of the covenant is exalted for His righteousness, mercy, and forgiveness. When we observe that a declaration of God's being righteous, merciful, and forgiving is the highest norm or standard, we are saying that this highest norm is established by countless passages in the Old and New Testaments. Revelation affirms of God: "Righteous and true are your ways" (15:3); "You are righteous, the one who is and the one that was, the Holy one" (16:5); "True and righteous are your judgments" (16:7). Righteousness characterizes God's ways, His personal being, and His judgments.

B. Background of the Book of Daniel

Since we are drawing materials from the Book of Daniel in our investigation of six major themes, we need to know a few things about the Book of Daniel.[1]

1. The man Daniel and the content of the book.

Although we usually think about Daniel as a great prophet (one who was a spokesman for God), Daniel is pictured primarily as a great statesman. When Nebuchadnezzar commanded that several young Jewish men (who had been carried into captivity) of royal family and nobility be given special training, Daniel was one of those chosen. He was educated in the "letters and language of the Chaldeans [Babylonians]" (Dan. 1:4). After three years of special training, the young men were given special tests. The results were that "in every matter of wisdom and understanding concerning which the king inquired of them, he found them ten times better than all the magicians and enchanters that were in all his kingdom" (Dan. 1:20).

Daniel's skills, particularly in interpreting the king's dreams, resulted in his becoming "ruler over the whole province of Babylon and chief prefect over all the wise men of Babylon" (Dan. 2:48). As a statesman he reached the top of the Babylonian administration.

Daniel's viewpoint and experiences as a statesman prevail throughout the book. In chapters 1 to 6, Daniel's and his friends' experiences, the dreams of Nebuchadnezzar, and the court intrigue reveal the world in which Daniel lived. We see what it was like for Daniel and his friends to live for God in a foreign country. We also find that the dreams clearly illustrate God was concerned for all nations, not only for Israel.

In chapters 7 to 12, the dream, visions, and narratives point to God's control over the kingdom of the earth, even though human rulers sought various means of demonstrating their own power.

2. Authorship of Daniel.

For more than one hundred years, commentators have debated the authorship of Daniel and the identity of the book's first readers. Since our primary purpose is to examine the teachings of Daniel and Revelation, we will not discuss in detail the varying views about author and readers. (The footnotes at the end of this chapter

11

provide sources for extended information about some of the viewpoints.) However, readers need some understanding of the arguments that have been presented to make Daniel only the hero, not the author, of the book bearing his name.

Many scholars believe that the Book of Daniel was written long after the occurrence of events such as Daniel's three friends in the fiery furnace (chap. 3) and Daniel's experience in the lions' den (chap. 6) that are associated with Nebuchadnezzar, Belshazzar, or Cyrus (605-530 B.C.). Some scholars believe that the Book of Daniel was composed and/or placed in its present form during the time of Antiochus IV Epiphanes (175-164 B.C.) because the events in the book seem to reflect the situation of the Maccabean era. Daniel 11:21-39 summarizes the career of Antiochus (as far as his activities with the Jews are concerned).

The following chart shows the prophecies in Daniel 11 and how they were fulfilled in the time of Antiochus:

ENIGMATIC PREDICTIONS IN DANIEL 11
AND THEIR POSSIBLE FULFILLMENTS

11:5-6
A. Kings of the South: Ptolemy I (305-285 B.C.),
Ptolemy II (285-246 B.C.)
Kings of the North: Antiochus I (280-261 B.C.),
Antiochus II (261-246 B.C.)
B. Contents and Possible Applications:
A marriage alliance between the king of the South and the king of the North proves ineffective.
Marriage of the Egyptian princess, Berenice to the Syrian king Antiochus II. Earlier wife of Antiochus II (Laodice) engineered the death of Antiochus II, Berenice, and their child.

11:7-9
A. King of the South: Ptolemy III (246-222 B.C.)
Kings of the North: Seleucus II (246-227 B.C.),
Seleucus III (227-223 B.C.)
B. Contents and Possible Applications:
Victory and vengeance of the king of the South over the king of the North.
Ptolemy II avenges his sister's death (Berenice) by defeating

Seleucus II (Syria). Seleucus II tried to invade Egypt, after waiting a couple of years, but suffered a disastrous defeat.

11:10-19

A. Kings of the South: Ptolemy IV (222-203 B.C.),
Ptolemy V (203-181 B.C.)
King of the North: Antiochus III, the Great (223-187 B.C.)
B. Contents and Possible Applications:
The king of the North was defeated by one king of the South, but later rose to win a victory over another king of the South. His strategy of intermarriage to weaken the king of the South failed. The king of the North pursued his plan to expand westward but was stopped by a powerful commander.

Encouraged by two victories in Palestine over Ptolemy IV, Antiochus III engaged Ptolemy IV in a decisive battle at Raphia (217 B.C.) where Ptolemy won a clear-cut victory. After the death of Ptolemy IV in 203 B.C., Antiochus III was able to defeat the Egyptian forces. Part of the strategy of Antiochus III was to give his daughter Cleopatra I to Ptolemy V. When Antiochus III tried to expand westward, the Romans stopped him at Thermopylae (191 B.C.). Under L. Cornelious Scipio they defeated Antiochus III at Magnesia in 190 B.C. But he gained control of Palestine in 200 B.C. at the battle of Panium and the Romans did nothing to take this from him. After she lost her fleet and all of Asia Minor, Syria was confined to the Eastern end of the Mediterranean including Palestine.

11:20

A. King of the South: Ptolemy V (203-181 B.C.)
King of the North: Seleucus IV (187-175 B.C.)
B. Contents and Possible Applications:
Another king of the North sent out a tax collector.
Seleucus IV did this and discovered quickly his unpopularity.

11:21-39

A. King of the South: Ptolemy VI (185-146 B.C.)
King of the North: Antiochus IV Epiphanes (175-164 B.C.)
B. Contents and Possible Applications:
A contemptible, cocky, seductive king of the North seeks to

destroy the Holy Covenant, but in due time comes to his own destruction.

Rise to power of Antiochus IV Epiphanes (11:21-24). Victory over the king of the South (11:25-28).

Antiochus IV successful invasion of Egypt (first invasion reported in the Book of Daniel). The king of the North defeated by the ships of Kittim (Romans) and the departure of the king of the South from the area. King of the North takes action against the Holy Covenant (11:29-30). Antiochus IV unsuccessfully invades Egypt (second invasion reported in Daniel). Antiochus IV crowned himself king in Memphis. Before he could annex the whole of Egypt, Rome sent an embassy to Alexandria led by Pupilius Laenus. He brought a decree from the Roman Senate which demanded Antiochus IV withdraw from Egypt. Laenus drew a circle in the sand around Antiochus IV and warned Antiochus IV not to leave this circle until he had made up his mind on leaving. He withdrew and returned homeward. After his defeat Antiochus IV gave himself solace by initiating and continuing a campaign to destroy the Jewish religion. He profaned the Temple, removed the continual burnt offering, persecuted those faithful to the covenant, and put many of them to death.

Description of the king of the North in terms of his arrogance, indifference to the God of gods and all other deities; his loyalty to his own deity and to his supporters (11:36-39).

Here we see a concise character analysis of Antiochus IV. We see his egocentricity, his antagonism to the covenant God of Israel, his abandonment of the national gods of Syria, his loyalty to a foreign deity (Olympian Zeus), and the favors he bestowed upon his friends.

11:40-45

Defeat of the king of the North and of another invader of the glorious land—picture of a composite prince (11:40-45). Defeat of Antiochus IV intertwined with the defeat of Titus and perhaps of some final opponent of God and of His people.

Another argument used to promote a late date for Daniel is the book's use of Greek names for musical instruments; therefore, the book would have to be written after the time when Alexander the

Great (337-323 B.C.) spread his rule over the entire area.

However, these arguments are not conclusive, and strong evidence points to the book's composition in its present form sometime between 535 and 450 B.C. Several factors suggest this earlier date: (1) The Book of Daniel was popular in the Qumran community where the famous Dead Sea Scrolls were found in 1947. This Jewish community apparently lived in the desert caves from about 135 B.C. to A.D. 135. Because almost all parts of the Book of Daniel were found among the materials in the caves, the original writing must have existed much earlier than the establishment of the community. At least two fragments of Daniel that were found in Cave 1 were in a handwriting similar to that of the Isaiah scroll found in the same cave. Because the Isaiah manuscript found at Qumran is generally considered to have descended from copies written several centuries before the founding of the Qumran community, the original writing of Daniel, like the original writing of Isaiah, could also have existed since an earlier time.

(2) The author of Daniel possessed an accurate knowledge of Neo-Babylonian and Persian history. He knew about Nebuchadnezzar, the builder of the new Babylon, and about his great power and pride in his accomplishments (Dan. 4:4-37). The writer also knew that Belshazzar functioned as king from the time Nabonidus, his father, took up residence in Tema. It is hard to imagine that a Jew living in Israel between 175 and 165 B.C. would know about the intricacies of lines of control in a period three hundred years earlier. Very few historical references to this period have been found.

Belshazzar was almost unknown in secular sources until 1854, when Babylonian inscriptions were discovered that illuminated Daniel's accurate record of Belshazzar's promise to make the interpreter of the handwriting on the wall "the third ruler in the kingdom" (Dan. 5:7, 16, 29). The Aramaic adjective *third* (*talthiy*) is used as a noun here. It means literally "one of three," or a "triumvir." Later in the Medo-Persian period, there was a governmental arrangement of three presidents (Dan. 6:2); but there is no evidence that the Babylonians followed this procedure. It is more likely that Belshazzar was thinking of himself, Nabonidus, and a third person not only wise enough to read the handwriting on the wall but also knowledgeable in other matters. Daniel heard the promise, interpreted the writing, and was given a presidential position. But the Babylonian Empire, governed by a triumvirate—Nabonidus, Belshazzar, and Daniel—was a doomed empire. Daniel had already pronounced God's judgment upon it in concise, graphic terms (Dan. 5:26-27). Daniel's appointment was one of the last gestures of a fading monarch.

(3) The use in Daniel of Greek names for musical instruments is not significant. Greek colonists inhabited Egypt around 650 B.C.(at Naucratis and Taphanhes), and Greek mercenaries fought for both the Egyptian and Babylonian armies and at the battle of Carchemish in 605 B.C. Wherever the Greeks went, their musical instruments would be sure to accompany them.

(4) Nearly half of Daniel is written in the Aramaic language, the rest in Hebrew. The Aramaic, in a section that runs from Dan. 2:4b to 7:28, is similar to that appearing in parts of the Book of Ezra and in the Elephantine papyri[2] discovered in Egypt in 1903. The papyri described practices and history of the Persian government about the end of the fifth century B.C.

The Hebrew in the Book of Daniel is similar in style and usage to that of Ezekiel, Haggai, Ezra (written about 500 B.C.), and 1 and 2 Chronicles (written about 400 B.C.). The Hebrew in Daniel is *not* like that in the apocryphal *Wisdom of Sirach* written about 180 B.C., and the Aramaic is *not* like that of the *Genesis Apocryphon* from Qumran Cave 1 (100 B.C.).

(5) One of the main reasons scholars assign such a late date to Daniel is their unwillingness to accept any supernatural predictive element in either prophetic or apocalyptic writings. Although there is much more in Daniel and Revelation than prediction, it is clearly a part of these books. The fact that some of the predictions were realized in Maccabean times, while others do not correspond with past history, is not an adequate reason for insisting on a later date. R. K. Harrison sees general statements rather than particular preciseness in Daniel 11—12: "If it is granted that there is a predictive element in prophecy, this factor, combined with the psychic powers of a visionary, could be more than sufficient to produce the rather general descriptions recorded in Daniel 11 and 12."[3]

(6) Seven times the Book of Daniel mentions a ruler named Darius the Mede (5:31; 9:1), who became ruler of the kingdom when he was sixty-two years old (5:31). He is mentioned by name several times in chapter 6 (6:1, 9, 25, 28) where he is called "king" twenty-eight times. He was said to be the son of Ahasuerus and by birth

was a Mede (9:1). The unnamed heavenly messenger who spoke with Daniel in chapter 10 told Daniel of his mission in the first year of Darius the Mede, to confirm and strengthen this important monarch (11:1). Since a Darius I (Hystaspes) occupied the Persian throne between 522 and 486 B.C., critics who hold to a late date for the writing of Daniel insist that the writer confused the two monarchs.

Donald J. Wiseman and his student, Joyce Baldwin, sought to identify Darius the Mede.[4] They examined the biblical evidence and the cuneiform historical texts. From their study, they have concluded that Darius the Mede is another name for Cyrus the Great. So Wiseman would translate Dan. 6:28, "So this Daniel prospered in the reign of Darius, that is, in the reign of Cyrus the Persian." Many conservative scholars perceive Daniel as a book written to encourage the Jewish people after Cyrus the Great had allowed a substantial group of them to return to their own land from their captivity in Babylon. This return took place in 539 B.C.(Ezra 1:1-4; Isa. 45:1, 13).

3. Evidence for the dates of each chapter of Daniel.

The narratives, dreams, and visions recorded in Daniel took place over a period of about seventy years. We know this because of the chronological statements such as "the second year of Nebuchadnezzar" (2:1). The last dated vision of Daniel is from the "third year of Cyrus" (10:1). When such time markers are not found, general indications in the contents point to certain periods in Daniel's long and productive career. The following chart shows what this writer believes is a defensible timeline.

Chap.	Date	Chap.	Date	Chap.	Date
1	605 B.C.	5	539 B.C.	9	539 B.C.
2	603 B.C.	6	537 B.C.	10	536 B.C.
3	600-590 B.C.	7	550 B.C.	11	536 B.C.
4	570-565 B.C.	8	547 B.C.	12	536 B.C.

If Daniel was fifteen years old when he was carried away captive in 605 B.C., he would be eighty-four years old by the time he received the last vision recorded in the book. Perhaps Daniel as an old man picked out the most representative narratives, dreams, and visions of his career and arranged them in a topical and chronological order something like the division below:

I. Mission of Daniel and his friends in the court of Gentile kings (chap. 1—6).
II. Message consisting of dreams, visions, and narratives concerning earthly kingdoms and eternal kingdom (chaps. 7—12).

The first six chapters consist mostly of a narrative involving Daniel and his friends, and the last six mostly of a dream and visions. There is a very little narrative material in chapters 7 to 12.

On the other hand, perhaps from 530 to 450 B.C. individuals who had supported Daniel in his illustrious career and survived him were guided by the Spirit of God to select and record certain narratives that Daniel had left behind in written form. These followers placed Daniel's experiences and visions into one book that would be particularly helpful to all Jewish people, both those who returned from exile and those scattered in foreign lands. This opinion means that the Book of Daniel would have been particularly helpful when the Syrian Antiochus IV Epiphanes invaded Israel (175-164 B.C.), but that the materials were composed at a much earlier time.

After some Jews returned from the Babylonian exile, they strove to have a national existence. Jews scattered in other places had to struggle to maintain their religious and cultural lives. So all Jews from the Babylonian exile to New Testament times would have found Daniel to be a model book. Daniel, the man with dreams, visions, and difficult crises, spoke to his people; his minority status was their minority status. The truths that God gave to him in his situation were truths that his fellow Jews needed to hear in similar situations. The book was a monumental testimony that the Jewish people could live in the world and not be swallowed up by it.

For these reasons we conclude, along with other scholars, that the Book of Daniel came from the early part of the Medo-Persian period (530-450 B.C.). Any later revisions or polishings of portions of the book would be the normal role of scribes who kept all biblical materials in a readable and understandable form. Canonical shaping (getting books ready to function authoritatively) is quite different from first writing down the material. The materials that we now read in the Book of Daniel were helpful to the Jewish people from Daniel's time until these writings were firmly fixed in the Old Testament canon about 100 B.C.

C. Background for the Book of Revelation
1. Author and contents of Revelation.

The Book of Revelation states that its author is John (1:4). Because John was a prophet (10:11), the book is a prophecy (1:3; 22:7, 10, 18-19). A prophet and a collection of his writings or oracles involve an oral and written proclamation that calls the hearers or readers to a holy life and sometimes offers statements about the future. Prophecy pleads with people to obey and honor God. Obedience will bring blessing; disobedience will bring judgment. So the prophet is involved with the past, present, and future of people's lives. The Book of Revelation as a whole, however, is a letter and contains seven other letters.

John is said to have been "in the Spirit," guided by the Spirit in what he experienced (Rev. 1:10; 4:2) and in what he wrote. But who is this John? Because of the prominence given to John the apostle in the Gospels, the name John was popular among Christians. Some commentators have projected this situation back into the first century. They speak of John the apostle (in connection with the Gospel of John), John the elder (in connection with the three epistles of John), and John the seer (in connection with the Book of Revelation.) If one John could be famous and well known, why could not two or three other Johns also become famous and well known? However, the name John is not that common in ancient times. If one person is involved with the writing of three different genres of literature (Gospel, letters, letter-prophecy-apocalypse), he would surely require help in such diverse literary undertakings. One John could be involved in all the writings, but their literary shaping and composing would also imply others who helped. In this way, the well-known John the apostle is also the seer of the Book of Revelation.

The contents of Revelation can be summarized as follows:

I. The source of John's visions for God's servants (1:1-8).
II. The description and declarations of the glorified Christ who walked in the midst of the seven churches (1:9—3:22).
III. The completion of God's program for His people, for those

in revolt, and for the rest of creation (4:1—22:5).
IV. Reactions to the revealed truths (22:6-21).

2. Original readers of Revelation.

The first readers of the Book of Revelation are described in some detail in the book itself.[5] In Rev. 1:10-11, John says he has been told to write what he saw to the seven churches in the Roman province of Asia: Ephesus, Smyrna, Pergamum, Thyatira, Sardis, Philadelphia, and Laodicea. In chapters 2 and 3, each of these churches is characterized in specific ways and given a message. It seems apparent, however, that these seven churches were chosen to be representative of all the churches of their day, especially those in the Roman province of Asia. The churches received not only particular messages from Christ but also a series of visions as to how God would judge evil, bring harmony to the world, and usher in the final state of sinless existence (chaps. 4—22).

In Rev. 22:16, Christ speaks to these churches and tells them that the whole book is for them as well as for other churches of their time who were under pressure: "I, Jesus, sent my messenger to testify to you [plural, the seven churches] these things [content of Revelation] for the churches."

The churches of that day faced serious threats to their Christian life and witness. Each city had gods and goddesses that received the loyal support of the people and involved many forms of sexual immorality. The cult of the emperor (emperor worship or respect to the emperor) was prominent.

Emperor worship in the Roman Empire was a composite of patriotism and idolatry. Since most people in the Roman Empire had their own idols, they had no difficulty in expressing loyalty to the ruler by forms of worship similar to their response to a particular idol. However, various emperors took different attitudes toward their venerations as a god. Julius Caesar was greeted as a god in Ephesus during his lifetime. Augustus wanted nothing of this in the city of Rome, but he had no objection to temples to himself in the provinces. Caligula, who seems to have been a supreme egotist, demanded homage to his statue. By the time of Domitian (A.D. 81-96), emperor worship and punishment for failure to comply had become official policy. The Romans hoped to make their civil religion a unifying factor. Since Christians would never say, "Caesar [any particular emperor] is Lord" (the capital "L" made this a title of deity), they were treated as disloyal citizens, persecuted, and sometimes put to death. The first readers of the Book of Revelation were acutely aware of this situation.

It may be difficult for us to appreciate the oppressive situation suggested in Revelation. In two of the seven churches, Christians were opposed by Jews faithful to Judaism and the synagogue and antagonistic toward the churches. Some of the churches were experiencing a false complacency caused by material prosperity. Furthermore, false teachers sought adherents in many Christian communities. The Christians' ever-present fear was that the Roman government would persecute them because they would not engage either in the cult of the emperor or in local demands for respect for all the gods. As long as people showed respect to the other gods, they could have their own favorite god and devote special attention to him or her. Christians, however, would acknowledge no other gods and consequently earned the contempt of their neighbors.

Some interpreters have maintained that the Book of Revelation shows the presence of the church only in chapters 1—3 and again after the account of Christ's return in 19:11—20:6. But the intervening chapters, they insist, do not belong to the "church age." The following outline gives a contrasting view of the situation of God's people in chapters 4:1—20:6.

I. Prayers of the saints have a prominent place in the picture of God's throne, 4:1-5:14.
II. Seals and trumpets are a symbolic picture of God's messianic judgments upon a world hostile to God's faithful people, a world devoted to self-centered living, 6:1—11:19.
   A. Some believers lose their lives for the Word of God and for the witness they have borne, chapter 6 (esp. 6:9-11).
   B. God seals His servants to protect them from His messianic judgments, 7:1-8; 14:1-5.
   C. Prayers of the saints are again prominent before the blowing of the trumpets, chapters 8—9 (esp. 8:3-4).
   D. God's secret announced as good tidings to His servants—the Old and New Testament prophets—will be completed with the blowing of the seventh trumpet, chapter 10 (esp. 10:7).
   E. When the present world's kingdom becomes Christ's

kingdom, God will reward His servants—prophets and saints (those fearing God's name), chapter 11 (esp. 11:18).

III. Satan puts pressures on the saints, but they respond with endurance and faith, 12:1—14:21.
   A. Satan's urgency after being thrown out of heaven at the time of Christ's ascension made life very difficult for the early Christians, chapter 12.
   B. John mapped out Satan's war on the saints and his strategy to further emperor worship, chapter 13.
   C. Warnings and promises highlight the destiny of obedient saints, chapter 14.

IV. Bowls of Wrath—final picture of messianic judgments—fall upon the harlot city and the kingdom of the beast, 15:1—19:10.
   A. Comforting picture of victorious saints shows the outcome of the struggle, chapter 15 (esp. 15:2-4).
   B. Individual Christians warned to be alert and not to be captured by moral evil in a time of judgments, chapter 16 (esp. 16:15).
   C. Hostility of the harlot city to the saints, chapter 17 (esp. 17:6).
   D. Invitation to Christ's people to leave the harlot city so that they do not experience God's messianic judgments upon her, chapter 18 (esp. 18:4, 24).
   E. A great multitude of Christ's people in heaven celebrate the judgment of God upon the harlot city, 19:1-10.

V. The second coming of Christ opens up the eternal realm, ends all revolt, and constitutes the saints as priests and kings who, in this capacity, reign with Christ, 19:11—20:6.

The approach that takes the church out of sixteen chapters of Revelation faces serious exegetical problems when we trace key expressions and their usage throughout the book. For example, consider the term *servants*, which is actually the word *slave* (*doulos*) in Greek. Those who hold that the church is absent in much of Revelation will agree that the servants in Rev. 1:1 and 22:3, 6 refer to Christians (those who are members of Christ's church). However, this term *servants* appears in many other places in Revelation where the church is supposed to be absent. For example, in Rev.

7:3-4, the "servants of God" are "sealed" for protection from the physical forces of judgment. These servants are described in Rev. 14:3-4 as being "redeemed" (from the Greek word *agorazo*, meaning "I buy or purchase").

In Rev. 5:9 this same term is translated "ransomed." It is used by Paul in 1 Cor. 6:20 and 7:23 as being "bought with a price." On what grounds then can we say that those who are "redeemed by God" since the time of Christ's incarnation, atoning death, and resurrection are not members of Christ's body, the church? There are no grounds.

In Rev. 10:7 and 11:18, the servants are the prophets who proclaim God's truth. Since John, the writer, is called a prophet, the term used here cannot exclude the Christian prophets of the New Testament.

Revelation 6:15; 13:16; and 19:18 are the only verses in the book where the term *servants*, or *slaves*, clearly does not refer to Christians; there a distinction is made between "slaves" and "free." From the beginning to the end of Revelation (22:6, 10), God's servants (believers in Christ, members of His church) are in the world, often under intense pressures.

The same conclusion follows from a study of the term *saints*. Throughout the New Testament, this term is often used to describe followers of Christ (e.g., Rom. 1:7; 1 Cor. 1:2; 2 Cor. 1:4; Eph. 1:1; Phil. 1:1; Col. 1:2; 1 Thess. 3:13; 2 Thess. 1:10). One of the best definitions of saints appears in both Rev. 5:8 and 8:3-4, where we have the "prayers of the saints." In Rev. 13:7 the beast is said to make war with the saints; the blood of the saints is mentioned in 17:6 and 18:24; reward for the saints is discussed in 11:18; the saints are commanded to rejoice at God's victory in 18:20. In Rev. 19:7-8, we see the saints invited to the marriage supper of the Lamb where they will appear as Christ's Bride, clothed in fine linen, bright and pure.

Thus, the first readers of Revelation would see this entire book as written for them and applicable to them. We can apply the Book of Revelation to Christians of every century until the first resurrection mentioned in Rev. 20:5-6. When Christ comes as King of Kings and Lord of Lords (Rev. 19:16), He will clarify things that are not now clear and give many further teachings. Until then, Revelation and Daniel are crucial books for Christ's people, and they must be studied for truths of living and serving.

D. Literary Forms in Daniel and Revelation

Daniel and Revelation differ in style and approach from most books in the Bible. Readers are often perplexed by sections that seem more like riddles than significant realities. How can we find their real meaning? In order to interpret them in the right manner, we must know what forms of literature we are interpreting.

1. Apocalyptic.

Both Daniel and Revelation are examples of *apocalyptic literature*. (*Apocalyptic* means "to uncover, disclose, reveal.") Daniel and Revelation are examples of a literary form often used in ancient times to disclose truth. Through visions and dreams, writers painted fantastic pictures of animals and beasts. Similes and metaphors were common as well. For example, the third beast of Daniel is "like a leopard, with four wings of a bird on its back and the beast had four heads" (7:6). In Revelation 12 a woman appears clothed with the sun; the moon is under her feet; she has a crown of twelve stars; she is pregnant, ready to give birth to a child. When another sign appears in heaven, John sees a great seven-headed red dragon with ten horns and seven diadems upon the heads. The dragon's tail sweeps away a third of the stars of heaven and casts them to the earth. The dragon then seeks to devour the Man-Child as soon as the woman bears him (Rev. 12:1-4).

Because modern writers rarely produce this type of literature, today's readers are ill-prepared to understand it. We can hardly cope with the allegory of *Pilgrim's Progress*, much less the apocalyptic nature of Daniel and Revelation. Perhaps the problem lies with our cultural limitations. If we learn to adapt our thinking to this kind of writing, its truths can make a deep impression on us.

The language of the Book of Revelation is highly imaginative, describing the conflict between good and evil, God and Satan, righteousness and unrighteousness. Against a dark background of unrest and the great power of evil, the victory of God and the triumph of His people are depicted. The imagery is brilliant, shocking or sometimes bizarre, but it rouses us from our dullness. Evil appears truly evil, and wickedness figures as an abominable perversion.

The apocalyptic view of history intends to instruct the readers about what lay behind the present and future events. History becomes a stage on which the conflict between good and evil is played out between God and Satan.

When Christ addressed the church at Pergamum (Rev. 2:13-17), He summarized what He knew about them. He knew (1) where they lived, (2) where Satan's throne was located, and (3) their faithfulness to Him—especially the faithfulness of Antipas who was martyred at the site of Satan's throne. The first readers believed Satan was behind emperor worship and his throne was its center. Such worship was no incidental gesture of patriotism but a denial of the lordship of Christ. Apocalyptic symbols made this clear.

Apocalyptic symbols not only reveal but also conceal. John wanted to prepare his first readers for whatever might come upon them. By using the term *beast* (which could cover both a hostile government and its ruler), he could alert his readers to potential dangers from Rome and its rulers without specifically naming them. His references to "the harlot city" (see Rev. 17) pointed out the seductive attractiveness of the lifestyle of Rome but did not designate the capital city, thus avoiding the charge of his being a traitor or a revolutionary. Outsiders reading these apocalyptic symbols could not decode them, and even if they did, they would not grasp the significance of God's movements in human history. Terms with significant content for Christians would say little to non-Christians. Thus apocalyptic literature was a vehicle to instruct Christians about what was, and is, really going on in the world, but a veil to those *in* the world.

We must admit, however, that the meaning of some imagery eludes us today even after careful study, and in those cases, we should not become dogmatic. The context and flow of thought clear up many obscurities. As a further help, the writers of both Daniel and Revelation sometimes identify and clarify their own symbols. Then we may concentrate on what the symbol depicts.

2. Prophecy.

Daniel and Revelation are also *prophecies*. The biblical use of the word *prophecy* differs drastically from modern usage of the word. Today *prophecy* usually means "prediction." But in both the Old and New Testaments *prophecy* refers to the call of people from idolatry to faithful service for God. In biblical times prophecy included exhortation, edification, encouragement, instruction, intercession, and confession (1 Cor. 14). Within the framework of announcing God's coming judgments and blessings, prophecy also involved prediction.

But prediction of events was subordinate to the proclamation about who God was, what He demanded of people, and how He would deal with sin. Although we like to distinguish between forthtelling (calling persons to obey God and serve Him) and fore-telling (prediction), the two elements in the Bible are part of one indivisible whole—prophecy. Usually the two elements are blended together; sometimes they are distinct. But whenever we discuss prophecy, we must not stress one element to the neglect of the other; do not omit forthtelling because of some overwhelming compulsion to peer into the future. We must see what the Bible tells us and distinguish carefully between what the Bible says and what some interpreters claim it says.

Daniel's primary calling was as a statesman, not as a prophet; therefore, the Book of Daniel is not found among the prophets in the Hebrew canon. The prophets in the Hebrew canon are divided between the "former" prophets (Joshua, Judges, Samuel, and 1 and 2 Kings) and the "latter" prophets (Isaiah, Jeremiah, Ezekiel, and the twelve minor prophets). The Hebrew classification known as "The Writings" included Psalms, Job, Proverbs, Ruth, Song of Solomon, Ecclesiastes, Lamentations, Esther, Daniel, Ezra, Nehe-miah, and 1 and 2 Chronicles. This miscellaneous collection of writings covered a long period of Israel's history.

The Book of Daniel gives us a few selected visions, dreams, and events in the life of this very successful statesman. However, Daniel *is* a prophecy as well as an apocalypse. The technical words for "vision" and "to see a vision" are often used in Daniel. Prophecy, in the biblical sense of calling people to God, is prominent in the book. The narratives in chapters 1 to 6 show God's protection of Daniel and/or his three friends and God's judgments against kings and other officials. These stories carry the prophetic note of God's involvement in human affairs. No more stirring prophetic words can be found than those directed to Belshazzar by Daniel before he translated the handwriting on the wall (5:22-23).

The Book of Revelation is specifically called a prophecy (1:3; 22:7, 10, 18-19). In Rev. 10:11, John's commission as a prophet is renewed, and he goes forth to continue his prophetic calling.

The dual nature of both Daniel and Revelation cannot be over-emphasized. Both are apocalypses (disclosures of significant changes in history) and prophecies (calling persons to God and announcing God's judgments). Our understanding of the distinctive characteristics of these two literary forms helps us to better interpret them. Prophecy frames the future in terms of the present historical situation. An apocalypse may begin the same way, but its images and symbols bring greater detachment from the present historical situation. Both prophecy and apocalypse are concerned with God's action in the historical, earthly sphere, whether that action is in the present or the future.

3. The letter format of Revelation.

The Book of Revelation is an apocalypse and a prophecy cast in a *letter* format. Just as our letters follow a common format, so also New Testament letters assumed a particular form. There was an opening greeting, often quite formal, in which the letter writer gave his name and the name of the person, persons, or group to whom the letter was written. Next would come some personal concerns or, in the case of the apostle Paul, a thanksgiving. Then the major reason for the letter and its contents followed. The letter would close with greetings or salutations and a final farewell. Adolph Deissmann's fascinating book, *Light from the Ancient East*,[6] is devoted mainly to papyrus letters that came from Egypt between 100 B.C. and A.D. 100-200.

The letter format in Revelation is much more complicated than that of 2 John or 3 John. In Revelation there are seven separate letters (chaps. 2—3) within one total letter. But unlike the style and contents of other New Testament letters (such as Paul's letters to the Thessalonians or the Corinthians), Revelation uses extensive apocalyptic and prophetic forms of literature in a rather unique combination. As stated earlier, without a knowledge of forms of literature, we could easily make the teachings of Revelation into something entirely different from their original intention. So the study of backgrounds and literary forms will open for us the contents that reveal a powerful message.

Daniel and Revelation: Riddles or Realities?

Notes for Chapter 1

¹For a careful study of all background materials to Daniel, see R. K. Harrison, "Daniel," in *Introduction to the Old Testament*, with a comprehensive review of Old Testament studies and a special supplement on the Apocrypha (Grand Rapids, Mich.: William B. Eerdmans, 1969), pp. 1105-1134. Brevard S. Childs, *Introduction to the Old Testament as Scriptures* (Philadelphia: Fortress Press, 1979). Professor Childs presents each book of the Old Testament in terms of: (1) its writing, (2) canonical shaping, and (3) theological and hermeneutical questions. For further background material on Daniel, see Edward J. Young, *The Prophecy of Daniel: A Commentary* (Grand Rapids, Mich.: William B. Eerdmans, 1949), pp. 15-29 and the appendices. John Whitcomb, "Daniel, Book of," in *The New Bible Dictionary*, ed. J. D. Douglas (Grand Rapids, Mich.: William B. Eerdmans, 1962), pp. 290-292. For an approach to the background of Daniel as coming from the second century B.C. as far as the present form of the book is concerned, see Arthur Jeffery, in "The Book of Daniel," in *The Interpreter's Bible Commentary*, ed. George Arthur Buttrick (New York and Nashville: Abingdon Press, 1957), VI:339-354. A recent English commentary is concise and helpful; see Joyce G. Baldwin, *Daniel: An Introduction and Commentary* (Downers Grove, Ill.: Inter-Varsity Press, 1978).

²Bezalel Porten, *Archives from Elephantine: The Life of an Ancient Jewish Military Colony* (Berkeley and Los Angeles: University of California Press, 1968). Porten discusses these papyri under three major headings: Part I, Political and Economic Life; Part II, Religious Life; Part III, Family and Communal Life. In Chapter IX, f.n. 5, pp. 479-480, Porten briefly comments on the late dating of Daniel 1—6: "The books of Tobit and Daniel 1—6 are usually ascribed to the Hellenistic period." Cf. R. H. Pfeiffer, *History of New Testament Times with an Introduction to the Apocrypha* (New York: Harper, 1949), pp. 258ff. Most recently, however, Y. M. Grintz, "Hebrew Literature in the Persian Period," (Hebrew) *Sefer hayovel lᵉrabbi Hanoch Albeck* (Jerusalem, 1963), pp. 123ff., has argued for a Persian date for these books; cf. also Y. Kaufmann, Tolᵉdot, IV/1, 405ff., 418ff.

³R. K. Harrison, *op. cit.*, p. 1130.

⁴Joyce G. Baldwin, *op. cit.*, pp. 23-28. Donald J. Wiseman, "Darius the Mede," in *The New Bible Dictionary*, ed. J. D. Douglas (Grand Rapids, Mich.: William B. Eerdmans, 1962), pp. 292-293.

⁵For a careful study of all the background materials to Revelation and its message, see these works by George R. Beasley-Murray: *Highlights of the Book of Revelation* (Nashville: Broadman Press, 1972); "Revelation," in *The New Bible Commentary*, ed. D. Guthrie, J. A. Motyer, A. M. Stibbs, and D. J. Wiseman, rev. ed. (Grand Rapids, Mich.: William B. Eerdmans, 1970), pp. 1279-1310; *The Book of Revelation*. New Century Bible (London: Oliphants, Marshall, Morgan, and Scott, 1974); "Pre-millennialism," in *Revelation: Three View Points* (Nashville: Broadman Press, 1977), pp. 11-70. See also William Barclay, *The Revelation of John*, 2 vols. (Edinburgh: St. Andrews Press, 1959), I:1-24. G. B. Caird, *The Revelation of St. John the Divine*, Harper's N. T. Commentaries, ed. Henry Chadwick (New York and Evanston: Harper and Row, 1966), pp. ix-x, 1-8. George E. Ladd, *A Commentary on the Revelation of John* (Grand Rapids, Mich.: William B. Eerdmans, 1972), pp. 7-17. Robert H. Mounce, *The Book of Revelation*, The New International Commentary on the New Testament (Grand Rapids, Mich.: William B. Eerdmans, 1977), pp. 18-60. Leon Morris, *The Revelation of St. John: An Introduction and Commentary*, The Tyndale N. T. Commentaries, ed. R. V. G. Tasker (Grand Rapids, Mich.: William B. Eerdmans, 1969), pp. 9-44. J. Ramsey Michaels, "Revelation—The New Prophecy," in *The New Testament Speaks*, ed., Glenn W. Barker, William L. Lane, and J. Ramsay Michaels (New York: Harper and Row Publishers, 1969), pp. 362-384. For an approach to the background of Revelation from historical-apocalyptic perspective, see Martin Rist, "The Revelation of St. John, the Divine," in *The Interpreter's Bible Commentary*, ed. George Arthur Buttrick (New York and Nashville: Abingdon Press, 1957), XII:345-365. For an approach to Revelation as a drama, see John Wick Bowman, "Revelation, Book of," in *The Interpreter's Dictionary of the Bible*, ed. George Arthur Buttrick (New York and Nashville: Abingdon Press, 1957), IV:58-71.

⁶Adolph Deissmann, *Light from the Ancient East: The New Testament Illustrated by Recently Discovered Texts of the Graeco-Roman World*, tr. Lionel R. M. Strachan, 4th ed. (New York and London: Harper and Brothers, 1927).

Chapter 2

How Big Is Your View Of God?

The more we learn about the Bible and the universe, the more we realize that our idea of God and our ways of describing Him are inadequate. When we learn that four distant quasars (starlike celestial objects that emit immense quantities of light or powerful radio waves) are estimated to be ten billion, four hundred million light years away from earth,[1] we recognize that we are part of an immense creation totally beyond our comprehension. Think of the power involved in keeping that amount of matter-energy functioning!

Daniel and Revelation expand our view of God's greatness, but they also stress God's personal concern for people. We see God dealing with nations and with individuals. We see God confronting leaders with who they are and what they do. Consequently, the greatness of God and His personal concern are inexhaustible themes.

I. What Is Daniel's Picture of Who God Is and What He Does?
Dan. 2:20-23; 4:26-27, 34-37; 6:19-27; 7:9-10; 9:2-23

God's dealings with Abraham the patriarch began at approximately 2000 B.C. By the time of the statesman Daniel (about 600 B.C.), some fourteen hundred years of God's deliverances and judgments of His people had passed. Daniel served God in the aftermath of a period of great judgment (Dan. 1:1-21; 2 Kings 24—25; 2 Chr. 36:5-23) in which many had been killed or carried away captive to Babylon. The captives were over a thousand miles from their home, Jerusalem. Against this background, the Jews saw renewed importance in the truths about the God of Abraham, Isaac, and Jacob and the God who had brought them out of Egypt. No longer did these people have a temple for security or even a promised land. But they did have God and what He had revealed to them about Himself. The Book of Daniel shows us the older truths of God becoming fresh again.

A. Greatness of God Himself

After Daniel learned the meaning of Nebuchadnezzar's dream about the four kinds of metals, Daniel praised God for revealing it to him. Daniel's hymn of praise celebrated God's ability and creativity (Dan. 2:20-23). Wisdom, might, strength, and power belong to God (2:20). God knows what is in the darkness (2:22), and the light dwells with Him (2:22); that is, God is the creator of light, and it is under His control. God would provide the very things that His people lacked in their situation. They needed wisdom and strength to live in a world different from that of their fathers. The darkness was foreboding, and the light revealed them to be vulnerable and defenseless. But wisdom and power, darkness and light are all fully at God's disposal.

God knows what is in the darkness just as He knew the dream that Nebuchadnezzar would not recount to his wise men. The king wanted to be sure they knew the dream's meaning, and to do that they were to tell him his dream as well as its meaning. But the wise men failed him. Only Daniel could provide the information the king wanted about the dream (Dan. 2:5-6, 19-23) because of God's revelation to him. The light dwells with God because God is its creator and He maintains His creation.

The Book of Daniel emphasizes God's importance. When Nebuchadnezzar's reason returned to him seven times later (Dan. 4:16, 23, 25, 32, 34), he blessed the Most High (4:34). Daniel's vision of the four beasts (chap. 7) described God as the Ancient of Days (7:9), which does not imply that God was an old man. This figure of speech merely points to God's dignity, importance, and value, in keeping with the ancient respect for old age. God's throne was flames of fire, its wheels burning fire. The flames stress God's brilliance and power to carry out judgment. The wheels of a chariot suggest that God has freedom of movement; He is not restricted to any one locale.

The Book of Daniel highlights God's uniqueness. When Daniel

survived being cast into the den of lions (chap. 6), King Darius (another name for Cyrus) ordered a decree to inform his subjects that the God of Daniel was unlike any other deity. Since Daniel apparently prepared this decree, the word choice is not that of a Gentile king, but of one of God's people. It said that the God of Daniel and his people is unique because He is the living God and He endures forever. Therefore, God's kingdom and His dominion are different from all earthly kingdoms and dominions.

Important as this great view may be, the character of God as a personal Being is a significant point to note in Daniel. We know that God does not have a literal throne nor does He have literal hair "like pure wool" (Dan. 7:9). But the allusion in Daniel 7 to thrones, clothing, and hair white as snow offers the readers a basis for understanding God as a personal God (7:9), in terms they can comprehend. Only as a personal Being with infinite power can God have fellowship with people. Although the throne imagery identifies God as a ruler, the apocalyptic language makes clear that God is different from any human ruler on an earthly throne. God's throne consists of "fiery flames" (7:9-10), and "a stream of fire issued and came forth from Him."

Daniel prayed earnestly and sincerely to God (Dan. 9:3-21), addressing Him as the Lord God (9:3). Daniel's prayer refers to God's personal greatness and the awe and reverence that it inspires (9:4). Yet God's greatness does not remove Him from His people. He faithfully keeps His covenant and steadfast love with those who love Him and keep His commandments. But where there is disobedience, the relationship is broken. In such a situation, the faithfulness of God is even more important. Because of His righteousness, uprightness, and justice (Dan. 9:7) God does not dismiss sin as some slight defect and continue to fellowship with people as if nothing had happened. Daniel prayed for the unfaithful, but his prayer also shows that sin broke fellowship with God and brought judgment.

Judgment is not the last word, however. To the Lord our God belong mercy, compassion, and abundant forgiveness (Dan. 9:9, 19). In Daniel 9, the prophet yearned for a forgiveness in which our sin is pardoned and a whole new course and way of life are established. Daniel does not tell us how God forgives, but he does assert the fact. Only in the New Testament do we glimpse the "how" of forgiveness (2 Cor. 5:21).

Though God judged His people, Israel, and they had been in

captivity in Babylon for almost seventy years (Dan. 9:2), they experienced no revival or widespread repentance (Dan. 9:13). According to Daniel, "They did not give heed or attention to thy truth" (9:13). People do not heed God's truth because their own duplicity makes them uncomfortable in its presence. But once they see the chaotic nature of falsehood, the firmness and surety of the truthfulness essential in the being of God attract them. We can rely upon God and turn to Him in faith because of His integrity.

B. Greatness of God's Action

In Daniel as in the rest of the Old Testament, God is known especially for His deeds. Although He does not carry out His actions as humans do, He may use human agents. Because these agents sometimes act in ways contrary to God's will, He operates by other means in the world. Habakkuk condemned the actions of the Babylonians who were God's agents (Ezek. 21:18-20; Hab. 1:6) but were cruel and violent (Hab. 2).

Daniel stresses God's control of the course of history. God changes the times and the seasons; He removes kings and sets up kings (Dan. 2:21). Whether a king dies of old age, a palace coup, or some fatal disease, God still guides the course of history. Our freedom and God's sovereign control are both realities in the ebb and flow of human affairs. If we stress only God's sovereignty, we may become indifferent to people, believing that everything is predetermined. If we stress our freedom, we may have total chaos—people's sovereignty resulting in God's being banished from His creation. Daniel saw God active in history, which meant that history was going some place (Dan. 2:44). Revelation likewise asserts God's control of history; after the seventh trumpet sounds, there is a thanksgiving that the Lord God, the Almighty One, has taken His great power and begun to reign (Rev. 11:17). We will understand this better when we see what Daniel and Revelation say about God's plan. Both books assert that, although God controls history, He does not assume full and direct control of all that takes place in human affairs until His own time.

The benefits God bestows were important to Daniel. God gives wisdom, knowledge, and strength (Dan 2:21, 23). He reveals deep and mysterious things (Dan. 2:22) to Daniel, such as Nebuchadnezzar's dream of the metallic images (Dan. 2:23). Daniel had no doubts that these things came from God. Daniel would scoff at the idea that he had a "sixth sense" or that his strength and knowledge were only a renewal of his natural physical and psychological faculties. The person who does not know God or who shuts God up in a box must accept any naturalistic and superficial explanation. Daniel knew he could not have wisdom, strength, and insight, unless God made them his. God's action is a reality for His servants because the gifts He gives change their situations.

The God who acted in behalf of Daniel is therefore the God who delivers. Daniel's three friends had this conviction before they were tossed into the furnace. They knew that God could deliver, but if He did not choose to deliver them, the king would know their steadfast purpose not to serve his gods or to worship the golden image that he had set up. After Daniel's experience in the lions' den, Daniel told Darius that God delivered him (Dan. 6:20, 22). Darius' decree, which told of God's intervention on Daniel's behalf, continued this emphasis: "God delivers and rescues. He works signs and wonders in heaven and on earth" (Dan. 6:27). The decree pointed to Daniel as an example of these signs and wonders. In Dan. 9:24 deliverance is raised to an even higher meaning of bringing in everlasting righteousness and atonement for sin. Even though certain parts of the Old Testament stress physical deliverance, the deliverance from sin is significant in Daniel's prayer for forgiveness (Dan. 9:3-19).

God not only delivers; He also rules. Daniel saw God's rule as both present and future. Even Nebuchadnezzar, when his mental balance was restored, acknowledged that the Most High rules the kingdom of people (Dan. 4:34-35). God's dominion is an everlasting kingdom that endures from generation to generation (Dan. 4:34). Darius' decree made a similar declaration: "His kingdom shall never be destroyed and His dominion shall be to the end" (Dan. 6:26).

The future may see some continuation of the present, but there will also be change. God now rules upon earth, but when His rule becomes total and complete (Dan. 2:44-45), all will be right with the world. God's rule means His active presence, which is quite different from the concept in Browning's poetic couplet:

God's in His heaven—
All's right with the world.

When Nebuchadnezzar's reason was restored at the close of his life, he praised and extolled the King of heaven because of God's

33

works and ways (Dan. 4:37). The term *works* refers to the acts of God, and the term *ways* refers to how God carries out His deeds. God's works are truth ("right," RSV), and His ways are justice ("just," RSV). In other words, God's works are genuine (without any false element), and His ways of dealing with people are fair, equitable, and right. Such a picture of God is comforting, but it does not suggest that God will pass over sin and ignore it. We can depend on God; His works and His ways testify to His continuing faithfulness. People, on the other hand, are fickle sinners. What they want today they despise tomorrow. They are not sure what is genuine and want justice only if it benefits them.

In Daniel, as in the rest of the Old Testament, God's greatness is the grounds for His openness to His creatures' prayers, especially the prayers of persons who worship Him. Daniel, as a true intercessor, wanted God to listen to him (Dan. 9:17), and he had no doubt that God heard his prayer. In this case, God answered immediately (Dan. 9:20-23), which is one of the wonders in both the Old and New Testaments: the infinite God entered into conversation with His people, individually and collectively. There are no boundaries to His ability, creativity, or presence; He is a personal rather than an impersonal God. He has a covenant relationship with His people, and in that relationship He both forgives and demands obedience to His truth.

Daniel drew this magnificent picture of God for a people dislocated from their individual and national lives. Because of the deportation of the northern kingdom in 722 B.C. and of the southern kingdom in 586 B.C., the Jewish people were alone wherever they were scattered. They could no longer rely on the outward signs of security—their temple and their land. The ones who did return to their land found everything in chaos. For these people, Daniel's picture of God portrays the only being who has the infinite will to hold life together. Daniel's belief in this God is apparent in his prayer: "O Lord, give heed and act" (Dan. 9:19).

C. Possible References to Christ in Daniel
Dan. 3:25, 28; 7:13-14, 27; 8:15-16

The Book of Daniel speaks of "an angel," "holy ones," "a watcher," and "ten thousand times ten thousands." Angelic beings, heavenly messengers, enter regularly into the narrative. They do not dominate the book, but they have special prominence. In certain passages interpreters differ as to whether specific language refers to an angel or to a preincarnate appearance of Christ. If in any place in the Old Testament Christ would have appeared, such an angelic appearance would certainly be likely in Daniel. Of course, if the interpreter should assume that Christ did not exist until the birth of Jesus in Bethlehem, this assumption would mean that all references in Daniel are to angels. But if we look carefully without presuppositions at what is said and judge the context, our conclusions cannot be dogmatic. Some references in Daniel may apply to the preincarnate Christ, but no one can really say what features could belong only to angels and what features could belong only to Christ. Perhaps because the messenger (named or unnamed) is a representative of the covenant God of Israel, he is described in terms of the Being he represents—the one who does signs and wonders, the one like a son of man, the presence of the Spirit of the holy God (Dan. 5:11, 14) in a particular man.

Nebuchadnezzar was present when Daniel's three companions were thrown into the furnace. In astonishment he asked, "Did we not cast three men bound into the fire?" His counselors answered him, "Undoubtedly, O king" (Dan. 3:24). Nebuchadnezzar added, "But I see four men loose, walking in the midst of the fire, and they are not hurt; and the appearance of the fourth is like a son of the gods" (Dan. 3:25). After the men were removed unharmed from the furnace, Nebuchadnezzar explained this fourth person by saying, "Blessed be the God of Shadrach, Meshach, and Abednego who has sent His angel and delivered His servants who trusted in Him" (Dan. 3:28). For Nebuchadnezzar the phrase, "a son of the gods," was an equivalent for "an angel." The Jewish expression, "an angel" and the Babylonian, "a son of the gods," both designate a higher being than man. Christian interpreters who perceive "angel," or "this one like a son of the gods" as the preincarnate Christ are not to be dismissed as quaint supernaturalists. The God of Israel was present with the three young Hebrews in their desperate need, and when He acted on their behalf, He showed Himself to be the Savior (cf. Isa. 45:15). The New Testament sees the Savior role in particular, historical surroundings, which does not negate many earlier historical actions where God was present (the preincarnate Christ being God) as Savior. If He appears as an angel or sends His angel, He is acting in both cases.

After Daniel's vision of the four beasts (Dan. 7:1-12), he had a night vision. With the clouds of heaven comes one like a son of man who is given everlasting dominion, glory, and a kingdom by the Ancient of Days. All peoples, nations, and languages pay reverence to this one (Dan. 7:13-14). Daniel completes the picture by saying that the kingdom and dominion and the greatness of the kingdoms under the whole heaven will be given to the saints of the Most High. Their kingdom shall be everlasting, and all dominions will serve them (Dan. 7:27). Some commentators have interpreted the one like a son of man as a Hebraic way of describing the saints of the Most High. But this interpretation would seem to mean that all nations will serve another people—the saints of the Most High. There is a step left out here that gives greater clarity. If we assume that the one like a son of man is Christ, then He receives the dominion, glory, and kingdom, which He shares with His people; He achieves the rule, and they participate in the ruling. The key to the saints' destiny lies in this unique person—a heavenly being as well as one like a son of man, whose heavenly and earthly characteristics qualify him to rule.

In chapter 8 Daniel sees a vision of a ram and a he-goat, images for Persia and Greece, respectively. A large horn stands for the most important king of Greece who we now know (from the advantage of historical distance) was Alexander the Great. Four horns represent four kings or kingdoms that would succeed him. A little horn symbolizes Antiochus IV Epiphanes. Initially Daniel had only the vision with no interpretation, but then he saw an "appearance like a man" and heard a man calling to Gabriel, commanding him to make Daniel understand (Dan. 8:15-16). If the one having the appearance of a man was an angel, then one angel commanded Gabriel, and another one clarified the vision for Daniel. But if this is the preincarnate Christ, He is conveying, through Gabriel, something else to Daniel about the pressures God's people will feel in a future crisis that will test their loyalty to God.

The final vision of Daniel covers the last three chapters. Daniel 10:1 states that the vision occurred in the third year of Cyrus, its contents were true, it spoke of great conflict, and Daniel understood it. Verses 10:2—11:1 relate how Daniel received this understanding, and verses 11:2—12:4 describe what the vision involved and some of its meaning. The book and the vision conclude by probing into the duration of this final period, the ultimate issue of these things, and the prospects that lay before Daniel (12:5-13).

36

Experiencing this vision left Daniel weak and shattered. On the banks of the Tigris he saw a man clothed in linen whose loins were covered with the gold of Uphaz. His body was like beryl, his face like the appearance of lightning, his eyes like flaming torches, his arms and legs like the gleam of burnished bronze, and the sound of his words like the noise of a multitude (Dan. 10:4-6). Only Daniel saw this vision, but the men who were with him experienced great trembling and fled to hide (Dan. 10:7). Afterwards Daniel fell into a deep sleep with his face to the ground (Dan. 10:8-9). A man came to strengthen Daniel, who discovered that this messenger is helped by Michael, an angel. Daniel also found that this messenger functions in the supernatural realm where he encounters angelic princes, the prince of Persia, and the prince of Greece (Dan. 10:13, 20), who supervised the activities of world powers. This picture raises a complicated question: "What does God allow, and what does God command nations to do?" From Daniel 10, we know that God is in control, but how His permissive will and His sovereign will are related is beyond our powers to know. Angelic beings are part of the picture of how God runs the world.

But who is this unnamed messenger? It could be a powerful heavenly being above, or equal to, Michael and Gabriel. It could even be the preincarnate Christ. Because the Old Testament view of God is incomplete (as is ours, although the New Testament teachings on Christ and the Spirit expand our view of God), the language of Daniel is sometimes ambiguous. The first hearers or readers may have thought the unnamed messenger was an angel. Certainly the parade of similes used in Dan. 10:4-6 seems to identify an exalted being. Are these given to angels, God's servants, because they represent Him? Or are they given to the preincarnate Christ who, after His incarnation, would represent God as no other being could? Two things are certain: when he communicated with this Being, Daniel was deeply affected (Dan. 10:9-10, 15), and the messenger showed great concern for Daniel and his people.

II. What Does Revelation Say About the Being of God?

The New Testament enlarges the pictures and ideas of God that we have in Daniel, but not in philosophical terms. Neither did the Old Testament writers view God in philosophical nor abstract theological terms. As we see God portrayed in the Book of Revela-

37

tion, we must not attribute to that portrait philosophical or theological abstractions that are not there. The New Testament teaches one God, one unique Being, who has revealed Himself to the church as three "persons" in one unified totality. Though we must sometimes use them, all analogies tend to distort. We have to recognize the limitations of language in dealing with a subject (God) that no one can adequately describe. We can appreciate the final accomplishments of New Testament writers in their works.

A. God Has a Relationship to Christ and Believers
Rev. 1:5-6; 21:7

The word *Father* occurs early in the Book of Revelation. John tells us of Christ's love for Christians and His loosing us from our sins by His own blood. John reminds us that Christ made us to be a kingdom and priests to His God and His (Christ's) Father (Rev. 1:5b-6). Believers therefore become part of a "Father-son" relationship, based on the prior Father-Son relationship between God and Christ (Rev. 1:6; 2:18; 14:1).

The Book of Revelation shows the opponents of God in conflict with Christians but emphasizes that each Christian is in the process of winning a victory. At the close of Christ's message to each of the seven churches, He makes a promise to those who are winning a victory ("to him who conquers," Rev. 2:7, 11, 17, 26; 3:5, 12, 21). The last time this expression of conquering appears (Rev. 21:6-7), the conquerors are promised that they will receive freely of the Water of Life. God uses the language of covenant promise when He says, "I will be God to Him and He will be Son to me." True faith is victorious faith. Hence Christians with a growing faith are winning an ongoing victory and will experience this Father-son relationship.

The term *Father* used of God describes a relationship either (1) between Christ and God, or (2) between the individual believer and God. We must remove from this term all human elements of imperfection and sin, or of procreation and mortality. The emphasis is on a loving and eternal relationship like that between Christ and His Father. The relationship between the believer and the Father begins when the believer puts faith in Jesus and obeys God's commandments (Rev. 14:12). That believers who live in obedient faith will have this Father-son relationship forever is the emphasis in the last two chapters of Revelation.

B. God Has Many Important Characteristics
Rev. 1:4, 8; 4:8; 11:17; 15:3; 16:5-7, 14; 18:8; 19:6, 15; 21:5-6, 22; 22:5-6

God is described simply but profoundly as the one who is, who was, and who is to come (Rev. 1:4, 8). God has no beginning; He simply was and is. The phrase about God's being the Coming One suggests that His full role in the affairs of human beings lies in the future. But in 11:17 and 16:5 the phrase "who is to come"[2] is absent because in these contexts John has described God's coming in a way that He has never come before. He will come to bring an end to the old dominant order and to bring in a new order of peace and harmony.

God is called the Alpha and the Omega (Rev. 1:8; 21:6), which are the first and last letters of the Greek alphabet. We usually think of "beginning" and "end" as chronological points of an event, but in the Book of Revelation "the beginning and the end" are God Himself. God completes life just as the opening and closing letters complete the alphabet. As Christians, we must reverse our pattern of thinking about life in terms of physical beginnings and endings and consider the beginning and the ending as God, not as events. Overcoming the tendency to be event centered is difficult. Even nations and empires begin and end with certain events. But God must be central in our larger relationship with Him. We must subordinate events to God; He is the originator and planner of the events of our lives.

The power of God is a dominant theme in the Book of Revelation. The expressions used of God's might, tell a great deal about Him. The phrase "the Lord God, the Almighty" appears in Rev. 1:8; 4:8; 11:17; 15:3; 16:7; 19:6; 21:22; the phrase "God, the Almighty" is found in 16:14, and 19:15; the phrase "the Lord God," or "the Lord, the God of" is found in 18:8 and 22:5-6. The word *Lord* characterizes God as the master, owner, ruler; the word *Almighty* stresses His supremacy over all things.[3]

As the apocalyptic portion of the book comes to a close, John sees no temple in the New Jerusalem, the Holy City, the final dwelling place of God's people (Rev. 21:22), because "the Lord God, the Almighty is the temple of it and the Lamb." Language that depicts God and the Lamb as a temple differs from philosophical language. Philosophically one might say, "God is a Holy Being whom, when we are aware of His presence, we ought to worship," or "The second member of the Trinity is holy and ought to be worshiped when we receive His presence." But apocalyptic language is not abstract, that is, theoretical and general. The apocalyptic symbols refer to certain known objects—a temple and a lamb—in new terms. We do not think that God is a literal building or that Christ is an animal that produces wool. For those with a Jewish background, the temple by association meant a holy place, the lamb an atoning sacrifice.

That both God and the Lamb are "temple" or "the temple" points to a unique relationship between God and the Lamb. The Father is pictured in terms of His holiness, the Son in terms of His atoning death and His defeat of all evil. The Father is the Holy One, and the Son is the Lamb. The oneness, holiness, and greatness of God—His qualities of immensity—demand this kind of language. The apocalyptic symbols of temple and lamb help us to discuss more fully God's glory and what rightfully belongs to God the Father. God is worthy of praise and honor and of receiving glory; we should acknowledge His renown, power, and sovereignty. However, sin prevents our recognizing His true worthiness; and we praise and honor ourselves, want renown for ourselves, and pretend we are the sovereign ones. True exaltation of God comes only from persons in right relationship to Him.

C. God Receives Worship
Rev. 4; 5; 7:9-17; 11:15-19; 14:1-3; 19:10; 22:9

To speak of modes or centers of God does not give sufficient distinctiveness to the Father, the Son, and the Spirit. Although the Father is Almighty, the Son also had to be all-powerful if His atoning death was to be effective against sin. We must accept the distinctive emphases in referring to the Trinity without nullifying the oneness or unity of God. If we "stutter" when we talk about the God of the Bible, it is because God is far beyond our present capacity to describe or define. In the ages to come we will understand more.

The Almighty Father is holy (Rev. 4:8 [three times]; 16:5) and righteous, and His judgments are true and just (Rev. 16:5, 7). We know that too much power in human hands often brings injustice, but power in God's hands means that good will be rewarded and evil will be punished. God knows the thoughts of a person who is committing evil (Christ searches the minds and the hearts, Rev.

40

2:23). Therefore, with God the Father there is power with justice and holiness. The four living creatures ascribe "Holy, Holy, Holy" (Rev. 4:8) to the Lord God, the Almighty. The term *holy* expresses dedication or consecration. God is dedicated or consecrated to all that He is—His righteousness, goodness, mercy, compassion, and justice.

D. God Initiates Revelation
Rev. 1:1-3

God initiates all disclosures about Himself; the truths declared in the Book of Revelation come from Him (1:1). He gave these truths to Christ who in turn showed His servants the things that must soon take place and what He wanted them to know, observe, keep, and practice (Rev. 1:3). Revelation is Christ's word as well as God the Father's word. It is important to remember that God, the Father, and Christ, the Son, provide John and his readers with the vital truths for living in a sinful, changing world heading for transformation.

E. God Is Sublimely Exalted
Rev. 4:2-6; 5:13

John depicts God's exaltation in several ways; he emphasizes the throne of God in Revelation 4 and the work of the Lamb in Revelation 5. Sometimes he attributes to the Father the physical qualities of a human, which is technically called anthropomorphism. Assigning human feelings and emotions to God is called anthropopathism. Such figures of speech do not mean that God the Father has actual physical parts (hand, arm, or ear) or human emotions (anger, grief, or joy). They simply guide us to a knowledge that God the Father is personal and has infinite power to do what no human can do. His boundless concern for people leads to holy wrath against the evil that destroys them.

In the throne scene (Rev. 4), John uses similes to picture God's exaltation. In appearance He is *like* the precious stones jasper and carnelian. A colored halo or rainbow *similar* to emerald was around the throne. These references stress God's beauty. The twenty-four thrones surrounding the throne of God the Father show that He shares His glory with His creatures. The flashes of lightning, voices, and peals of thunder (4:5) indicate reverential awe as beauty and immense power are brought together; God is not under man's control. The seven lamps burning before the throne are the seven spirits of God, that is, God's Spirit in His sevenfold completeness (4:5, see pp. 53-57). In front of the throne was something like a sea, transparent as glass, similar to a rock crystal (4:6). All these figures magnify for us the beauty and majesty of the Father.

At the close of the fifth chapter, John describes the response of myriads of angels, the four living creatures, and the twenty-four elders. They show how worthy is the Lamb, the one slain to receive all that belongs to Him (Rev. 5:12). Then every creature in all creation ascribes blessing, honor, glory, and might forever to the one who sits upon the throne and to the Lamb (Rev. 5:13). These qualities and responses belong to the Father (and to the Lamb) because of who He is.

F. God Is Active and Creative
Rev. 21:5-8

This passage continues the throne imagery of chapters 4—5. God the Father upon the throne summarizes His actions since He first sent His Son into the world: "Lo, I am making all things new" (Rev. 21:5). This process is climaxed with the new heavens and the new earth (Rev. 21:1-4). But the action of God centers in Himself: He is making all things new, working continously, although creation still groans and evil is yet undefeated (Rev. 21:8). An example of His efforts on our behalf is in Rev. 21:6; anyone who is thirsty for life is invited to take the Water of Life without price. God satisfies people's thirst for Him, and He grows closer to His creatures.

To the one who conquers Revelation 21:7 promises a Father-son relationship that will transcend the present Father-son relationship existing in a state of conflict. Although God desires to renew all things through involvement with His people, His actions do not make an individual's actions and willingness unnecessary. When people are thirsty, they must turn to God, who will satisfy their thirst (Rev. 21:6; 27:17). When a person determines to come through the conflict victorious, a Father-son relationship is established that will last forever. Though God has all power, He does not overwhelm His people or destroy their freedom of choice. Mutual cooperation brings the blessings of a true Father-son relationship.

G. God Receives Worship
Rev. 4; 5; 7:9-17; 11:15-19; 14:1-3; 19:10; 22:9

Revelation is a great book of worship as evidenced by its hymns and songs. The vision of the throne (chaps. 4—5) emphasizes group worship and ends with a universal response to God. Angels play an important part: "the voice of many angels, numbering myriads of myriads, and thousands of thousands" (5:11). This awe-inspiring picture of true worship was essential for the first readers, who were surrounded by false gods and the emblems of emperor worship. Like us, they had much to learn about true worship.

At the close of Revelation, John twice was tempted to forget God in the midst of all the splendors he witnessed. As he heard about the wedding banquet of the Lamb and of the fellowship with Christ, he fell down to worship (show respect), somehow directing his worship (respect) toward his guide who sternly rebuked him. "You must not do that! I am a fellow servant with you and your brethren who hold the testimony of Jesus. Worship God" (Rev. 19:10).

A little later John thought of all that he had seen in these visions. He heard Christ's words declaring that He is coming soon (Rev. 22:6-7). Overwhelmed, he fell down to worship (show respect), again directing his worship (respect) toward his guide. Again he was rebuked: "You must not do that! I am a fellow servant with you and your brethren the prophets, and with those who keep the words of this book. Worship God" (Rev. 22:9).

John's experience is an example for each of us today. We too can become so involved in the magnificent splendor of what lies ahead, in the details of events that will defeat and eliminate evil, that we forget God. More subtly, we may exalt the small part of God's plan that we have glimpsed and forget God Himself. What God has disclosed to us should induce us to worship. These disclosures were never meant to focus attention upon themselves; true worship focuses our attention upon God.

III. What Does Revelation Say About the Person of Christ?

Christ is both earthly and heavenly, but the Book of Revelation says little about His earthly life. Chapter 12 pictures the small messianic community of Jewish people from which Jesus came, but it notes only Christ's birth (12:2, 4-5). We must know the Gospels to recognize that the antagonism of Satan and his attempt to "devour her child" refers to the attempt of Herod the Great to rid himself of all rivals. (This paranoid monarch ordered the slaying of all infants in Bethlehem, two years and younger [Matt. 2:12-18].) Revelation 12 immediately moves to the Ascension, war in heaven, the banishment of Satan from heaven, the conflict between Satan and the Palestinian church, and Satan's extension of the conflict "to the rest of her seed," which apparently refers to believers throughout the empire. Apart from these few historical references, the Book of Revelation centers upon the glorified Christ. But this powerful, dramatic presentation of Christ never wanders into theoretical language understandable only to theologians.

A. The Effects of Christ's Death Are All-Encompassing
Rev. 1:4, 17-18; 5:5-12; 7:14; 12:11; 13:8; 14:3-4

If we only superficially read the Book of Revelation, we probably are unaware of how much is said about Christ's death. But in the picture of the throne, the image of the Lamb is central: "...on the center of the throne and among the four living creatures and in the midst of the elders there was a lamb standing as if it had been slain" (5:6). John's words focus on Christ's atoning death.

There are many other references to Christ as "Lamb," and each one carries a connotation of his death. The term *Lamb* refers not only to Christ's atoning death but also to His rule, power, and holiness. The Lamb is said to be the final temple (Rev. 21:22). The concept of atonement, however, is always there, and the death of Christ, which has a central position in Revelation, is essential in dealing with moral evil at the close of history as we know it.

The phrase, "by His own blood," occurs often in the book. The blood stands for Christ's life—an infinite, unique life poured out to put in motion God's power to deal with sin. Christ is pictured as loving us, "loosing us from our sins by or in His blood" (Rev. 1:5). When people respond to the Savior who gave His life for them, power comes that frees them from the bonds of sin. The God-Man, Christ, experienced the destructive power of sin. Having entered into our human predicament, Christ conquered sin both by living free from it and by setting in motion through His death this new power that breaks its hold.

He breaks the power of canceled sin,
  He sets the prisoner free;
His blood can make the foulest clean;
  His blood availed for me.   Charles Wesley

This released power must be applied constantly. John says he saw a great, victorious throng which no person could number from all nations, tribes, peoples, and tongues (languages) (Rev. 7:9). They came from an earthly setting where they had been under great pressure. But they washed their robes and made them white in the blood of the Lamb (Rev. 7:14). When Satan is denied access to heaven (Rev. 12:7-12), he returns to earth full of wrath because he knows that his time is short (Rev. 12:12). The brethren conquer Satan by (1) the blood of the Lamb, (2) the word of their testimony, and (3) their capacity to love not their lives unto death (Rev. 12:11). John calls his readers "blessed" who are constantly washing their robes (Rev. 22:14, any translation except KJV). The death of Christ is not only a historic occurrence but also an event that set in motion a present power. That is why Paul exclaims that when sin abounded, grace abounded much more (Rom. 5:20).

The Book of Revelation stresses three times the Lamb "who has been slain" (5:6, 12; 13:8). Here we have the perfect tense in Greek that emphasizes an act has occurred and its effects continue. The Christ who was slain has conquered death and is alive. Because His death is effective now, He is worthy to receive power, wealth, wisdom, might, honor, glory, and blessing (Rev. 5:12). The RSV translates Rev. 13:8, "...every one whose name has not been written before the foundation of the world in the book of life of the Lamb that was slain." This translation is possible, but I think it is not in accord with the Greek word order. In the Greek, the participle, "has been slain," is followed by the phrase, "from the foundation of the world." The Greek order would produce the idea: "of the Lamb's book of life, the Lamb who has been slain from the foundation of the world" (cf. Rev. 13:8, KJV). This idea is more difficult, but that very fact warrants our consideration. Interpreters, as well as the scribes who copied the Book of Revelation century after century, tend to prefer an easier reading rather than a more difficult one.

In the plan of God, the Lamb—God's eternal Son—is to play a central role in redemption. Since God created each person with a will, an individual's decision to try to make it on his own is no surprise to God. But in God's plan, God and man have come together in the Incarnation (Christ becoming man), in Christ's death and resurrection, in the use and application of the power set forth by His death, and in the time when that power will bring about the complete destruction of evil. Christ has been slain from the foundation of the world because the remedy for sin was conceived before the results of sin were experienced.

Peter writes the same thing to Christians who lived in Pontus, Galatia, Cappadocia, Asia, and Bithynia. He tells them they were not redeemed by silver or gold but "with the precious blood...of Christ who was foreknown from before the foundation of the world but manifested in the last of these times because of you" (1 Pet. 1:19-20). Both in Rev. 13:8 and 1 Pet. 1:19-20, Christ's atoning death is said to be a vital part of God's plan from before the foundation of the world. Those who are joined to Christ become part of the remedy for moral evil, not the means for furthering the chaos that moral evil brings.

The term *purchase* is used to stress the value of people and to show that, although they were created by God, they really do not now belong to Him. Instead, they have given themselves to the cause of evil and belong to a highly organized system of evil beings. In Rev. 5:9 the four living creatures and the twenty-four elders celebrate in song that Christ was slain and that He purchased ("ransomed," RSV) people for God by His blood. This verse does not mean that God paid some price to Satan or that God paid some price to Himself. Rather the image of making a purchase points to the value of those who were bought and to their special relationship of belonging to God as His possessions. But these persons have the freedom to respond to the one who made this possible (Rev. 22:17). The 144,000—who are the new Israel, consisting of Jews and Gentiles who acknowledge Jesus as the Messiah—are twice spoken of as purchased or bought. They "have been purchased from the earth" (Rev. 14:3); they "were purchased from people to be a firstfruit to God and to the Lamb" (Rev. 14:4). They are a firstfruit because John sees Christ as coming soon (in a short time, Rev. 1:1, 3; 12:12; 22:6-7, 10, 12, 20). When Christ reigns upon earth (Rev. 20:1-6), the earth will be filled with the knowledge of the glory of the Lord as the waters cover the sea (Hab. 2:14; Isa. 11:10). Believers coming to Christ before this time are a

46

"firstfruit" of countless numbers who will then acknowledge Christ's lordship and saving power.

John declares that Christ died but lives forever and forever. Through death, Christ acquired the keys of death and Hades (Rev. 1:17-18), which means that He has the keys of eternal destiny (Rev. 1:18) and knows firsthand what death is. Death and Hades are personified as the captors of all people, but with their keys (in this metaphor *keys* equal "confine and loose") Christ now controls the realms which hold people and do not allow them to return to life. The future lies in Christ's hand because He experienced death and conquered it; through His death He will conquer sin. Since death threatens every person's future, our deliverance lies with the one who controls the future, the one who defeated both death and sin.

B. The Resurrection of Christ Is a Central Fact
Rev. 1:17-18; 2:8

When Christ speaks to the church of Smyrna, He describes Himself as the one who was dead and became alive again (Rev. 2:8). When He says to John, "I was dead and lo, I am living forever and forever" (Rev. 1:18), He clearly asserts His resurrection. The statement in Rev. 1:18 follows a paragraph liberally sprinkled with similes and metaphors describing the glorified Christ (Rev. 1:12-16). That Christ has a bodily form is made clear by this exalted language. Indeed, the Book of Revelation is concerned with the living, resurrected Christ. What is He now doing? What will He be doing? Who is He, and why is He so central? The Resurrection is recorded as fact, but unlike Christ's death, it is not a recurring theme in the book.

C. The Person of Christ Is Distinctly Disclosed

The Christ depicted in Revelation is a person of majesty. Throughout the book He is involved in God's communication with humankind, in the defeat of moral evil, in a rule that overcomes the limitations of human government, in the salvation of God's people, and in the climax of history. Let us examine some of the features illustrating His capabilities for these immense tasks.

1. Christ appears to John. Rev. 1:10-20

John's vision of the glorified Christ, described in the first chapter of Revelation, occurred on the island of Patmos where John had

47

been banished. John, in the Spirit on the Lord's Day, heard behind him a loud voice like a trumpet. This voice commanded John to write what he saw (literally, what you are seeing) and to send the written material to seven churches of the Roman province of Asia.

John turned to see the voice. First he saw seven golden lampstands, and in their midst he saw one who was like a Son of man. But the description shows that He was more than a man. The same things said of Him are said of God the Father. He was truly man, but He was the God-Man: (1) He was clothed with *a robe* reaching to His feet; (2) He was girded with *a golden belt* around His breasts; (3) His *head* and *hair* were as white as wool and snow; (4) His *eyes* were like a flame of fire; (5) His *feet* were similar to fine bronze made red hot in a furnace; (6) His *voice* was as the sound of many waters; (7) He had *the seven stars* in His right hand; (8) from His *mouth* proceeded *a sharp two-edged sword*; (9) His *face* was like the sun shining in its strength; (10) He described Himself as *the First* and *the Last*; and (11) twice (Rev. 1:18) He emphasized that He was *the Living One*. He was dead, but now He lives forever and has the keys of death and Hades.

The seven stars in His right hand show His closeness to His people—believers in the churches. These seven stars have been interpreted variously as: (a) seven angels, each of whom was assigned to oversee the work of one church; (b) seven messengers, each of whom brought a copy of the Book of Revelation to one church (they would interpret and apply the things each church needed; obviously they would spend some time there); and (c) the leader, or chief minister, of each church who was to work strenuously for the changes Christ asked. The last interpretation is perhaps the easiest to visualize because some of the churches' needs would demand action for an extensive period of time. A messenger who stayed for only a short time could accomplish little, but if he stayed for a longer time and perhaps returned, he could really strengthen the church. Least likely is the angelic supervising spirit because such a being would have to work through the leadership of each church. The last two possibilities (b and c) are the most likely. However, the last—a single pastor for each church—does not agree with the evidence we now have about church government in the first century. Each church seems to have had a plurality of leaders. The best interpretation for the first-century situation is that of seven messengers who each brought a copy of the book and remained for a time to strengthen the church.

With a sharp two-edged sword proceeding from His mouth, the Lamb comes with authority and power to deal with moral evil (Rev. 1:16; 2:12, 16; 19:15). Without great force in the hands of Christ, anarchy and chaos would take over. The whole book shows why this does not happen.

The face of Christ is compared to the sun shining in its full strength. This image refers to the breadth of the effects of Christ upon people. Just as no one is hidden from the rays of the sun upon the earth, so no one is hidden from the person of Christ, either now or at His return when He will visibly act in human affairs.

Christ is "the first and the last"; the boundaries of life and history are not events but a Being. Christ is preeminent (the First), but He is also the Last—He will bring to completion God's plan for history. When sin is forever banished, a whole new epoch will dawn. As the "first" and the "last" in this great drama of history, Christ puts a personal stamp on all of creation. Creation is not some blind force of matter-energy. Neither are we pawns under some impersonal force. We are a creation controlled by a personal God, and His eternal Son is the commander of a world destined for harmony and wholeness.

Because Christ is "the living one," He is able to carry out God's plan. By His experience of death He shows He is involved with man's predicament. Christ lives to banish sin, destruction, and death.

2. Christ stands in the midst of the seven churches.
Rev. 2:1, 8, 12, 18; 3:1, 7, 14

Of the fourteen things said about Christ in the titles of His addresses to each church, all but five have been mentioned in chapter 1. But here they are repeated because of their special significance for a particular church with particular needs. Note the description of Christ who speaks to the messenger of the church in Ephesus. He *holds* or *holds fast* in His right hand the seven stars, and He *walks* in the midst of the seven golden lampstands (Rev. 2:1). Because Ephesus had lost its first love (love for one another and for God [Rev. 2:4]), the members of this church needed to know that Christ *was walking* in *their* midst. Christ saw their lack of love in the manner they tested persons who claimed to be apostles but were not. They uncovered liars in the process, but they seemed to be losing their power to love. Christ *was holding* the messenger and all their leaders firmly in His hand. Were these leaders so intent upon delivering the church from evil people (especially those making false claims) that they forgot the badge of Christianity, namely love? In view of what Christ says to this church, that seems to be the case (Rev. 2:5).

In chapters 2 and 3 of Revelation, seven distinctive things are said about Christ that are not mentioned in chapter 1. For example, when God's unique Son addresses the church at Thyatira, Rev. 2:18 says, "the words of the Son of God" (RSV). Literally we read: "The Son of God says the following things." The use of "Son of God" exalts Christ in His special relationship with His Father.

The Christ who addresses the church at Philadelphia is called the Holy One (or Consecrated One) and the True One (or Genuine One) (Rev. 3:7). Christ is dedicated completely to all that He is. He has no divided loyalty; He hates iniquity. When we succumb to moral evil, we are not being true or genuine. But Christ responds to evil with all that is proper for the righteous, holy deity and for the upright, consecrated man; He is truly the God-Man.

In Rev. 3:7 Christ has the "key of David," symbolizing His messianic role. In the context of Rev. 3:7-9, the church of Philadelphia is promised an open door to win converts and success in its mission to its Jewish opponents: "Behold, I will make those of the synagogue of Satan who say that they are Jews and are not, but lie—behold, I will make them come and bow down before your feet, and learn that I have loved you" (Rev. 3:9, RSV). Because they do not acknowledge the true Messiah, John speaks of Jewish people as belonging to the synagogue of Satan. Christ promises that persons ("those," "many," "them" [KJV], "some") from this synagogue will come and acknowledge that God loves Christians in Philadelphia. Ignatius of Antioch certainly seems to confirm the success of this church's mission to reach Jews.[4] Writing approximately twenty years later to the Philadelphians, he says, "If anyone interprets Judaism to you, do not listen to him; for it is better to hear Christianity from the circumcised than Judaism from the uncircumcised. Both of them, unless they speak of Jesus Christ, are to me tombstones and sepulchres of the dead, on whom only the names of men are written."[5] Evidently there must have been some Jewish converts there! Christ's "opening and closing" involves His control of the mission of the church, His earthly reign, His banishment of all evil, and His judgment of all people and the determination of their destiny.

The distinctive things said about Christ in Revelation 2—3, that are not mentioned in chapter 1 conclude with the titles (1) the Amen, (2) the Faithful and True Witness, and (3) the First Cause or Originator ("Beginning," RSV) of God's creation (Rev. 3:14). These titles are used when Christ deals with the self-sufficient church at Laodicea. This church claimed wealth and need of nothing while in reality it was wretched, pitiable, poor, blind, and naked (Rev. 3:17).

The titles "Amen" and "Faithful and True Witness" belong together (Rev. 3:14b). Christ is called the Amen because He so frequently made firm declarations: "Truly, truly [amen, amen], I say to you, unless a grain of wheat falls in to the earth and dies, it remains alone; but if it dies, it bears much fruit" (John 12:24). Christ's being called the Amen means that both He and His declarations are firm and sure. The next title, "the Faithful and True (or genuine) Witness," emphasizes the character of the one who testifies. Most people learn about God through testimony or witness, not by scientific experiments. They do not analyze or discover God in a telescope, microscope, or atom smasher. The witness par excellence, faithful and genuine as no other witness, was Christ the Messiah.

Christ is also described as the "First Cause and Originator" of God's creation (Rev. 3:14c). The RSV and the KJV translate this phrase as "the beginning of God's creation," or "the beginning of the creation of God." The Greek word arche carries the meaning of the "beginning" but it also means "origin," "first cause," or "ruler." 6Considering the context, the best meaning here seems to be either Originator of God's creation, or Ruler of God's creation, or both ideas blended into one title. The bestower of true gold (or wealth), true clothing, true eyesalve to enable people to see, and the reprover and chastener of His people (Rev. 3:18-19) is the Originator and Ruler of God's creation (Rev. 3:14c).

3. The Christ is at the throne.
Rev. 4:1-5:14

The importance of the throne in Revelation 4—5 cannot be minimized. Its affinity to the descriptions of God the Father is clear.

These chapters depict both the human—the one who died—and deified—the one in control of His people's destiny—aspects of Christ's person. The twenty-four elders, the four living creatures, and a chorus of innumerable angels all sing about the worthiness of the Lamb. He completes redemption by bringing His people to reign upon the earth, and also He receives power, wealth, wisdom, and might (Rev. 5:12). Because of all His qualities, He is worthy to receive the worship of created beings—honor, praise or glory, and blessing (Rev. 5:12).

The picture of the throne shows both the Father and the Son as deity, but there is still only one divine Being. The one main throne surrounded by twenty-four thrones illustrates the unity of God (Rev. 4:2-4). Through the imagery of the throne we learn about (1) the Being of God, (2) the people of God (twenty-four elders), and (3) the totality of nature (four living creatures). The Father, who sits upon the throne, and the Lamb carry out the activities of God to bring all of creation into one positive response to Him (Rev. 5:13). The concept pictured here is so vast it is almost impossible to comprehend. There is mystery in beholding the greatness of God.

D. Special Features Mark the Christ Who Returns
Rev. 22:12-13, 16

Christ comes to reward each man according to his works. Some interpreters forget that He rewards and recognizes good deeds because they emphasize Christ as commander and judge, the one who destroys every vestige of evil. People are not saved by doing good; they are saved by faith, trust, and commitment of their lives to Christ. But their deeds are the evidences of genuine faith and of their identity. When Christ rewards a person for the deeds done, He is not inflating that person's ego. Rather He is showing His approval of the person who uses the power that God bestows to spread deeds of kindness. Christ is a recompenser who does not forget.

Christ is also "the Alpha and the Omega, the first and the last, the beginning and the end" (Rev. 22:13). In Rev. 1:8 the Father is the Alpha and the Omega; in 21:6 the Father is the Beginning and the End. In 1:17 and 2:8 Christ is the First and the Last. But in 22:13 all three expressions are used of Christ. In our scientific age, we ask: "How did things begin?" and "How will things end?" A more biblical question would be: "*Who* began things?" and "*Who* will end them?" In Revelation, beginning and ending are concerned neither with the "how" nor with an unknown "who" of beginnings and endings. Rather, beginning and ending are absorbed into the person of Christ who came and is coming again. The boundaries of life are not temporal, spatial, or psychological. To limit our thinking about life imposes a mental blinder that allows people to think only in terms of physical birth and death. Life instead is bounded by God. When we know Him, we do not think of ourselves as being locked into a brief span of years with all of the future concealed in mystery. Instead, the future, the end, and the forever are all to be identified with Christ.

Yet the Christ described at the end of the Book of Revelation came into the human sphere as the root and offspring of David (Rev. 22:16); He is much more than a philosophical principle. He came from a chosen family of the human race, and He speaks to His churches as the fulfillment of all God's promises.

The last title of Christ, "the bright morning star," shows that God's promises have come into a dark world (Rev. 22:16). Christ is the dawn, the herald of a whole new day. As the bright morning star, He will initiate a day that will have no night (Rev. 21:25; 22:5), and He will make what is hoped for a reality, a city that has no sun or moon. Then Christ will no longer be the morning star. The Being of God will be light: "The glory of God is its [the final city's] light and its lamp is the Lamb" (Rev. 21:23). The morning star has become the eternal light resplendent in its brilliance.

IV. What Does Revelation Say About the Spirit—in Heaven and Upon Earth?

In each previous section we have affirmed the unity and oneness of God. Many non-Christians, such as adherents of Judaism or Islam, insist that Christians really believe in three Gods but will not admit it. The imagery and manner by which the Spirit is described in Revelation make clear that He is part of the Being of God, but He is also distinct. The Book of Revelation more strongly emphasizes certain functions of the Spirit than do other New Testament books.

A. Who Are "the Seven Spirits"?
Rev. 1:4; 3:1; 4:5b; 5:6b

When John writes to the seven churches, he brings grace and peace to them from the Father (who is, who was, and who is coming), from Jesus Christ, and from "the seven spirits who are before his [Father's] throne" (Rev. 1:4, RSV; "seven Spirits," KJV). The text literally says "seven spirits," but there is no differentiation between capital or lower case letters in the Greek text. The context must determine whether "spirit" refers to (1) man's inner being, (2) angels or spirit beings, or (3) the Spirit of God, or Holy Spirit. Here, whether one writes the "seven spirits" or "seven Spirits," the context shows that the expression refers to the Spirit of God in His completeness. When Christ addresses the church at Sardis, He describes Himself as having the seven spirits (Rev. 3:1). In the great picture of the throne we find "seven torches of fire burning [brilliantly] which are the seven spirits of God" (Rev. 4:5b). The next chapter depicts the Lamb with seven eyes that are "the seven spirits of God, eyes that have been sent forth into all the earth" (Rev. 5:6b)

In pointing out specific details of this imagery, we must be careful not to lose sight of the whole picture. Although Christ addressed each individual church, He wanted all the churches to hear whatever He said to each one. A common refrain is found in the personalized note to each church: "Hear what the Spirit says to the churches" (2:7, 11, 17, 29; 3:6, 13, 22).

How can "seven spirits" equal "the Spirit"? The emphasis on the number seven points to wholeness or completeness,[7] the perfection of deity in action. The Spirit of God is the fullness of God in action toward His people; He brings them grace and peace (Rev. 1:4).

In discussing the seven spirits and seven churches, language poses a problem for us. Since there were seven actual churches in seven geographical locations, the reader may be tempted to conclude that there must be seven angels and seven spirit beings. But this conclusion overlooks the significance of apocalyptic language. We must look at the total context of the phrase "seven spirits" and compare it with the singular, "the Spirit." The number seven modifying the "Spirit" says something different when it modifies "churches" or "messengers" ("stars"). When Spirit is applied to the covenant God of Israel, the word is clarifying a unique Being whose presence and power can be felt or perceived.

Christ "has the seven Spirits of God and the seven stars" (Rev. 3:1). The speaker (Christ) to the church at Sardis has the Spirit as the other Helper, Counselor, or Comforter (John 14:16). He also controls the messenger and leaders of each church as well as the church itself. Christ "has" the Spirit in the sense that He sends the Spirit to fulfill His mission in the world among His people. For the reader, the Spirit and Christ are united to God the Father by means of the throne in chapters 4 and 5 of Revelation. The Lamb takes the scroll from the Father who sits upon the throne (Rev. 5:7). The Spirit is also in the presence of the throne and is described as seven torches of fire burning continuously before the throne (Rev. 4:5a), as the seven Spirits of God (Rev. 4:5b), and as the seven eyes of the Lamb (Rev. 5:6). Just as God is a "consuming fire" (Heb. 12:29) and a "devouring fire" (Deut. 4:24), the seven torches point to the Spirit as revealing God's active holiness. The torches show the Spirit's purifying role. Dedicated to righteousness, the Spirit also illuminates and consumes all that is evil. As the eyes of the Lamb, the Spirit sees beneath the deceit and concealment characteristic of moral evil. The seven eyes indicate that the Spirit sees everything completely. What a vivid picture! These eyes are sent forth into all the earth, indicating that the Spirit is not confined to any single site.

Seven torches, seven eyes, and seven spirits point to the completeness and perfection of God. Because the Spirit is by the throne and is sent into all the earth, this third "person" of the Godhead vividly describes in Revelation God's heavenly and earthly sides. The number seven, when used of the Spirit, epitomizes the perfect completeness of God brought into constant interaction with people.

B. What Is the Spirit's Message to the Churches?
Rev. 2:7a, 11a, 17a, 29; 3:6, 13, 22

In chapters 2 and 3 of Revelation the glorified Christ speaks to seven churches. Through the messenger He addresses the leaders and all the members of each church. There is a brief description of Christ, then a statement of particulars about each church. There are no criticisms or statements of defects for two churches (Smyrna and Philadelphia), but the other five are censured and warned to be faithful. Each church also receives a promise from

Christ. At the end of each message there is an identical refrain: "He who has an ear, let him hear what the Spirit says to the churches."

Obviously, Christ's message is also the Spirit's message. These seven, actual churches located in Asia Minor were chosen because their problems and strengths represented all the churches of John's day. Any church of the first century could find something in each letter pertinent to itself. All were exhorted: "Any individual who has an ear, let him hearken to [obey] what the Spirit is saying to the churches." The Spirit described in a sevenfold fashion is the Spirit of the churches (or groups of Christians), an emphasis also found in Paul's writings. But we often miss this corporate aspect and individualize the commands without recognizing that Paul addresses them to groups. "You [plural]—the church at Thessalonica—stop quenching the Spirit" (1 Thess. 5:19). "You [plural]—all the Christians addressed at Ephesus—stop grieving the Holy Spirit of God in which you [plural] were sealed unto the day of redemption" (Eph. 4:30). "You [plural] be in the process of being filled with the Spirit" (Eph. 5:18). The individual members of Paul's churches and of John's churches were to respond to the message of the Spirit. But they were to respond in full awareness that the Spirit was addressing with authority the whole group.

This leaves no room for false individualism. Whoever does not grieve the Spirit, is filled with the Spirit, and hearkens to and obeys the Spirit and makes his influence felt throughout the group. Of course, he may also make an impact individually, but the stress of the New Testament—especially Revelation—is on what groups of Christians can do when they listen to what the Spirit is saying to churches. The individual remains important, for in the promise made to each church, it is "he who conquers" or "the one who is in the process of winning a victory" to whom Christ grants certain blessings. But this individual is not detached from the group with whom he struggled to overcome Satan, the deceiver (Rev. 12:9; 20:10). In association with all other groups the final victory was obtained (Rev. 12:11).

C. How Concerned Is the Spirit for Believers Under Pressure?
Rev. 14:13

Prior to the depiction of harvest and judgment in Rev. 14:14-20, two important announcements are proclaimed. The first calls for the endurance of the saints. Who are the saints? They are the people who keep God's commandments (especially difficult in a lawless age) and maintain their faith in Jesus (Rev. 14:12). We are told that God will judge anyone loyal to the beast (the kingdom and ruler opposed to God).

The second announcement speaks of the future of the saints. A voice out of heaven tells John to write: "Blessed are the dead— those who die in the Lord from now on; indeed, the Spirit says this: 'they are blessed seeing that in dying they will rest from their toils; for their works or deeds are following with them' " (Rev. 14:13).

The ones who die under this pressure are blessed because of their loyalty to God. They have considered the question: "Will you identify with God and bear His name upon your forehead (Rev. 7:3; 9:4; 14:1; 22:4), or will you identify with an anti-God government and bear the hostile ruler's mark" (Rev. 14:9-11)? And their deaths in fellowship with the Lord Jesus answered for them. The Spirit has comforting words for them: "They will rest from their toils; further, their works which showed their fidelity continue with them." The persons faithful to Christ at death will rest, but their works, or deeds, will continue as the overwhelming evidence of the Spirit's interest in the activities of the saints. Some of these "works" are probably actual people following the ones who showed them the way to God. The Spirit says that noble works of all kinds are to have an enduring effect because they are still a part of those who did them and they remain influential to those who were benefited.

V. The Trinity Is a Reality and a Mystery
Rev. 1:4-5a; 5:6; 22:16-21

Revelation begins and ends by talking about God and His people. We have God, Christ, and the Spirit all active in revealing truth, bestowing grace and peace, protecting the truth, inviting persons to take the Water of Life, and breaking through into our world to inaugurate a new epoch.

Grace and peace come from (1) the one who is, who was, and who is to come, (2) the seven Spirits who are before God the Father's throne, and (3) Jesus Christ, the faithful witness, the firstborn of the dead, and the ruler of the kings on earth (Rev. 1:4-5a). The Father, Spirit, and Son are involved here, but they are not discussed in theoretical, philosophical terms such as "the Godhead." In heaven their functions involve one throne (Rev. 4—5).

In heaven as well as upon earth the Father, Son, and Spirit have distinct yet similar activities. In chapters 2—3 we find the Spirit reenforcing and reaffirming what Christ said to the churches. In Rev. 22:16, Jesus sends His angel, also mentioned in 1:1, to testify these things to the seven specific churches that were meant for all churches. The Spirit and the people of God (the Bride) invite each person to take the Water of Life (Rev. 22:17). God the Father, on the other hand, will act in a final judgment against anyone who adds or subtracts from the message of the Book of Revelation (Rev. 22:18-19). John's closing prayer asks that the grace which the Lord Jesus bestows be with all readers (Rev. 22:21).

Although the Spirit and the Bride can both invite persons individually to take the Water of Life, the Spirit is also called the seven eyes of the Lamb (Rev. 5:6b). He sees within each person while the people of God can invite only by looking at the outward person. Christ reveals truth and announces His return to complete His earthly work as the morning star of a new epoch (Rev. 22:16, 20). The Father protects the truth disclosed (Rev. 22:18-19). The persons of the Trinity contribute to the unified purpose of God.

Specific statements in Revelation about God the Father, Christ, and the Spirit make the triune God a valid conclusion from a study of this book. There is *one* throne (4—5), *one* temple (21:22), and *one* light (21:23-24; 22:5). These metaphors point to the oneness or unity of God. Of course, one God. Surely angels are around the throne (Rev. 4—5), and an innumerable company of believers is before it (Rev. 7:9-10). Their nearness to the throne makes neither angels nor believers to be God, however; the throne is that of God and of the Lamb (Rev. 22:1, 3). In 5:1 God the Father is seated on the throne. But in 5:6 we read: "And I saw on the center[8] of the throne and among the four living creatures and in the midst of the elders a Lamb standing as if it had been slain." This Lamb has seven eyes (the seven Spirits of God) that have been sent forth into all the earth (5:6). Thus, the Spirit through the Lamb is in the middle of the throne as well as in all the earth.

Who can fully understand this? The unique being of God does not fit into human categories of thought. We use language drawn from human life to provide metaphorical pictures of God. Such words and phrases as King, Judge, Shepherd, Lover, Rock, Fortress, Potter, Shadow of His Wings, and Shadow of the Almighty enable us to think and talk more meaningfully about God. The Christian doctrine of the Trinity does not try to explain fully the mystery of God, but it does stress His unity. It also shows the inadequacies of any physical analogies about oneness. For example, the Trinity is not like a molecule of water that has two atoms of hydrogen and one of oxygen. Once the two hydrogen atoms are separated from the oxygen the substance is no longer water. Unlike the three atoms in a molecule of water, the three members of the Trinity cannot be separated from their union, but they can be more clearly distinguished than the elements of water.

Despite its mysterious nature, the doctrine of the Trinity testifies to progress in revealed truths about God. We see in the New Testament how God must be bigger and more profound than the magnificent pictures we have of Him in the Old Testament. The Book of Revelation contributes to this enlargement.

VI. The Plan (Will) of God Centers in His Kingdom

Both Revelation and Daniel emphasize God's personal involvement in human affairs. People of every generation must face certain universal questions. "What is the destination of history? What will happen to the strange, incredible power of evil or to the world created by the God of Daniel and Revelation?" These questions point to God's plan to deal with evil, to eradicate sin and its effects, and to bring about a new order where there is no chaos or revolt. Sometimes mentioned explicitly and sometimes symbolically, an unmistakable theme runs through Daniel and Revelation: God's plan will reach its goal because God with His infinite power will bring to actuality what He has promised. That is why the kingdom of God is central in both books.

A. What Is the Scroll in the Hands of Christ and John?

There are two prominent scrolls in Revelation. The most important one has seven seals and Christ alone can open it (chap. 5). In Revelation 10 there is a little scroll opened in the hands of an angel who verbally delivers his own message concerning the completion of God's mystery when the seventh angel sounds his trumpet (Rev. 10:7). But the little scroll pertains to John and his prophetic ministry.

1. Worthy is the Lamb to take the scroll and to open its seals.
Rev. 5:1-10; 6:1-16; 8:1—9:21; 11:15-19; 15:1—16:21

In Revelation 4—5 there is a dramatic picture of the throne in heaven. The one who sits upon it is similar to jasper and carnelian; a rainbow that looked like emerald was around the throne. Surrounding the throne were twenty-four elders, four living creatures, seven torches of fire, a sea of glass like crystal, and the Lamb who showed the marks of His atoning sacrifice. At the right hand of the one upon the throne was a scroll written on both sides and sealed with seven seals. A strong angel asks, "Who is worthy to open the scroll and to loose its seals?" (5:1-2). In all creation no one is found worthy to open the scroll and to break its seals, which caused John to weep (5:4). Finally, one of the elders tells John to stop weeping because the Lion of the tribe of Judah has conquered and will open the scroll and its seven seals (5:5). The four living creatures and the twenty-four elders celebrate this unique role of the Lamb: "Worthy are you to take the scroll and to open its seals because you were slain and purchased people to God by your blood..." (5:9).

What does this scroll mean? To answer this question, we must see what happens when Christ breaks the seals, which is described in Revelation 6. The first four seals involve four horsemen: militarism, war, famine, and death and Hades.

When Christ breaks the fifth seal, He sees the persons who had been slain because of the word (message) of God and their witness to it. After they ask God to vindicate them, they are told to rest for a little time "until both the number of their fellow servants and their brethren should be complete, who were to be killed as they themselves had been" (Rev. 6:11). The first hearers or readers in these seven churches of Asia Minor knew that Nero had put to death many Christians some twenty or thirty years earlier. They knew of others, like Antipas (Rev. 2:13), killed in their own times. These martyrs experienced their version of the great tribulation and remained faithful. Soon Christ would come and vindicate them.

The sixth seal depicts upheavals in the physical universe that bring a sense of foreboding to both the lowly and the great. All people will know that God is angry and no one can stand before His wrath (Rev. 6:16-17).

When the seventh seal is broken, there is silence in heaven for about half an hour (Rev. 8:1). Then John sees that the seven angels who stand before God have seven trumpets.

The seals illustrate Christ's control of destiny, and when He breaks each one, the world moves closer to its final climax. The seven trumpets, the seven bowls of wrath, and the explanatory visions depict what the climax involves. The pause with the seventh seal is like the change of scenes in a drama and indicates that we move from what was written on the seals (the outside of the scroll) to what was written within (the scroll's contents). The section covered by Rev. 8:2—22:5 discloses some of the contents of the scroll that Christ took from the hand of the Father (Rev. 5).

What we have here are "Highlights in the Plan of God" that might be outlined as follows:

I. Setting the Stage for the Climax of the Age: the Seven Seals, 6:1-16; 8:1.

II. Participants in the Climax of the Age: God, People, Angels, Physical Creation, Satan, and Evil Angels, 7:1—19:10.

   A. Sealing of God's Servants upon their foreheads—scene upon earth, 7:1-8.

   B. A great multitude that no person can number has achieved final victory—scene in heaven, 7:9-17.

   C. The Seven Trumpets, 8:2—9:21; 11:15-19—judgments involving nature, demonic forces, and the completion of God's confrontation with moral evil's attempt to control the world.

     1. The Angel and the little scroll, 10:1-11.

     2. The temple and the two witnesses, 11:1-14.

     3. The Woman clothed with the Sun, the Man-Child, and the Dragon—Satan's behind-the-scenes strategy, 12:1-17.

     4. The Two Beasts (Antichrist and the False Prophet) who oppose God and His people, 13:1-18.

     5. The Lamb and the People of God (144,000) in the heavenly Zion, 14:1-5.

     6. Proclamations of good tidings, judgments, and final harvest, 14:6-20.

   D. The Seven Bowls of Wrath, 15:1—16:20—judgments involving nature, demonic forces, and the completion of God's confrontation with moral evil's attempt to control the world.

1. Defeat of political powers, especially the capital city of the federated world government, 17:1—18:24.
2. Heavenly rejoicing over the defeat of the harlot city and over the prospects of the Bride and the Lamb entering a whole new stage of fellowship, 19:1-10.

III. Second Coming of Christ brings to a climax the present evil age, revolutionizes human history with the first resurrection, and inaugurates Christ's earthly reign, 19:11—20:6.
IV. Banishment of Moral Evil, Final Judgment, and Sketches of Life in a deathless, harmonious existence, 20:7—22:5.

There is no blueprint of how God is going to remove moral evil, bring in everlasting righteousness, and expand life into new spheres. But there is enough revealed to give us confidence in God and show the magnitude of His plan. God will make what we see dimly become a spectacular reality.

2. The little scroll: effects upon John. Rev. 10:1-11.

If the scroll in the hands of Christ represents God's plan for the whole of history, the little scroll represents God's will and plan for His servant John. Of course, John's ministry is part of the larger plan to which the angel's announcement pertains. But the little scroll is for John alone and becomes a renewal of his call. John was commanded not only to take the scroll but also to eat it. He had to appropriate the message and make it a part of his very being so that he could deliver it. In his mouth, the message, or scroll, was as sweet as honey, but in his stomach it became bitter. In this dramatic form John's message becomes clear. The bright side of hope and wholeness for people and creation is represented by the sweetness while the dark side of temporal judgments and final judgment is represented by the bitterness. After this symbolic action, the angel says, "You must again prophesy about or to many peoples and nations and tongues and kings" (Rev. 10:11).

John may have been banished to the island of Patmos (Rev. 1:9), but God had not forgotten him. He had much more to do. In prophesying about and to peoples and nations, John would confront them with their destiny which would have its bitter or its sweet side, depending upon their response. In delivering the message, John carried out God's will for him and fulfilled his part of God's total, comprehensive plan. The little scroll and the seven-sealed scroll emphasize the truth that life in the world is not haphazard. God will carry out His will, and He has tasks for each of us to do.

B. *The Kingdom of God Is a Present and Future Reality*

Both Daniel and Revelation acknowledge the present and future aspects of God's kingdom, or reign. To think of only a future reign of God fails to recognize God's present activity. But to think of only the present action and reign of God is to ignore a vital part of Christian hope:

Thy kingdom come,
　Thy will be done,
　　On earth as it is in heaven
　　(Matt. 6:10).

This balance between the present and the future aspects of God's reign makes for tension between "the already" and "the not yet." What we now possess in partial form is certainly real, but it is not the full reality. Hence we long for that full reality even though we thank God for what we have already experienced of the powers of the age to come.

1. *God's kingdom is contrasted with earthly kingdoms.* *Dan. 2:34-35, 44-45; 4:1-3, 25-27, 34-37; 6:23-27*

In chapter 5 (on human government) we will discuss at greater length some of these passages, but here we will discuss God's kingdom.

Nebuchadnezzar had a dream in which he saw an image made of four metals (Dan. 2). The head was of gold, the breast and arms of silver, the belly and thighs of bronze, and the legs of iron. The feet, regarded as part of the legs, were of both iron and clay. Then a stone was cut out by no human hand and struck the image on its feet. The image collapsed, and all the metals broke into pieces, which became like chaff on the summer threshing floor to be carried away by the wind. The stone that struck the image became a great mountain and filled the earth (Dan. 2:32-35). Daniel explained that Nebuchadnezzar was the head of gold, and the other three metals represented the world kingdoms that would follow him.

However, the stone stood for God's rule and God's kingdom. In the days of these four world empires and their rulers God will set up a kingdom that will never be destroyed or leave its sovereignty to another people (Dan. 2:44). His coming kingdom will break all earthly world powers and will stand forever. There is a sharp contrast between this future kingdom and the dominant world powers. Daniel assured Nebuchadnezzar that his dream described this change in human history: "Just as you saw that a stone was cut from a mountain by no human hand, and that it broke in pieces the iron, the bronze, the clay, the silver, and the gold, a great God has made known to the king what shall be hereafter. The dream is certain, and its interpretation sure" (Dan. 2:45). This passage stresses the future aspect of God's reign.

After God's deliverance of Daniel's friends from the fiery furnace (Dan. 3), Nebuchadnezzar wanted to issue a statement to all his subjects (Dan. 4:1-3). As a high government official, Daniel probably was asked to formulate this decree. Nebuchadnezzar acknowledged that the Most High God wrought signs and wonders that amazed him by their greatness and might: "His kingdom is an everlasting kingdom and His dominion is from generation to generation" (Dan. 4:3). Note that God's kingdom is present as well as future. The fact that God can intervene in human affairs as He wishes shows that His kingdom is permanent and His rule "is from generation to generation."

The same emphasis on God's present rule or dominion continues thoughout Daniel 4. Nebuchadnezzar is warned that he will be deprived of his rule and will live among the beasts of the field. He will lose his mental balance and act like a domesticated animal. (These bizarre symptoms have been noted in some mental patients in our times.) This judgment would come upon Nebuchadnezzar until he knew "that the Most High *rules* the kingdom of men, and gives it to whom He will" (Dan. 4:25, 32). Here the present rule of God is asserted again. However, Daniel promised Nebuchadnezzar that his unstable mental condition would be only temporary and his reign would continue as before. When Nebuchadnezzar was restored and put this trying episode behind him, he blessed the Most High and praised and honored Him. Then he acknowledged the true Ruler: "His dominion is an everlasting dominion, and His kingdom endures from generation to generation" (Dan. 4:34).

When Daniel was delivered from the lions' den, the monarch

Darius published for his subjects his convictions about the true God he had come to know because of Daniel. The wording of this decree is probably adapted to the Hebrew audience that would read and hear the message. Darius proclaimed that God lives, and "His kingdom shall never be destroyed and His dominion shall be to the end" (Dan. 6:26). Above, and yet parallel to, all human kingdoms is God's reign, rule, or kingdom. This present reality can easily be forgotten. Human power and the insidious workings of evil seem to push God's actions and rule into the background. Yet certain crises like the ones recorded in Daniel show that human power is limited and moral evil will be defeated. Even now, God rules.

2. One like a son of man, the saints, and the kingdom. Dan. 7:13-14; 15:18, 22, 27.

The seventh chapter of Daniel bears some similarities to the second chapter. The second chapter uses an image of four metals, and the seventh portrays four kinds of beasts that are like a certain combination of animals or parts of animals. Both chapters deal with coming world empires, about which scholars disagree. Some have said the fourth empire points to Syria, with Antiochus IV Epiphanes as the Antichrist. Others believe the fourth empire is Rome because Syria never had the world influence of Babylon, Medo-Persia, Greece, or Rome. But beyond the issues of world empires and the final Antichrist, Daniel 7 talks about (1) God the Father exercising judgment and presiding over judgment, (2) the one like a son of man to whom was given dominion, honor, and the kingdom, and (3) the saints of the Most High who receive the kingdom.

In the picture of God's acting in judgment and defeating the final Antichrist, Daniel speaks of what he saw "in the night visions" (Dan. 7:13; the vision is described in 7:13-14). With clouds of heaven, the coming world ruler (one like a son of man) comes to the Ancient of Days whose throne was fiery flames (Dan. 7:9). He comes before the Father, the Lord of the Old Testament. At this moment some outstanding things happen: (1) the Ancient of Days gives Him dominion, honor, and the kingdom; (2) all peoples, nations, and languages pay reverence to Him; and (3) His dominion is declared to be everlasting, His kingdom will not be destroyed. In

65

the light of the New Testament, the one like a son of man is Christ, both a suffering servant and a coming king (see pp. 52-53).

The kingdom is given not only to one like a son of man but also to saints of the Most High who possess it "until perpetuity, until the ages of the ages" (Dan. 7:18). Many interpreters say that the one like a Son of Man is another way of speaking of the saints because both receive a kingdom; these designations are merely two ways of describing the same thing. But the New Testament provides a more adequate interpretation. What the saints themselves could never accomplish, Christ accomplishes for and with them. He receives the kingdom (by virtue of who He is and what He accomplished), and because of the saints' identification and relationship with Him, they too possess the kingdom. The "one like a son of man" is Christ, and the saints of the Most High are those who are related to Him—Christ's people, flock, household, or family. Therefore, it can be said of Christ and His people: "Their kingdom shall be an everlasting kingdom, and all dominions shall serve and obey them" (Dan. 7:27). In Daniel this reign is future, but those who will reign are already active in the earthly and heavenly realms.

3. The present aspects of the kingdom are constantly felt.
Rev. 1:6, 9; 5:10; 12:10

The Greek word translated "kingdom" also means "reign," "kingship," "royal power," or "royal rule." In the New Testament the word most frequently means "the royal reign or kingdom of God."[9] In the first chapter, John brings grace and peace to the seven churches from the triune God. He speaks of Christ who "continually loves us and who loosed us from our sins in His blood" (Rev. 1:5). This Christ "made us to be a kingdom and priests to God even His Father" (Rev. 1:6). Individuals who are Christians are now "a kingdom" because they have come under Christ's royal power or rule. Because the next phrase states that we are also priests for God, those who are a kingdom must be more than "subjects"; they must have both kingly and priestly qualities. This kingly role will become clearer in the future aspect of the kingdom.

Christians are said to be persons who have been purchased for God by Christ's blood from every tribe, language, people, and nation (Rev. 5:9-10). Christ's purchase of them made them a kingdom and priests, and they will reign upon the earth. Those who are now a kingdom will also reign (some ancient manuscripts read "are reigning"). Some commentators question whether the verb "to reign" should be in the present or the future. The Greeks sometimes used their present form of a word to refer to action in the future that was very certain. If the present aspect is correct, it would reveal John's expectancy that God's people were so close to Christ's coming and their reigning with Him that it was stated as a present reality. To be redeemed or purchased by Christ constitutes a radical change for the ones redeemed. They are a kingdom, and they acknowledge Christ's royal power over them. They are priests who represent God to the people around them, and they talk to God for other Christians, for those outside Christ's fold, and for themselves and their own needs.

John himself exemplifies this new role. He describes himself as a brother, a fellow sharer in the tribulation and kingdom and patient endurance (Rev. 1:9). Since he had been exiled to Patmos because of the message God gave him and the testimony Jesus communicated to him, he knew how to share tribulation and patient endurance with his fellow believers. He and they also shared the kingdom of Christ in their lives. The importance of God's message and Jesus' testimony caused believers to endure banishment and imprisonment; these Christians must have had a vital relationship to their king. His rule they knew; His presence they did not yet see.

As soon as Christ ascended to heaven, the effects of His atoning death were felt. The picture of a war in heaven and of Satan's being cast out (Rev. 12:7-13) indicates that Satan's sphere of influence was restricted. He can no longer accuse the saints before God day and night. With this turn of events a great voice in heaven exclaims, "Salvation has just now come, both the power and the kingdom of our God and the authority of His Christ" (Rev. 12:10). What is true of the heavenly sphere where God dwells is not yet true of earth. Satan came down to earth having great wrath because he knew that he had little time (Rev. 12:12). The rest of the Book of Revelation (chaps. 12-22) shows how God the Father and Christ banish Satan from earth just as he has been banished from heaven and how they initiate a whole new quality of existence. Of course only the highlights of this future panorama are unfolded in these chapters, but for the present the reign of God is complete in heaven and is dominant in the lives of the redeemed. God's plan is in vital relationship to His kingdom.

4. The future aspect of the kingdom will inaugurate a whole new era.
Rev. 1:15; 12:5; 15:3-4

In chapter 7 of this book we will carefully examine what we know about the end of history from Daniel and Revelation. Here we want only to observe that when the future aspect of the kingdom starts to function, it will be a radical change.

The sounding of the seventh trumpet (Rev. 11:15-19) summarizes major occurrences that will accompany the emergence or breakthrough of God's reign. Loud voices in heaven announce the inauguration of this new and final epoch: "The kingdom of the world comes to be, becomes the kingdom of our Lord and of His Christ, and He will reign for ever and ever" (Rev. 11:15). The future aspect of the kingdom does not take place in the heavenly sphere or in some ideal realm. Rather, the kingdoms of the world (as in Dan. 2; 7) feel the impact of God's action. When God annihilates the ones who are destroying the earth (Rev. 11:18), He will assert His great power and begin to reign (Rev. 11:17).

In the one chapter of Revelation that alludes to the birth of the Man-Child (Rev. 12), Christ the Son is the one "who is to rule all the nations with a rod of iron" (Rev. 12:5). Here the future aspect of the kingdom of God is celebrated in terms of the King who will shepherd, lead, and rule the nations. The need for force (a rod of iron) indicates that God's kingdom has opposition. Christ's reign will bring about the defeat, removal, and transformation of anything that opposes God.

Those who sing the song of Moses and the song of the Lamb extol God's works and His ways (Rev. 15:3). They address the Lord God Almighty as King of the nations (or in some manuscripts, the King of the Ages, Rev. 15:3). The next verse (v. 4) certainly seems to support the expression "King of the nations": "Who will not fear, Lord, and who will not glorify your name? Because you alone are holy, because all the nations will come and will worship before you." The nations come before Him in awe to worship and glorify His name, not because they are struck down in terror before some absolute monarch, but because they are responding to the one who is the true and everlasting King, the unique sovereign whose plan to bring harmony in His universe has reached its goal.

VII. How Can We Expand Our Limited View of God?

To the question "How big is your view of God?" we must answer, "Not big enough. Our view of God makes Him far too small." This reply underlines the central task of the whole Bible, which is to tell us who God is and why images and all forms of idolatry give us a false picture of Him. But if we humbly admit the inadequacy of our statements or pictures about God, how can we progress to better statements and pictures?

A. Meditate on God's Uniqueness: Who He Is and How He Acts

The pictures and statements in Daniel and Revelation concentrate on *who* God is and *how* He acts. As we meditate on them our view of God constantly enlarges. God, Christ, and the Spirit will be for us one Being so unique that language and pictures cannot possibly bind or frame Him. Yet our inadequate language and pictures are essential for our progress. We gratefully use them and grow in our view of God.

B. Humbly Celebrate the Certainty of God's Plan

We do not celebrate how much (or how little!) we know of God's plan. We do not celebrate the superiority of our presentation of God's plan. God has told us very little about His plan, and we may not sufficiently comprehend the part that He has disclosed. But God has a plan, and because He is God we celebrate His kingdom or reign. God's present and future reign will mean harmony and the realization of His plan. The world never has been, is not now, and never will be out of God's control. With an expanding view of who God is, we also have expanding confidence in God's plan. The God who is and the God who acts is the God whose plan will come to completion.

The more we learn about the Bible and the universe, the more we realize the shortcomings of our views and ideas about God. Neither Daniel nor Revelation depict God abstractly, theologically, or philosophically. Instead, these books speak in concrete terms to encourage and enlighten both their original readers and today's readers. Their apocalyptic language, rich in symbols, furthers the communication of profound truths.

Summary

What does Daniel tell us about God?

The hymn of praise in Dan. 2:20-23 celebrates God's ability, creativity, wisdom, strength, power, and light in the midst of darkness. God endures forever. Daniel points to the integrity of God's character. He is the personal Lord, faithful, upright, and just, who gives wisdom and strength to His people. But their sin breaks fellowship with God and brings His judgment upon them. However, Daniel asserts that God also forgives, although we do not learn *how* He does. God controls history, and He is active in human affairs through human agents He uses to carry out His will. Some of His agents are good, but others are wicked and violent. Our human freedom to do good or ill and God's sovereign control are both real. God is able to deliver His people from trials and death if He chooses.

What does Revelation teach about God?

Revelation teaches that God is a Father to believers. The term *Father* in Revelation describes a loving relationship between God and His Son, Jesus, and between God and and believers. God has no beginning or ending; He is not event-centered, as we are. God is Lord God, the Almighty. John sees no temple in the New Jerusalem because "the Lord God, the Almighty is the temple of it and the Lamb" (Rev. 21:22). God initiates revelation; He discloses Himself. Only God is almighty, holy, righteous, just in judgments, and worthy of worship. Revelation describes God in human terms, with both physical and emotional qualities, to show His infinite power and concern for people. God is continually renewing His people, but He does not destroy their freedom of choice.

What does Revelation tell us about Christ?

The Book of Revelation concentrates on the glorified, resurrected Christ, not the earthly Christ. He has a bodily form and is a person of majesty. But Revelation also says much about Christ's death. The phrase "Lamb who was slain" speaks of His atoning death; "His own blood" refers to the means by which He loosed His people from their sins. Because Christ died for our sins, He has the keys to death and Hades—the eternal destiny of all people. John describes Christ as like a Son of man but then uses language

70

similar to that for God the Father (Rev. 1:10-20)—one with great power and authority, the First and the Last. In the letters to the seven churches, Christ is called the Son of God (2:18), the Holy One (3:7), and the Amen, the originator of God's creation, the faithful witness (3:14). Revelation 4 pictures Christ at the throne. In Revelation 5, Christ receives praise from the twenty-four elders, four living creatures, innumerable angels, and every creature. Christ rewards persons on the basis of their individual works. In Revelation 22 Christ is the root and offspring of David, the "bright morning star."

What does Revelation say about the Holy Spirit?

Revelation speaks of the Holy Spirit as the "seven spirits"; the number seven points to wholeness or perfection. Revelation 4—5 employs several images to illustrate how the Spirit and Christ are related to God the Father by means of the throne. The Lamb (Christ) takes the scroll from the Father who sits upon the throne (5:7). The Spirit is described as seven torches burning continuously before the throne (4:5) and as the seven eyes of the Lamb (5:6). Therefore, the throne, the Lamb, the seven torches, and the seven eyes symbolize how the Spirit fits into the Being of God. The Spirit is the Spirit of the churches, and the messages in the letters to the seven churches are for groups of people.

Importance of the Trinity

All that is said about God the Father, the Son, and the Holy Spirit in Revelation points to the unity of the triune God. There is one throne, one temple, one light. The concept of a triune God is a mystery beyond our comprehension.

Importance of God's kingdom, reign, or royal rule

The plan or will of God centers in His kingdom, a theme central in both Daniel and Revelation. God's kingdom, reign, or royal rule is both present and future, posing a tension between "the already" and the "not yet." Although God rules now, what we possess in partial form today is not the full reality. Human power continues to be limited. God's coming kingdom will break all earthly powers and will stand forever.

God's kingdom is given to one "like unto the son of man" and to the saints of the Most High who possess it until the ages of the ages

71

(Dan. 7:18). Christians are now "a kingdom" because they have come under Christ's royal rule. The ones who are now a kingdom will also reign. As soon as Christ ascended to heaven, the effects of His atoning death were felt. Satan was cast out of heaven (Rev. 12:7-13), and his sphere of influence was restricted. Satan could no longer accuse the saints before God. The rest of Revelation shows how God the Father and Christ exclude Satan from earth just as he had been excluded from heaven. The future aspect of God's kingdom will inaugurate a whole new era. God will destroy those who are destroying the earth.

How can we expand our limited view of God?

We can meditate upon the uniqueness of God as revealed in the Bible and recognize how little we really understand of God's plan. Yet we can celebrate the certainty of what we do know—God is definitely in control of this universe and He will complete His plan for it. We can rejoice that our knowledge of God will continue to grow forever.

How Big Is Your View Of God?

Notes for Chapter 2

[1]Kenneth Brecher, "Astronomy: Galaxies and Cosmologies," in *Britannica Book of the Year, 1978* (Chicago: Encyclopedia Britannica, Inc., 1978), p. 207.

[2]This phrase appears in the KJV but not in the best Greek texts (not in the RSV, NEB, NIV, and other versions based on those texts).

[3]*Pantokrator*, Wilhelm Michaelis, *Theological Dictionary to the New Testament*, ed. Gerhard Kittel, trans. and ed. Geoffrey W. Bromiley (Grand Rapids, Mich.: Wm. B. Eerdmans Publishing Company, 1965), III:915.

[4]"Ignatius to the Philadelphians," in *The Apostolic Fathers*, ed. and trans. Kirsopp Lake (Cambridge, Mass.: Harvard University Press, 1912, I:244-245. This is chapter six, verse one.

[5]*Ibid.*, p. 245.

[6]Walter Bauer, *A Greek-English Lexicon of the New Testament and Other Early Christian Literature*, ed. and trans. William F. Arndt and F. Wilbur Gingrich; 2nd ed. revised and augmented by F. Wilbur Gingrich and Frederick W. Danker from Walter Bauer's 5th ed., 1958 (Chicago and London: The University of Chicago Press, 1979), pp. 11-12.

[7]Karl H. Rengstorf, *"hepta"* (seven), in *Theological Dictionary to the New Testament*, II: 628, 632-633.

[8]Bauer, *op. cit.*, 2., p. 508; *New English Bible*, "in the very middle of the throne"; J. B. Phillips, *The New Testament in Modern English* (New York: MacMillan, 1958), "in the very center of the throne."

[9]Bauer, *op. cit.*, pp. 134-135.

Chapter 3

Has God Really Communicated With His People And To The Rest Of Humankind?

The Bible assumes two things: (1) the existence of the covenant God of the Old and New Testaments, and (2) this covenant God chose to communicate in special ways with certain people who proclaimed and transcribed these special communications. The Bible emphasizes what God said to these people of the past, and if we properly interpret this material, we can rightly apply it to our situation today.

Daniel and Revelation disclose a great deal about "how" God communicates. The individuals to whom God communicated made it very clear that their experiences were not always easy or enjoyable, but the importance of having God "talk to" and "deal with" them outweighed any personal difficulty.

In order to know whether or not God has communicated, we need to learn more about the "how" and the "why" of His communication. In the Old Testament books of the exile, the central characters are important members of kings' courts: (1) Daniel and his friends, (2) Esther and Mordecai, and (3) Nehemiah.[1] God communicated with Daniel and his friends in a Gentile setting to benefit all His exiled people living far from their homeland. But this communication affected powerful non-Jewish leaders, and their truths continue to have meaning in a world much larger than the one Daniel knew.

I. How Did Outsiders in Daniel React to God's Acts and Disclosures?

Daniel and his friends were not ordinary courtiers. Daniel re-

mained at the king's court (Dan. 2:49), but the king appointed
Shadrach, Meshach, and Abednego over the province of Babylon
(Dan. 2:49). Among the king's officers, only Daniel and his three
friends were Jews—members of God's covenant people. Their co-
workers were "outsiders" or, as Paul says, "strangers to the covenants of promise" (Eph. 2:12). Yet, these same outsiders testified
that the covenant God of Israel does communicate, and what He
had to say was significant for them, too.

A. Nebuchadnezzar
Dan. 2:46-47; 3:24-25, 26-30; 4:1-3

Nebuchadnezzar had a forty-three or forty-four year career as
king of Babylon (605 B.C. to 562-561 B.C.), and Daniel served him
for forty years. He assigned Daniel and his three friends to a three-
year course in the book learning and language(s) of the Chaldeans.
When the four of them finished their training, they were ten times
better than others in the same program (Dan. 1:3-4, 17-20). Chapter 1 gives the approximate dates for some of the events or visions
in the other chapters. Of the events or dreams in Daniel, the ones
reported in the first four chapters happened during the reign of
Nebuchadnezzar, who was an absolute monarch. He made decisions on the facts available to him and often tried to get beneath
the surface of situations. He named Daniel "Belteshazzar" after his
Babylonian god (Dan. 4:8), but Nebuchadnezzar evidenced a
growing realization that there was a Supreme Ruler over him.
Nebuchadnezzar was a strong political ruler, even after he was
banished and then restored to his throne. His reactions to the God
of Daniel are not to be taken lightly.

When Daniel first interpreted to Nebuchadnezzar the dream of
chapter 2 (about 603-600 B.C.), the king was moved by the ability
God gave Daniel (Dan. 2:46-47). Here was an official who could
tell the king both the dream and its meaning! Nebuchadnezzar declared, "Of a truth it is that your God is God of gods and Lord of
kings, and He is revealing secrets in as much as you were able to
reveal this secret." Nebuchadnezzar paid tribute to Daniel, but he
also spoke of the superiority of Daniel's God in revealing mysteries.

When God delivered Daniel's three friends from the fiery furnace, Nebuchadnezzar was watching. He had been incensed because they refused to obey his edict. While he looked through the

opening at the bottom of the furnace, he said he saw "four men loose, walking in the midst of the fire, and they are not hurt; and the appearance of the fourth is like a son of the gods" (Dan. 3:25). Immediately, he shouted to these three Hebrews who had been faithful to God: "Shadrach, Meshach, and Abednego, servants of the Most High God, Come forth, and come here!" After the men emerged unharmed from the furnace, Nebuchadnezzar talked with them: "Blessed be the God of Shadrach, Meshach, and Abednego, who has sent His angel and delivered his servants who trusted in Him, and [they] set at nought the king's command, and yielded up their bodies rather than serve and worship any god except their own God" (Dan. 3:28).

The question arises: "Who was the fourth person in the furnace?" Christians have often conjectured that this fourth one was either the angel of the Lord or the preincarnate Christ. There is no way to know for sure, but Nebuchadnezzar as an observer said, "God sent His angel" (Dan. 3:28). What was sure for Nebuchadnezzar and the three Hebrews was that God acted. Before being thrown into the furnace, the three Hebrews had told the king of their confidence in God and their commitment to Him. They knew that God could act, but they did not know if He would in this case (Dan. 3:17-18). There is no magic in this narrative; it simply has a surprising outcome. God revealed Himself through an act of deliverance.

Nebuchadnezzar then issued a proclamation (Dan. 4:1-3) that celebrated the signs and wonders that the Most High wrought: "His signs, how great and his wonders, how mighty." Through these the king became aware of God's kingdom. However, Daniel never suggested that King Nebuchadnezzar, because of the fiery furnace experience, became a convert to Judaism. Most of Daniel 4 describes a proud and independent monarch needing severe discipline by God. It is significant when this king testifies that God communicates and acts. But this acknowledgment was only intellectual assent; he did not change his ways or actions until later.

B. The Queen Mother and Belshazzar
Dan. 5:10-12, 13-16

Daniel has a striking account of the final hours of the Babylonian Empire (539-538 B.C.). During a banquet, the guests watched as a hand wrote on the wall: MENE, MENE, TEKEL, UPHARSIN

(Dan. 5:5, 25). Everyone was severely disturbed, and Belshazzar nearly fainted in fear. His alarm grew when none of his wise men could tell him what the writing meant.

In came the queen or, more likely, the queen mother (Dan. 5:10). (Since King Belshazzar's wives were already at the banquet, this woman was probably Nebuchadnezzar's widow. Nebuchadnezzar was the "father" of Belshazzar [5:11] in the sense of being his predecessor. We are uncertain of their exact relationship.) The queen told Belshazzar about Daniel and his ability to interpret dreams and riddles (Dan. 5:11-12): (1) in him was the spirit of the holy gods; (2) he had illumination; (3) he had insight; (4) he had wisdom like the wisdom of the gods; (5) he had an excellent spirit or attitude; (6) he had the power of knowing; and (7) his insight gave him the ability to interpret dreams, (8) declare the meaning of riddles, and (9) loosen knots, i.e., solve problems or difficulties. Here an outsider (a non-Jew) described how God prepared Daniel to communicate His truth.

When Daniel was brought to him, Belshazzar repeated some of the things the queen mother had said: "The spirit of the holy gods is in you." Belshazzar's intense fright when he saw the handwriting on the wall may indicate he had premonitions that his career was ending. He needed a genuine word from someone with fresh ideas, someone who did not share his own ideas. It is significant that Belshazzar, an outsider, wanted a word from God, even though that word turned out to be one of dark foreboding. In light of Daniel's message, Belshazzar's rewards did not amount to much. He promised Daniel the highest position he could offer—the third ruler in the kingdom. (Belshazzar was only the second-ranking ruler.) Very likely Daniel's message brought him recognition from Cyrus and the Medo-Persians who took over when they defeated Belshazzar and the Babylonians. Nonetheless, God had communicated with Belshazzar.

C. Darius the Mede
Dan.6:16-18, 19-24, 25-27

When Daniel was an old man of eighty-one or eighty-two, he witnessed the defeat of the Babylonian Empire by the Medo-Persian Empire. Daniel was apparently welcomed with favor into the new court, but in the turnover of power he became the victim of the court intrigue and petty jealousy common in ancient times.

Daniel customarily prayed three times a day in his own quarters. Jealous men in the new government coerced the king to forbid any such religious activities for thirty days. However, Daniel continued his lifelong practice, and as a result, he was thrown into a den of lions.

Darius had not intended that Daniel be the victim of his edict because he respected Daniel's religious beliefs and practices. Darius' comment, "May your God, whom you serve continually, deliver you!", shows how an outsider viewed God's acts and relationship with His people (Dan. 6:16-18). The next morning, Darius went to see for himself what had happened to Daniel. Daniel was not only still alive, but he also proclaimed that God had sent His angel to deliver him. Darius issued a new edict proclaiming that the God of Daniel lives forever, His kingdom shall never be destroyed, and He delivers and rescues and works signs and wonders in heaven and on earth (Dan. 6:25-27). Even though Daniel summarized this edict so it would be clear to a Jewish readership, the language indicated the impact of God's action on Darius. Darius perceived Daniel's God to be different from any other deity he knew.

However, some scholars reject the authenticity of these accounts. They say they are merely stories created to raise the status of Daniel and his friends so that the spirits of people under foreign oppression would be lifted. Many times behind such an assertion is an aversion to miracles. Throughout the Bible—from Abraham to Christ's servant John—there are long periods when there were no recorded miracles. During the time when miracles were more frequent, God gave them not to satisfy a desire for spectaculars but to do something special for His people. There seem to be four clusters of miracles in the Bible: (1) the Exodus from Egypt (the Book of Exodus); (2) the inauguration of the prophetic period with Elijah and Elisha (incidents in 1 Kings 17—2 Kings 13); (3) the Babylonian exile (Daniel); and (4) the birth, life, death, resurrection, and ascension of Jesus Christ with the birth of the church at Pentecost (the New Testament).

Of the four, Daniel is unique because we find recorded in this book the responses of outsiders to the miraculous. The authenticity of these responses is certainly supported by the rarity of this kind of thing in the Bible. The Bible condemns magic because it is considered demonic. Perhaps that is why the powerful deeds of

God are not common occurrences, but they are carefully inter-twined into the regular course of events.

II. How Did God Communicate to Daniel and How Did It Affect Him?

The contents of Daniel are so interesting that the reader may not notice exactly how God disclosed the truth to Daniel. When we take time to study how God revealed Himself, the amount of material will surprise us.

A. Expressions for Disclosing Truths
Dan. 2:19, 21-23, 28-30; 7:1-28; 8:1-4, 7, 13, 15-17, 19, 27

In Daniel 2, King Nebuchadnezzar decided to test the skill of his wise men—magicians, enchanters, sorcerers, and Chaldeans. The test was simple but almost impossible to pass. The king's wise men were to tell him the contents and the meaning of his latest dream. It wasn't that the king had forgotten the dream. Rather, he con-structed this test to convince himself that their interpretations were valid. If they were right in telling him the dream, he would be sure that the meanings they gave to it were even more correct.

When the wise men failed to recount the dream or its meaning, the king angrily ordered all his wise men to be killed, including Daniel and his three friends. When Daniel heard what was hap-pening, he asked "from the king that time be given to him and that he would declare to the king the interpretation" (literal translation from Aramaic text of Dan. 2:16). He then went home and asked his three friends to pray to the covenant God of Israel (who was called in Babylon "the God of heaven") for merciful intervention "concerning this mystery" so that they would not perish (Dan. 2:18). The rest of chapter 2 is filled with expressions showing how Daniel received truth.

Nebuchadnezzar's dream and its meaning are called "a mystery." "Then the mystery was revealed to Daniel in a vision of the night" (Dan. 2:19). These two words *reveal* and *vision* are common both in the Aramaic and Hebrew portions of Daniel. What is revealed varies from context to context. When Daniel had a vision, he was not sleeping; his mental powers were so sharp that he saw and heard things. In a vision that took place at night, Daniel learned the interpretation of Nebuchadnezzar's dream, and immediately he praised God for His wisdom and might (Dan. 2:20). Daniel's praise to God proclaims that the God who disclosed these particular truths to Daniel changes the times and seasons; He removes kings and sets up kings; He gives wisdom to the wise and knowledge to those who have understanding (Dan. 2:21). He is constantly revealing deep and hidden things (Dan. 2:22). Nothing is too profound for God; nothing is hidden from Him. He knows what is in the darkness, and the light dwells with Him (Dan. 2:22). Daniel praised God for causing him to know what he and his friends had asked of Him (Dan. 2:23). He was also thankful for the gift of wisdom and strength that prepared him for God's revelation.

When Daniel later told Nebuchadnezzar all about the dream, he stated clearly that he was God's instrument: "The God who reveals mysteries has made known to King Nebuchadnezzar what will be at the end of the days, what will be hereafter, what is to be" (Dan. 2:28-29). Daniel did not say that the picture was complete. He simply said that God had revealed important truths to Nebuchadnezzar.

Daniel 7 discusses Daniel's dream that came about fifty years after the dream of Nebuchadnezzar cited in Daniel 2. At this time God communicated to Daniel both in a dream and in visions as Daniel lay upon his bed (Dan. 7:1). Daniel wrote the dream—that is, he put down in writing the dream with its central symbols. His other visions seem to have been explanatory and supplementary to the symbols in this one dream.

Daniel 7:1 also says he related the essential content of the matter. To whom would Daniel tell his dream and visions? Earlier in his life he consulted with his three friends in exile; now near the end of his life he probably served as a leader for some fellow Jews. (In chap. 9 he prays for all his people in exile.) Daniel was close to his people as well as to his diplomatic associates.

Throughout chapter 7 we find allusions to his visions: "I was beholding in visions during the night" (7:2, 7, 13) and "I was beholding" (7:6, 9, 11 [twice]). Daniel was obviously concentrating on what he was seeing. Naturally, his next question would be: "What does all this mean?" When he asked one of the angels the meaning, the angel responded and "caused him to know the interpretation of the matter" (7:16). Perhaps a modern analogy would be a closed circuit television in which God programmed what Daniel should see, hear, and understand.

Daniel has another vision, and the language of the opening verses of chapter 8 is saturated with vision words: "...a vision appeared to me, Daniel...and I saw in the vision; and when I saw ...and I saw in the vision...I raised my eyes and saw" (8:1-3a). In this vision Daniel sees (8:4, 7, 15) and hears (8:13, 16). The verbal message came to him through Gabriel who was commanded to "make this man understand the vision" (Dan. 8:16). Note that Gabriel said to Daniel, "I am making known to you," or "I am causing you to know..." (8:19). These verses indicate how God disclosed truth to Daniel and how Daniel understood what he saw and heard. But Daniel was very honest and knew his understanding was very limited: "I was appalled by the vision and did not understand it" (8:27). Although Daniel understood parts of the vision, he did not understand it as a whole.

B. Incidents, Strange Turns of Events
Dan. 4:4-28 (esp. v. 25); 5:23-24

Most of chapter 4 is devoted to Nebuchadnezzar's strange dream and its even stranger outcome. King Nebuchadnezzar dreamed of a huge tree, visible to the end of the whole earth, whose top reached to heaven. The animals found shade under the tree; the birds dwelt in its branches; all creatures were fed from it. An angel came and ordered the tree cut down, leaving only the stump in the earth. The ones cutting down the tree were to put a band of iron and bronze around the stump. Then, suddenly the stump is treated like a person (4:15). It, or he, was to be wet with the dew of heaven; he was to have his lot with the beasts and to have the mind of a beast. Seven "times" were to pass over him. All of this was to occur so that people may know that the Most High rules the kingdom of men (4:10-18).

Called to interpret the dream, Daniel reluctantly told Nebuchadnezzar what would be happy news for the king's enemies. Nebuchadnezzar was the tree, and as the tree was cut down, "they" would drive Nebuchadnezzar from his throne. This indefinite "they" refers to neither foreign enemies nor to rivals in the palace who might plot to overthrow the king. Rather, this action was to be carried out by his friends and officials! They were to feed him grass like an ox. This warning came to Nebuchadnezzar twelve months before the onset of his disease.

R. K. Harrison believes that the illness of Nebuchadnezzar

would be diagnosed today as a pathological obsession known as boanthropy. The patient imagines that he is a cow or bull, and he eats grass. Harrison documents a case in a British mental institution during 1946 and 1947. The man's sole diet consisted of grass that he plucked and ate from the hospital's lawns. He was careful not to eat weeds, and the institution provided him with clear drinking water. He remained in good physical condition. Since many of this man's habits paralleled those attributed to Nebuchadnezzar in Daniel 4, his stable physical state might explain how Nebuchadnezzar was able to endure the rigors of being a monarch after his recovery.[2]

When Daniel interpreted the dream, he told Nebuchadnezzar that it was a communication from God: "It is a decree of the Most High which has come upon my lord the king" (Dan. 4:24). He explained that the effects will remain "till you know that the Most High rules the kingdom of men and gives it to whom he will" (Dan. 4:25). The length of the period is designated as "seven times," that is, a complete length of time to bring about what God intended. The Aramaic word for "time" means "periods involving specific conditions."[3] How long or short the period was, no one knows. If it meant seven months, the period would be very short. Some commentators have interpreted the time to be longer—even seven years—but there is no way of knowing. Seven months would surely be sufficient for Nebuchadnezzar to learn that false pride is distasteful to God. When he was restored, his whole personality changed. He found new delight in his work, but he fully recognized that God was the real ruler. God's word through Daniel in Daniel 4 was powerfully effective. The events that Daniel predicted, when they took place, underscored the fact that Daniel's words were also God's words. God communicated to Nebuchadnezzar, and this old king heard God when he heard Daniel.

With the handwriting on the wall (Dan. 5), Daniel prophetically drove home the truth to Belshazzar who had failed to honor the God controlling his very life's breath. As God's spokesman, Daniel made it abundantly clear that God had written this message: "Then from his presence the hand was set, and this writing was inscribed" (5:23-24). The mental illness of Nebuchadnezzar and the handwriting on the wall were both ways in which God communicated, and Daniel was an essential link in His communication. We may hear God communicating to us, too, through these events demonstrating that God speaks and conveys what He wants. If we are indifferent to His voice, we will suffer great loss.

C. Psychological Effects Upon Daniel When He Received Revelation Dan. 7:28; 8:17-18, 27; 10:1—11:1, esp. 10:1, 2-3, 7-9, 10-12a, 15-19

In our time we place great emphasis on how people feel: "How did you feel when your husband won the golf tournament?" "How did you feel when you successfully crossed the Atlantic in a balloon?" Rarely, however, do we find people asking: "How did Daniel, Paul, or John feel after they received revelation from God?" Daniel himself supplies an answer.

Daniel's dream and visions in chapter 7 involved four beasts, the other little horn, the Ancient of Days upon a throne of fire, the one like a son of man, the nature and power of the fourth beast, and the saints of the Most High. After all of that, Daniel said, "As for me, Daniel, my thoughts greatly alarmed me, and my color changed, but I kept the matter in my mind" (7:28). The truth that he received from God caused him such great alarm that he turned pale. He knew he was seeing some of the intense struggle between God and moral evil. The overview he received of an important segment of history perplexed him, although he glimpsed only some of the features of destiny and a fraction of the immensity of God's plan. It was still enough to make any serious thinker reel.

In Daniel 8 the prophet had a vision of a ram and a he-goat, which stand for Medo-Persia and for Greece, respectively. The great horn of the he-goat is called "the first king" (Daniel 8:21). Although Alexander the Great was first in importance, he was not the first ruler of a succession of the Greek kings. The four horns stand for the four kingdoms into which the empire of Alexander was divided after his death: (1) Macedonia, (2) Thrace, (3) Syria, and (4) Egypt. Out of one of these kingdoms a little horn was to rise, whom Daniel 8 and 11 describes as Antiochus IV Epiphanes (175-164 B.C.). This Syrian tyrant ordered the cessation of the continual burnt offering in the temple at Jerusalem, and he set up a statue of the Greek god Zeus in the Jewish temple area (Dan. 8:13; 9:27; 11:31; 12:11; 1 Maccabees 1:41-64; 2 Maccabees 6:1-11). Daniel and the first readers of his writing could not have known as we do about the acts of Antiochus IV Epiphanes and the desecration of the temple, because these events took place hundreds of years after Daniel. But today's readers can view Daniel in the light of (1) the books of 1 and 2 Maccabees and (2) the writings of the historian Josephus (A.D. 37—100) as well as (3) other Greek or Roman historians.

The vision was terrifying for Daniel, and the angel Gabriel was ordered to make him understand it. Daniel wrote, "I was frightened and fell upon my face" (Dan. 8:17). Gabriel awakened Daniel from a deep sleep, set him upon his feet, and began to explain what the vision meant (Dan. 8:18). Daniel had been in control of his rational faculties, but when it was all over, "I, Daniel was overcome and lay sick for some days; then I rose and went about the king's business; but I was appalled by the vision and did not understand it" (Dan. 8:27). This declaration shows how intense was his experience of receiving revelation from God. If we would ask Daniel how he felt after God sent these visions, he would say: "I felt exhausted, confused, and ill." No one should seek vision experiences from God. It took a man as strong in faith as Daniel to stand the shock of the experience.

One might expect that Daniel would eventually become accustomed to such experiences, but he never did. The last visions reported in Daniel cover chapters 10—12 and came when Daniel was approximately eighty-four years old.

Chapter 10 graphically describes Daniel's last vision experience. The first verse summarizes the content of the vision that he saw and heard, and the rest of the chapter demonstrates that this experience of revelation was a rather lengthy process. It began during a three-week period of mourning, during which Daniel ate no meat, wine, or delicacies; and he did not anoint his skin with oil (Dan. 10:2-3). The text provides no clue as to the reason for his mourning.

Sometime during those three weeks, Daniel had a vision that he was standing on the banks of the Tigris River. He saw either a brilliant angel or a preincarnate appearance of Jesus Christ (Dan. 10:4-6). The men with him began to tremble violently, and they fled to hide (Dan. 10:7). Therefore, Daniel was alone when he saw this great vision (Dan. 10:8). The effects of this vision were even more profound than those of his previous ones: (1) he had no strength left; (2) he was weak and exhausted; and (3) he fell with his face to the ground into a deep sleep when he heard the words of the messenger (Dan. 10:9). Only after total emotional exhaustion did relief come to him.

Then Daniel tells how he came out of this exhaustion and received God's communication. A hand touched him and set him trembling on his hands and knees (Dan. 10:10). The supernatural being encouraged Daniel and asked him to pay careful attention to the words that he would speak: "Fear not, Daniel" (Dan. 10:12). The message praised Daniel for his humility and his desire to understand. The vision took the form of what we would call a lecture given by the angel, and it referred to Daniel's people in the end of the days, that is, in times when God would act for His people in a decisive manner (Dan. 10:12-14).

Even with this encouragement, Daniel turned his face to the ground and could not say a word (Dan. 10:15). When "one in the likeness of the sons of men" touched Daniel's lips, Daniel was able to relate his predicament: because of the vision, pains had come upon him, and he had no strength (Dan. 10:16). How could the Lord's servant talk with him since Daniel had neither strength nor breath (Dan. 10:17)? Then the one having the appearance of a man again touched Daniel and strengthened him (Dan. 10:18) and spoke further words of encouragement: "Fear not...peace be to you...be strong and of good courage" (Dan. 10:19). Finally, Daniel was able to say, "Let my lord speak because you have restored me to strength" (Dan. 10:19).

Daniel's testimony was that of a veteran, but he never became accustomed to receiving direct communication from God. He could only be strengthened by it.

Some interpreters disregard these materials explaining the psychological effects from receiving revelation as apocalyptic literary imagery used to heighten the message's importance. They imply that the effects Daniel described are no more real than the sun being turned into darkness or the moon into blood. Perhaps both are real.

The language about physical changes in the sun and moon point to actual physical upheavals in the balance of nature even though we do not know exactly what they will be. Daniel's psychological condition following the direct revelation brought on real physical symptoms, real pain, real exhaustion although we cannot render an exact psychosomatic analysis of what happened. When the

Maker of a ten billion, eight hundred million light-year-universe (the size of the universe at the three-quarters mark of the twentieth century) communicates in a direct way, there must be side effects. It would be very strange if there were no such reactions! The Book of Daniel shows the reality of not only the visions but also their effect upon Daniel.

III. How Did God Communicate in Revelation and How Did It Affect John?

Revelation and Daniel, as we have said, belong to apocalyptic literature, which involves many symbols, visions, and spectacular dramatic productions. Since both John and Daniel had the experiences accompanying apocalyptic visions, we find many similarities between the two books.

A. Expressions for Disclosing Truths
Rev. 1:1-2, 9-12, 17, 19-20; 4:1-2; 22:6, 8-9

Four frequently used expressions in the Book of Revelation show how John came to know God's truth. The first is the Greek word *deiknumi*, meaning "to show" or "to point out" (1:1; 4:1; 17:1; 21:9-10). In each context there is a sense of urgency, implying there is something important to understand. What John has been shown in a vision, he uses to further understand the meaning.

The second expression is the phrase "in the Spirit" (*enoipneumati*) or "in spirit" (*en pneumati*; 1:10; 4:2; 17:3; 21:10). In each context John changed his normal way of functioning. Both by God's Spirit and in his own spirit, John was freed from certain limitations of bodily existence. He saw new things and came into a new realm through the power of "the Spirit."

The third term (*horaō*) means "to see." It appears about fifty times, including 1:1-2, 12, 17, 19-20; 4:1; 5:1-2, 6, 11; 7:1-2, 9; 8:2, 13; 9:1, 17; 10:1, 5; 13:1-2, 11; 14:1, 6, 14; 15:1-2, 5; 16:13; 17:3, 6, 8, 12, 15-16, 18; 18:1; 19:11, 17, 19; 20:1, 4, 11-12; 22:1-2, 22. In each instance John tells about some specific thing, person, or place that he sees, and the reader begins "to see" the vision. What is happening here is that our imagination has specific content for what we picture. *Imagination* must not be confused with *imaginary*. Something imaginary means that it exists only in our imagination; for example, hands change to wings and we fly. However, our imagination is a distinctive feature of our mind that has the power not only to create things that do not exist but also, more frequently, to call up a mental picture of what really exists in the world of reality. John paints pictures with words. We "see" a throne; the one on the throne has a scroll in His right hand; we "see" Christ as the only one who is worthy to take the scroll, break its seals, and open it. Christ goes up and does the very thing that He is worthy to do (Rev. 5:1—6:17; 8:1). John's vision of the throne dealt with a reality that we can "see." The more we "look" at it and think about it the more the picture and the reality grow within us. This is true of every vision to which we give careful attention.

The fourth expression is closely associated with the third because John not only "saw" things; he also "heard" (akouō) things. We find the verb "to hear" in these contexts: 1:10; 4:1; 5:11, 13; 6:1, 3, 5-7; 7:4; 8:13; 9:13, 16; 10:4, 8; 12:10; 14:2, 13; 16:1, 5, 7; 18:4; 19:1, 6; 21:3; 22:8. John hears a voice, the living creatures, certain facts, angels, sounds of music, and a great throng.

All of John's senses were alert when God communicated with him (Rev. 1:9-20). God gave the revelation to Christ to show to John. Then Jesus Christ set the revelation in motion by sending it through His angel to His servant (literally, "slave") John, who in turn testified to God's message and Christ's witness to humankind. John's testimony involved "as many things as he saw" (1:2).

The setting for John's visions was the island of Patmos in the Aegean Sea just off the coast of present-day Turkey. With other Christians John was a "fellow-sharer in the tribulation and kingdom [reign] and endurance in Jesus" (Rev. 1:9). The tribulation and endurance were because of the message from God and the testimony that Jesus brought to him. John tells us that on one eventful Lord's Day (Sunday), by the Spirit and in his own spirit, he received a vision from God that would be followed by many more. The first vision was of the glorified Christ. John both heard and saw: "I heard behind me a great voice as a trumpet saying, 'What you see, write in a scroll and send it to the seven churches'" (Rev. 1:10-11). John turned to see the voice (the person speaking to him) but instead saw seven golden lampstands (Rev. 1:12).

John relates his reactions to this first vision: "When I saw him, I fell at his feet as though dead" (Rev. 1:17). Christ put his right hand upon John and spoke: "Write the things you saw, both the things that are and the things that are about to be" (Rev. 1:19). Some of what John saw in the visions was already past, other things were in the present, and more were about the future. The visions were complicated by this moving back and forth in time—past, present, future; or future, present, and past. The language and imagery were usually drawn from the past and present, but the content may concern the unknown future.

After the vision of the glorified Christ, John received from Christ a message for each of seven churches in Asia Minor. In each message Christ analyzes the conditions of the specific church. The commendations, the criticisms and warnings, the promises and exhortations should be read with the picture of Christ in Revelation 1 clearly in mind. The glorified Christ is speaking to His people in these particular churches and, by application, to all other groups of Christians.

Revelation 4:1-2 serves as a transition; John explains that the powerful voice (being) who spoke to him earlier (Rev. 1:10, 12) continued to speak and to lead him to another vision. John saw an open door in heaven, and the first voice, like a powerful trumpet, spoke to him again. He commanded John to come hither (into the heavenly realm) where John would see things that must take place in the near future. John moved into the heavenly realm by being "in spirit," or "in the Spirit." Note how God is communicating with John. John is taken out of his oppressive setting on the island of Patmos, and he sees marvelous visions (chaps. 1—5) that are vital for him, the seven churches, and all other Christians of his time. This was not escapist literature to help early Christians forget their miserable surroundings. For the first readers, as for us, the message of Revelation is to enable God's people to live more fully and faithfully for Him. The visions of John confirm this message. John first saw the throne, the creatures surrounding this throne, and the Lamb who was worthy to take the scroll from the hand of the one who sat upon the throne (chaps. 4—5). If John's first vision was spectacular, the second was even more so. More visions would follow to encourage and give hope to the saints—central visions, explanatory visions, and one final climactic vision of a "new heaven and new earth" (Rev. 21:1—22:5).

How did all of this affect John? Being a messenger of God had a strong, positive effect, but he was so overwhelmed by what he "saw," "heard," and experienced that twice he momentarily forgot that he had an angelic guide (Rev. 19:10a; 22:8-9). John described his conduct this way: "And I am John, the one hearing and seeing these things. But he says to me: 'Take care! Don't do that! I am your fellow servant and one of your brothers, the prophets, and one of those who keeps [observes or practices] the words of this book [scroll]. Worship God'" (Rev. 22:8-9). Worship of God was not optional; worship of Him was central. John soon discovered that his brief worship of his angelic guide was wrong. Yet it was not nearly as bad as our temptation to entirely lose sight of God while we debate furiously about some small detail upon which we sincerely differ.

B. Renewal of John's Call
Rev. 10:1-11

This chapter is primarily an account of an explanatory vision. In John's vision a mighty angel announces that the seventh angel and the seventh trumpet (see Rev. 11:15-19) signal the completion of God's plan that He announced as good tidings to the prophets. God will destroy evil and bring harmony to His world (Rev. 10:1-7). The mighty angel also had a little scroll open in his hand, which was a special message for John from God (Rev. 10:8-11).

The way God communicated to John is significant. God told him: "You are not finished with your work as a prophet; you are to prophesy again to [or about] many peoples and nations and languages and kings" (Rev. 10:11). God renewed John's call as a prophet, but in the process He did much more.

God asked John, through the voice from heaven, to take the little scroll from the angel. John obeyed. The angel then told John, "Take it and eat; it will be bitter to your stomach, but sweet as honey in your mouth" (Rev. 10:9). John did as the angel ordered, and the results were exactly as predicted. After that, John is told to whom and about what he is to prophesy (Rev. 10:11). The account does not explain the symbolic action of his eating the scroll, but it is obviously part of God's communication to him. Although we cannot be dogmatic here, the little scroll probably stands for John's part in God's plan. God's message will become a part of him, and he will become an effective prophet. The sweet taste depicts his joy in proclaiming God's message; the bitterness in his stomach represents his inner feelings when he sees people turn away from the message. A prophet not only dispenses informa-

89

tion; he is also a part of the people to whom he brings God's message. He suffers or rejoices in their response.

Like Daniel, John knew that divine revelation affects the person who receives it. This remains true for us today. Although God does not impart new revelation to be added to the New Testament canon, what He has already given us—through His chosen servants who did produce the New Testament—can be sweet or bitter depending on *our* response. The same concept applies to the Old Testament. Although we carry God's message to others, we cannot compel them to take the right road. As we see them choose to obey or disobey God, we experience the sweetness or bitterness of the message and the results of their response.

C. Warnings About Altering the Written Form of the Message
Rev. 22:18-19

We have seen that God really communicated with His servants Daniel and John, and they recorded their visions and revelations so that today we can read their books for ourselves. However, in the years immediately after John wrote Revelation, early Christians had to hear it read to them. The ones who could read and write might carefully pass around the scroll. Some others would painstakingly copy it by hand for others to read and discuss. John warns that in this process nothing should be added, omitted, or changed in what he had written: "If anyone adds to these things, God will add to him the plagues that have been written in this book [scroll]; if anyone takes any things away from the words [those written in this scroll]; if anyone takes any things away from the words of the book of this prophecy, God will cut off his share from the tree of life and from the holy city" (Rev. 22:18-19).

Because of this warning, we can see the authority of the contents of Revelation. Only by practicing what is written in it (Rev. 1:3; 22:7) can we really demonstrate that the Book of Revelation is authoritative for us and will bring the promised blessing to its readers.

However, more interpretive schemes have been spun around the books of Daniel and Revelation than around any other biblical books. Most have been sincere attempts to understand the books. Rarely has anyone tried to subtract, but many interpreters, seemingly oblivious to the warning above, have piled addition on addition for a seemingly plausible reason: they believe other teachings of the Old and New Testaments should be fitted into these books.

Here the interpreter must work with great care. He must be certain that what he thinks is in Revelation is also taught elsewhere in the Bible. He must distinguish between God's highest ideals, norms, or standards and the regulations that God often gave for people where they were in time, maturity, and history.

For example, the Old Testament often speaks about the sacrifice of lambs. Should these passages about Old Testament Jewish sacrifices determine the meaning of "the lamb standing as if it were slain" (Rev. 5:6)? Of course not. The Old Testament sacrifices were only shadows of Christ's final sacrifice. The highest idea, or norm, of atonement is the death of the Messiah. We must determine what "the lamb standing as if it were slain" means in Revelation. The context and our understanding of the New Testament indicate that it refers to Christ—not to an Old Testament sacrifice.

Yet there are interpreters who want to make the Book of Revelation a manual for some revised form of Judaism rather than a handbook for Christians under pressure from hostile world powers. John's readers lived on this side of Calvary. They knew that the book was not some concealed form of Judaism. They knew the truth that the Book of Hebrews clearly teaches. Christ was the total fulfillment of the Old Testament system of sacrifices. This knowledge was and is basic to becoming a Christian. The Book of Revelation is a Christian book from the first verse to the last.

Interpretation of the Book of Revelation must fit the book itself. It must not force upon itself something from outside it.

IV. How Did the Servants of God Communicate His Message?

The books of Daniel and Revelation are both a prophecy and an apocalypse (a book rich in symbols that disclose truth through many figures of speech). In these books we learn not only how God communicated to the men, Daniel and John, but also how these men communicated the divine truths to others.

A. Foretelling (Prediction)
Dan. 9:1-2

There are two aspects to prophecy in the Bible. The most important is that God's servant calls people to a holy life. The prophet urges people to leave their idolatry and self-centeredness and focus their lives on the Being of God. The second aspect involves how people respond. If people obey God, the prophet promises blessing. If people turn away from God, he announces judgment, both in this life and beyond.

This second part of prophecy is also called prediction, or foretelling. Daniel mentions this kind of prophecy in Dan. 9:1-2. In the first year of Cyrus the Great (Darius is either another name of Cyrus or one of his generals), Daniel was reading some words of Jeremiah the prophet:

Therefore says the Lord of hosts: Because you have not obeyed my words, behold I will send for all the tribes of the north, my servant, and I will bring them against this land and its inhabitants, and against all these nations round about; I will utterly destroy them, and make them a horror, a hissing, and an everlasting approach. Moreover, I will banish from them the voice of mirth and the voice of gladness, the voice of the bridegroom and the voice of the bride, the grinding of the millstones and the light of the lamp. This whole land shall become a ruin and a waste, and these nations shall serve the king of Babylon seventy years. Then after seventy years are completed, I will punish the king of Babylon and that nation, the land of the Chaldeans, for their iniquity, says the Lord, making the land an everlasting waste (Jer. 25:8-12).

For thus says the Lord: When seventy years are completed for Babylon, I will visit you, and I will fulfill to you my promise and bring you back to this place (Jer. 29:10).

Daniel recognized that these words had foretold that God would send His people into captivity under Nebuchadnezzar because of their disobedience (Jer. 25:8). There would be no more joy in the land—no sounds of the millstone or the pleasant glow of lighted lamps (Jer. 25:10). The judgment would last for seventy years.

Daniel prayed (Dan. 9:3-19) because he realized that the seventy years that God had allotted for judgment would soon be over. His prayer includes confession and a call to repentance. This case illustrates how the foretelling aspect of Jeremiah's prophecy prepared the way for the forthtelling aspect of Daniel's prophecy.

B. Forthtelling (Prophetic Preaching or Praying: Man/God Relationship)

The forthtelling aspect of prophecy concerns people and their relationship to God. Are their lives focused on God, or are they forgetting God as they pursue other things? In prophetic preaching or praying, the prophet expresses his concern. Sometimes he instructs; other times he condemns, pleads, encourages, or commands. As God's spokesman, he can say with authority, "Thus saith the Lord." In praying, he is also a spokesman for God and represents the people to God. He can express what the people feel in their plight and how they should feel.

1. Prayer as confession. Dan. 9:3-23

Through Daniel's prayer, we see him as a prophet praying for his people. (The overall content of this prayer will be discussed later.) Here we are concerned with the opening part of the prayer in which Daniel functions in a priestly role: he is representing his people to God. A priest usually carried out this role through offerings intended to do or say specific things to God. Ezekiel was both a prophet and a priest, but Daniel was only a prophet—and a part-time one at that, since his main calling was as a statesman. As a prophet, he represented God to people and people to God, not through offerings in the temple, but in other areas of Israel's life. Daniel had been a man of prayer all his life (Dan. 6:10), but in this instance he prayed with the burden of his people weighing down upon him. He was concerned for individuals, families, and the nation.

He sought God by prayer and supplications with fasting, sackcloth, and ashes: "I prayed to the Lord my God and made confession" (Dan. 9:3-4). He addressed God as the great God who inspires reverence and keeps covenant and steadfast love with those who love Him and keep His commandments. His next dramatic words are, "We have sinned and done wrong and acted wickedly and rebelled" (Dan. 9:5). Forthtelling usually involves God's speaking through the prophet to His people, urging them to turn back to Him. But here the prophet Daniel speaks for the people: "We have sinned." This is what God wanted to hear. The prophet spoke, and God listened.

2. Prophetic preaching to an audience of one.
Dan. 5:17-28

Chapter 5 of Daniel describes a banquet where a thousand of Belshazzar's lords, wives, and concubines drank wine and feasted, using the gold and silver vessels that Nebuchadnezzar had taken from the temple in Jerusalem. In the midst of the banquet the famous handwriting appeared on the wall: MENE, MENE, TEKEL, UPHARSIN. When none of the king's wise men could read it, Daniel was called. Before Daniel told Belshazzar the meaning, Daniel did some prophetic forthtelling (preaching). We do not know whether the guests fled when the handwriting appeared, or if some of them were still in the banquet hall when Daniel spoke. Although others may have been listening in on what Daniel said, the prophetic preaching (forthtelling) was really for Belshazzar alone.

Daniel reviewed for Belshazzar what had happened to his predecessor, Nebuchadnezzar. He said the Most High God gave to Nebuchadnezzar all his greatness, power, and influence. However, when he became proud, the Most High God judged him. He had to live among the beasts and eat grass like an ox. He endured this tragic experience "until he knew that the Most High God rules the kingdom of men, and sets over it whom he will" (Dan. 5:21).

Then, turning to Belshazzar, Daniel offered a powerful prophetic analysis of him: "You...have not humbled your heart, though you knew all this" (Dan. 5:22). Belshazzar showed the same pride that had brought Nebuchadnezzar's downfall. Daniel revealed to him that his indifference to God was evident on the very evening when the handwriting appeared on the wall. He had used the vessels of God's temple in Jerusalem to celebrate the gods of silver, gold, bronze, iron, wood, and stone—gods that could not see, hear, or know.

Daniel concluded his forthtelling: "But the God in whose hand is your breath, and whose are all your ways, you have not honored" (Dan. 5:23). The Aramaic word *hadar* means "to honor or glorify." It is an intensive form (*hadareth*), implying that true giving of honor, glory, or praise involves response deep within the giver. Belshazzar had made no such response.

After Daniel delivered his prophetic word, he told briefly the meaning of the writing: MENE—God has numbered the days of your kingdom and He has finished it (the kingdom); TEKEL—you have been weighed in the scales and found lacking (wanting, deficient); PERES—your kingdom has been broken in two and given to the Medes and Persians (Dan. 5:26-28).

That was all. There was silence. A dramatic prophecy came to a close, and so did an empire.

C. *Foretelling and Forthtelling Together*
Rev. 1:19; 2-3; 22:6-22

In Rev. 1:19, Christ commands John to write what he saw, both what is and what is to take place later, which John carried out in the messages to the seven churches (Rev. 2—3). The format of these letters involved (1) a greeting to the messenger of each church, (2) a title describing Christ, (3) a commendation, (4) a criticism, (5) a warning of what would happen if there was no repentance, (6) a promise to the individual who overcomes, and (7) an exhortation to hear what the Spirit says to the churches.

Forthtelling and foretelling are inextricably woven together in this format. The descriptions of Christ, the commendations, and the criticisms are all part of forthtelling. Foretelling, on the other hand, contains the warnings of what will happen if there is no repentance, the promises to the overcomers, and the exhortations to hear what the Spirit says to the churches. Some prophetic writings are characterized by more forthtelling than foretelling; in others, the balance is reversed; in still others we have only one or the other. Prophecy is a "thus saith the Lord" that calls people to learn about God, to obey Him, to know that He announces judgment and blessing, and to have faith in His plan to abolish evil and set up everlasting righteousness. This remarkable balance between present and future, between who God is and what He will do, makes Daniel and Revelation profoundly relevant books.

The last chapter of Revelation shows the power of prophecy as both forthtelling and foretelling. As part of foretelling, God shows His servants things that must soon take place (Rev. 22:6). The next verse states that Christ is coming soon and there is blessing for the one who keeps (practices) the contents of the Book of Revelation (22:7); this verse includes both foretelling and forthtelling. Then the angel stops John's attempt to worship his angelic guide (Rev. 22:8-9), another case of forthtelling. The angel tells John not to seal up the words of this book because "the time is near." The one involved with evil is capable of more evil, and the one involved with righteousness can still act in righteousness. These verses (Rev. 22:10-11) include some foretelling, but mostly forthtelling.

Other verses in chapter 22 include both forthtelling and foretelling. Christ speaks for Himself in Rev. 22:12-13: "Behold I am coming soon, bringing my recompense to repay everyone for what he has done. I am the Alpha and the Omega, the First and the Last, the Beginning and the End." John writes of a blessing for Christians who apply the atonement to their own lives and thus have the right to the tree of life, to enter the city by its gates (22:14-15). Outside this city are the ones whose actions show they were living and acting a lie by living for themselves. Jesus speaks again by declaring He has sent His messenger to help the churches and He, as an ancestral member of the family of David, is the morning star of a new epoch for all people (22:16).

The same pattern is repeated in the next verse (22:17). The Spirit, the Bride (the body of Christians), and the one who hears all invite sinners to come and take the Water of Life as a gift (without payment). John warns that those who might add to or subtract from what is written in his book will receive severe judgment (foretelling). Christ's closing message to John is that He is coming soon, and John responds with "Amen, come, Lord Jesus." John ends the book with a prayer that grace will be with all Christians. Both elements of prophecy are present in the book's conclusion as well as in its opening.

D. Two Prophets Proclaim God's Truth During the Time of the Final Form of Antichrist
Rev. 11:3-13a

Three main visions occur between Revelation 6:1 and 19:10; and they involve the seven seals, the seven trumpets, and the seven bowls of wrath (also called the seven last plagues). The other visions in this section are explanatory. In one, God addresses all people through John's vision of the two prophets.

The two prophets are given a huge task to accomplish in 1260 days (forty-two months, or three and a half years), which symbolize a short period of time rather than an exact time measurement (see Rev. 7). The two prophets somewhat parallel Elijah and Moses (2 Kings 1:10-12; 1 Kings 17:1; Exod. 7:14-24; 9:24)—they have power to bring down fire, withhold rain, and turn waters into blood (Rev. 11:5-6).

The second and third trumpets (Rev. 8:8-11), and the second and third bowls of wrath (Rev. 16:3-7), seem to indicate that these two prophets are God's representatives. God uses them to disturb the balance of nature and thus judge people who insist on their own way.

When the two prophets finish their ministry (surely one of

forthtelling), the beast kills them. The beast is the final form of Antichrist, typifying many earlier forms that have been equally desperate to destroy God's servants.

The people on earth refuse to bury the two dead prophets. Instead they "make merry and exchange presents" in their delight to be rid of the men who had tormented them with messages and judgments (Rev. 11:10). These two prophets are the climax in a line of noble prophets who, like the Savior, endured hostility from the ones they sought to help.

However, the rejoicing quickly ends for the people hostile to the gospel. After three and a half days, God vindicates the two prophets by raising them from death. As their enemies watch, they ascend to heaven in a cloud, which makes clear God's sovereign control. Then a great earthquake kills 7,000 people. The survivors are terrified and give praise (glory) to God (Rev. 11:13). Apparently the prophetic message brought conversion to many people.

Although this passage is about the future (foretelling), the effects are those of forthtelling (prophetic preaching)—people turn to God. God communicates to His servants who in turn communicate to the people. The result is either rejection of the prophetic message or repentance by the people.

Summary

Through the books of Daniel and Revelation, readers might think that God's revelations to Daniel and John were everyday experiences, but that is not so. Long periods of divine silence separated the times of powerful deeds or miracles.

Direct revelation from God has traumatic psychological effects on its recipients. God is powerful. As sinners, we do not want to get close to Him. Even as redeemed sinners, we still have dross to be burned out, and we are hardly in a condition to receive much direct revelation. Both divine speech and divine silence make us aware that we must preserve the genuine communication we have from God, which is sufficient to guide us through our earthly pilgrimages.

The Old and New Testaments contain materials preserved by God's people. We find history, poetry, and proverbs; we discover people burdened by despair and uplifted by joy. But most important we find God speaking both directly and indirectly to His people.

In a sense, all revelation is indirect for us today because it came to others in earlier times. Yet when we respond to it, it is as effective as direct revelation, because God's Spirit is present. When we do not grieve or quench that Spirit, the powerful revelatory word comes to us in its transforming power and wonder.

God communicated both to His own covenant people (Israel) and to "outsiders" (Gentiles). However, His communication to the outsiders usually came through prophets among His own people. Through Daniel, God spoke to Nebuchadnezzar, Belshazzar, and Darius the Mede, each of whom acknowledged that "the Most High God" was speaking through Daniel.

A. How Did God Communicate to Daniel and John?

Both Daniel and John received visions from God. Usually these were not like the dreams of a sleeping person whose conscious mental powers are turned off. Rather, in these visions, the mental powers of Daniel and John were sharpened, and the prophets were able to respond to them. (God's communication to Daniel about Nebuchadnezzar, however, did come in a dream and a vision as "Daniel lay upon his bed" [Dan. 7:1]. Daniel asked the angel who appeared in the dream-vision what it meant, and the angel "caused him to know the interpretations of the matter" [Dan. 7:16].) The visions of John in Revelation were both "seen" and "heard." The revelation or communication was said to come from God to Christ through an angel to John, who was exiled on the island of Patmos.

B. What Effects Did God's Communications Have on Daniel and John?

Daniel writes about the traumatic effects the visions and dreams had upon him: "My thoughts greatly alarmed me, and my color changed" (Dan. 7:28). After Daniel had the vision recorded in Daniel 8, he wrote, "I was frightened and fell upon my face" (8:17). He was physically ill for several days and had to go to bed until he could recover. Daniel's last recorded vision came when he was about eighty-four years old; during a three-week period of mourning he ate no meat, wine, or delicacies. He saw a brilliant angel or messenger of God. His strength left him, and he fell with his face to the ground into a deep sleep (in other words, he experienced total emotional exhaustion). When the angel or messenger of God touched him, he was unable to speak until the angel touched his lips and spoke words of strength and encouragement (Dan. 10:16-19).

When John received his visions from God, the effects were somewhat similar. "When I saw him [the glorified Christ], I fell at his feet as though dead" (Rev. 1:17). Then Christ put his right hand on John and told him to write the things he saw. At one point in John's vision, he was so overwhelmed by what he saw and heard that he fell down to worship before the feet of the messenger who was showing him these things (Rev. 22:8-9). The messenger rebuked him and told him that only God was to be worshiped.

C. How Did God's Servants Communicate the Messages They Received from God?

Prophecy involved two important aspects. One is foretelling (prediction), and the other is forthtelling (prophetic preaching or praying). Although foretelling no doubt received greater attention at the time it occurred (as well as at the present time), it was not the major aspect of God's prophetic communication because it usually indicated God's judgment on a person or a nation for their disregard of Him and His commandments.

The forthtelling aspect of prophecy focuses on people and their relationship to God. As a part of forthtelling, Daniel prayed a prayer of confession on behalf of his people (Dan. 9:3-23). He also proclaimed God's judgment—sometimes to an audience of one, as he did with Belshazzar.

Revelation embodies a persistent mixture of forthtelling and foretelling, as in the letters to the seven churches. Revelation 22 points to what must soon take place and promises blessings for the ones who keep the contents of the book. Much of the rest of the book shows what will happen (foretelling) to persons who refuse to follow God's commands (forthtelling).

Divine revelations such as the ones John and Daniel received were not everyday experiences. There were also long periods of divine silence. However, when we respond to the revelations that came to others in earlier times, God's Spirit can use them with transforming power in our lives.

Notes for Chapter 3

[1]W. Lee Humphreys, "A Life-Style for Diaspora: A Study of the Tales of Esther and Daniel," *Journal of Biblical Literature* XCII, no. 2 (June 1973), pp. 211-223.

[2]R. K. Harrison, *Introduction to the Old Testament*, pp. 1115-1117.

[3] Brown, Driver, and Briggs, *A Hebrew and English Lexicon of the Old Testament*. (Oxford: Clarendon Press, 1959), p. 1105.

Chapter 4

Why Does Moral Evil Deceive And Destroy?

Today people hesitate to label any conduct as evil or sinful; they prefer instead to think of right and wrong in relative terms. We say, "What's okay for me may be wrong for you," or "People from different backgrounds see things differently." The whole concept of sin and moral evil is uncomfortable to us.

But sometimes things happen among our friends or in society at large that smash our make-believe world. We may be confronted by Auschwitz or a cold-blooded dictator who orders the killing of anyone who opposes him. We see friends destroyed by alcohol or drugs, families ripped apart by cruelty or selfishness. Sin cuts an appalling swath, leaving behind a hideous toll. Then the full effects of moral evil turn into sober, cold facts. Why are innocent people so often victims?

The books of Daniel and Revelation say much about moral evil. These books portray individuals and groups ignoring God and what He has revealed that is good and worthwhile. They set up their own gods and turn to acts harmful to themselves and many others. The true nature of moral evil is revealed through symbols and figurative language in Daniel and Revelation to show that moral evil is no mirage. Moral evil is a reality to be confronted and overcome through the power of God.

I. Moral Evil Joins Hands with Worldly Wisdom
Dan. 1:20; 2:1-13; 5:5-9, 13-16; 6:4-13, 24

In Daniel 2:12, King Nebuchadnezzar became angry when his

wise men could not tell him his dream and its interpretation. Whom did Nebuchadnezzar consider to be wise men? Magicians and enchanters are mentioned (Dan. 1:20), along with sorcerers and Chaldeans (Dan. 2:2). In Daniel the term *wise men* referred to these advisors to the king.

Daniel and his friends were trained in all the book learning and wisdom of the Chaldeans. Such learning is not attacked in the Old Testament in the same way that sorcery is attacked. Daniel and his friends were "ten times better" in terms of wisdom and understanding than the Babylonian magicians and enchanters (Dan. 1:20), and Nebuchadnezzar addressed Daniel as the chief of the magicians (4:9).

What was the difference between the wisdom of the believing Hebrews and the worldly wisdom of the followers of pagan religions? Wisdom is "worldly" when it is used to deny God and to exalt people to places that belong only to Him. In Daniel, the wise men could not interpret dreams or read the handwriting on the wall. But God revealed His truths to Daniel, a truly wise and learned man.

After Daniel revealed the king's dream and its interpretation, Daniel's three friends were appointed over the affairs of the province of Babylon (Dan. 2:49), which indicates that individuals receiving such political appointments were also considered to be "wise men" although they were not technically palace advisors. Daniel and his friends needed a very practical wisdom.

In the Babylonian Empire under Nebuchadnezzar and Belshazzar, and later in the Medo-Persian Empire under Cyrus (another name for Darius), subordinate rulers were extremely competitive. Darius' men (who sought to destroy Daniel because he faithfully worshiped his God three times a day) had the following titles: president, satrap, prefect, counselor, and governor (Dan. 6:6-7). Because they were jealous of Daniel, the elder statesman, they persuaded the king to sign an edict stating that no one should petition or ask anything of any god or man except the king for thirty days. They were certain that Daniel would continue to worship his God, thus disobeying the king's unchangeable law, and would have to be thrown into a den of lions as the law specified.

Although these men were wise and successful, they were not wise enough to resist evil. Instead, they devised a plot to destroy a truly wise man who, through his faith, escaped their plot. Intelligence alone is no defense against evil. History has shown repeatedly that intelligence can be used for either good or evil causes.

II. Moral Evil Destroys by Emphasizing Self

The strategy of evil is quite simple: break down a person's or group's loyalty to God, distract people from giving God the attention He deserves, and encourage them to be totally occupied with themselves. When life revolves around self or one's own group, God is quietly excluded.

A. Pride Usually Emphasizes Self
Dan. 4:22-26, 28-30, 37

Not all boasting, glorying, and pride is evil, but these things must be in God, not in ourselves (Jer. 9:23-24; 1 Cor. 1:31; 2 Cor. 10:17). We are to glory in the cross of Christ (Gal. 6:14) because through Christ's death we gain victory over sin and the worldliness of a life that excludes God and what He has willed. As Christians we can be proud of one another—of the assistance, the service, and the love that help us to share the day of Christ's triumph (2 Cor. 1:14). Usually the Bible refers to pride in a negative sense; the proud person gives no credit to God or anyone else for his achievements, and he delights in his independence.

In Nebuchadnezzar's dream, recorded in Daniel 4, a tree grew and became great. The tree stood for Nebuchadnezzar, who had become great and strong, with a far-reaching influence. In the dream, a "holy one" commanded that the tree be cut down, leaving only its stump, all of which symbolized the sudden change that would come to Nebuchadnezzar. He would be driven from people and would live like the beasts. Seven times (or periods) would pass over the king "until he knew that the Most High rules the kingdom of men, and gives it to whom he will" (Dan. 4:25). But the stump also bespoke Nebuchadnezzar's eventual status. He would return to his kingdom "when he knew that heaven rules" (Dan. 4:26).

Daniel urged Nebuchadnezzar to repent by "breaking off your sins by practicing righteousness" or "breaking off your iniquities by showing mercy to the oppressed" (Dan. 4:27). Although Nebuchadnezzar heard Daniel's warnings, he did not heed them. He continued his usual patterns. A proud person like Nebuchadnezzar finds it hard to be concerned for others unless his own importance is furthered.

By both past and present worldly standards, Nebuchadnezzar was a success with many achievements to his credit, but was a victim of his own self-sufficiency. He gave no thanks to God or anyone else. As a result, the center of his life collapsed, and he became subhuman.

About a year after his famous dream, Nebuchadnezzar reflected on his own importance: "Is not this great Babylon, which I have built by my mighty power as a royal residence and for the glory of my majesty?" (Dan. 4:30). Then God spoke: "The kingdom has departed from you..." (Dan. 4:31). Nebuchadnezzar was to be separated from people until he "learned that the Most High rules the kingdom of men and gives it to whom he will" (Dan. 4:32). Like many proud people, Nebuchadnezzar forgot that God has the last word. At the end of a period of separation, God restored Nebuchadnezzar, who then "blessed...praised...honored" the Most High God. A new conviction became part of his outlook, for he had learned that "those who walk in pride, He [God] is able to abase" (Dan. 4:37).

B. Jealous People Are Afraid of Losing Prominence
Dan. 3:8-12; 6:1-9, 12-13

When we live for ourselves, we fiercely resist any threat to our importance. The story of the three Hebrews being thrown into the fiery furnace is an example of the extremes to which jealous people may go. Shadrach, Meshach, and Abednego had been appointed over the affairs of the province of Babylon. Shortly thereafter, Nebuchadnezzar set up a golden image in the plain of Dura and ordered everyone to worship the image. Some of the Chaldeans knew this observance would be contrary to the Jews' religious convictions, and they "maliciously accused the Jews" for not complying (Dan. 3:8). A literal translation is, "They ate the pieces of the Jews."

In order to put these three Jews in the worst possible light, the Chaldeans told Nebuchadnezzar that (1) "they pay no heed to you," (2) "they do not serve your god," and (3) "they do not worship the image which you set up" (Dan. 3:12). The Chaldean accusers achieved their purpose, and Nebuchadnezzar exploded in rage. Not bothering to hear the Jews' side of the story, he announced to them: "Comply or be cast into a fiery furnace." The three men were later delivered, showing that jealousy at its worst cannot thwart God's purpose.

This same kind of jealousy later set Daniel on a collision course with certain government officials. In his early eighties, Daniel was still intellectually sharp, and his lengthy experience was a great asset to the new Medo-Persian Empire. These qualities did not go unnoticed, and he was appointed one of three presidents. Later, as the king observed Daniel's great leadership abilities, he planned to set Daniel over the whole kingdom (Dan. 6:3). But the intense jealousy of the other two presidents and the satraps caused them to be obsessed with Daniel's extinction. God frustrated their plot, however, and Daniel was unharmed in the den of lions (Dan. 6:22-23).

Such jealous acts show how evil deceives and destroys the persons preoccupied with self. Proud people who give no credit to God or to other people are often beset by irrational fears that someone else may get more attention or recognition. They plot to nullify the threatening persons and, as a result, their own sensitivity is obliterated. The stories of Esther and Daniel illustrate this consequence: Haman died upon the gallows he had erected for Mordecai (Esth. 7:9-10), and the conspirers of Daniel's death were themselves killed by the lions that Daniel survived (Dan. 6:24). False pride and bitter jealousy bring their own judgment.

C. Idolatry Encourages Self-Indulgence
Dan. 1:8-16; 3:4-7; 5:1-4

Students of the Bible sometimes wonder why Daniel and his three friends were so meticulous about their diet during the three-year training period for their work in the Babylonian court. They asked for a simple diet of vegetables and water in place of the king's rich food and wine (Dan. 1:8-16).

Because parts of food and wine were often offered to various idols, Daniel and his friends did not want to participate in idolatry.[1] Of course, they also observed the Levitical laws on food (Lev. 11), but if we overemphasize that aspect, we will lessen the severity of the threat that idolatry posed to Daniel and his three friends as they lived in Babylon. Ancients had many gods because they thought each deity specialized in a particular sphere, such as farming or the weather. These gods received sacrifices of food and wine at meals, banquets, and other festive occasions. Worshipers presented these offerings not to some kind of stone statue but to the deity represented by the statue. Daniel and his three friends' refusal to eat the king's food made clear their rejection of these idolatrous practices; but, at the same time, they complicated life for believers in the covenant God of Israel. How should they react when banqueting with Gentiles?

Daniel 1 tells how Daniel requested a Spartan diet of vegetables and water. At the end of a ten-day test of the king's diet versus the Hebrews' diet, the Hebrews were in better health than those who ate the king's rich food and wine (Dan. 1:15-16). The men were allowed to continue on this diet during their training in the book learning and language of the Chaldeans (Dan. 1:4).

Rich food and wine were associated in ancient times as in our own with the lifestyle of success and prosperity. Beyond that, self-indulgence had religious meaning; it was considered a kind of toast to the gods. With such a convenient religion a person could please himself and at the same time piously toast the gods for their contribution to his happy state of affairs.

The fifth chapter of Daniel graphically portrays how idolatry contributes to self-indulgence. Belshazzar made a great feast for a thousand of his lords and for his wives and concubines. He drank wine in front of them, that is, he offered toasts to the deities for various worthy goals that were making the country run smoothly. He then brought in his antiques (the gold and silver vessels that Nebuchadnezzar, his predecessor, had brought back from the temple in Jerusalem) and used them in another round of drinking as they "praised the gods of gold and silver, bronze, iron, wood and stone" (Dan. 5:4).

It was in this setting that "the fingers of a man's hand" appeared and wrote on the wall. God does not usually make such dramatic outward moves to point up self-indulgence, but in this case He did. Daniel translated the writing for the king to mean that the self-sufficiency and self-gratification of Belshazzar and his lords would come to an end (Dan. 5:25-28). Judgment was coming. Belshazzar and his lords, wives, and concubines learned that no attitude of independence from God alters any person's accountability to Him.

III. Moral Evil Involves Both Individuals and Groups

The books of Daniel and Revelation show clearly that moral evil operates in both groups and individuals who contribute to its growth as well as suffer its effects.

A. Group Loyalty to Idols
Dan. 5:1-4; Rev. 9:20-21

Belshazzar and his lords, wives, and concubines apparently lived agreeably with each other and with the various idols to which they were devoted. Sometimes everyone in a group was loyal to the same idol but other times some members worshiped one idol to the neglect of deities favored by other people. They agreed, however, to respect each other's idols.

As modern people, we often give ourselves to pleasure, to the accumulation of things, or to success in business and career. Like the ancients, we ask only that no one question to what we are giving our loyalty. Hedonism (living for pleasure) and materialism (living for things) are two popular lifestyles that often overlap. But they are both considered legitimate purposes for living. In ancient and modern times, tolerance for all forms of idolatry has been regarded as essential to the smooth functioning of society.

Such tolerance is evident in the conclusion of the accounts of the trumpets in Revelation. Seven angels blow their trumpets in turn (Rev. 8:6—9:21). After each of the first four trumpets sounds, terrible changes occur in the balance of nature, bringing death and destruction, which are part of God's judgment against persons who behaved as if the world were their private property.

The fifth and sixth trumpets involve demonic armies. The demonic, locustlike creatures that come after the fifth trumpet inflict their punishment only on those loyal to the beast—those who "have not the seal of God upon their foreheads" (Rev. 9:4). With the sixth trumpet a demonic cavalry brings plagues of fire, smoke and sulphur (Rev. 9:18-19) that kill a third of mankind. In these judgments, God shows His hatred for idolatry and His willingness to judge idolaters in this life.

Yet idolatry and demon worship in John's vision remained attractive to the people who were left. Survivors of the plagues "did not repent from the works of their hands nor give up worshiping demons and idols of gold and silver and bronze and stone and wood which cannot see, hear, or walk" (Rev. 9:20). Likewise, they "did not repent from their murders, or their sorceries or their immorality [sexual immorality] or their thefts" (Rev. 9:21).

Both the rich and the poor had their idols. The rich made theirs of gold and silver; the poor used wood or stone. Their attachment to these gods did not make them better people. They murdered anyone who got in their way; they used magic and sorcery in an attempt to control supernatural powers; they practiced sexual immorality; they stole rather than worked for what they wanted. These activities were true of them as individuals and as a group. In all societies, the group influences the individual, and the individual influences the group.

B. What Sin Is and What Sinners Need
Dan. 9:3-20

Daniel's prayer in the ninth chapter reveals some important truths about sin and some of his insights into its nature. Daniel was aware that the period of the Jews' exile away from the land of Israel was drawing to a close (Dan. 9:2; Jer. 25:11-12; 29:10). He saw that the exile had not brought his fellow Jews to a vital faith in God.

Speaking to God on behalf of his people, Daniel says (1) we have sinned (9:5, 8, 11, 15-16, 20) because we missed the goal that God desires and acted instead to please ourselves; (2) we have done wrong (9:5, 13, 16) in that we are involved in the guilt, pollution, and consequences of iniquity; (3) we have acted wickedly (9:5, 15); (4) we have rebelled against God (9:5, 9); (5) we have turned aside from God's commandments and ordinances (9:5, 11), although He made them clear; (6) we have not listened to His servants, the prophets (9:6, 10-11, 14); (7) we have acted treacherously (9:7), and we have been unfaithful to God and His covenant; (8) all Israel has transgressed God's law (9:11), overstepping the covenant or command of God (we know what God wants, but our conduct is contrary to our knowledge); and (9) sin is both individual and national, involving both persons and groups: "While I was speaking and praying and confessing my sin and the sin of my people Israel" (9:20).

Nearly all these phrases describe individuals' determination to do just as they desire. Their will becomes what is right. The fact that God, their Creator, has made known His good and perfect will makes no difference to most sinful people. They separate themselves from God by asserting their own will.

But what do they need? They need the righteousness that belongs to the Lord (Dan. 9:7). Because people insist on doing what they please instead of following God's commands, they suffer from what Daniel called "confusion of face" (Dan. 9:7). (The word literally means "shame of face.") When we live in revolt against God, we have no sense of direction. God's mercy and forgiveness are available to people who confess they have pursued the fantasy that they are free to do as they please, but people who persist in that pursuit increase their bondage to sin (Dan. 12:10).

Daniel's words show the way back to God. (1) When we confess our sins, God hears, forgives, and acts on our behalf (Dan. 9:19). (2) God's gracious response is "for His sake"—the basis lies within Him (Dan. 9:17, 19). (3) We must pray for forgiveness on the ground of God's great mercy not on our righteousness (Dan. 9:18). (4) God and His people reaffirm together the covenant "because thy city and thy people are called by thy name (Dan. 9:18).

Because sin involves doing as we please and disregarding what God desires, sin makes fellowship with God impossible. Daniel and Revelation assert that repentance is the only way out of the predicament of sin (Dan. 9:4-20; Rev. 2:5, 16, 21-22; 3:3, 19; 9:20-21; 16:9, 11).

With repentance comes conversion or restoration: "And the rest became afraid [startled] and gave glory to the God of heaven" (Rev. 11:13). When people do not repent, they become more deeply entrenched in their evil: "But they did not repent to give Him glory" (Rev. 16:9).

IV. Moral Evil Conceals Its True Nature by Appearing to Be Good

The most consistent quality about moral evil is that it rarely looks like evil. It often looks like truth; its falseness appears only when the results of the sin it causes become apparent. One example may be seen in the phenomenon of chemical dependency. Pushers of drugs promise increased awareness through chemicals, which is really an illusion, and the deterioration caused by the drugs relentlessly takes hold. Moral evil is basically deceptive.

A. The Harlot City Is Very Attractive
Rev. 17:1-6

The Book of Revelation contrasts two cities: the harlot city and the holy city. At the end of Revelation 17, John identifies the harlot city as Rome and says the beast is the empire of which she (Rome) is the capital (Rev. 17:16-18). We could see in the Roman Empire an early version of a final world empire or in the city of Rome an early version of a final capital city. But when the first readers of Revelation came to the end of Revelation 17, they knew that John was writing about the Rome of the first century.

Revelation 17 discusses the judgment of the great harlot. When John wrote of the kings of the earth committing fornication with the harlot (Rev. 17:2), he referred symbolically to an idolatry that has increased in the nineteen hundred years since his time. It is an idolatrous lifestyle wrapped up with materialism, pleasure, selfishness, and sensuousness. The harlot offers an intoxicating wine that represents the ecstasy of our doing what we want and the bombardment of sensations that demand another round of the same sensations to maintain the mood of the moment.

The harlot (the capital city) rides on a beast (the empire and/or its rulers) that was full of the names of blasphemy. The golden cup in the harlot's hand is full of the abominations and impurities of her lifestyle. As the mother of harlots, she encourages other cities and countries to live as she does. Most of all, she is drunk with the blood of the saints, and she puts to death anyone who opposes her kind of living. This is her true character.

But she first appears beautiful, elegant, rich, and royal. She is clothed not only in purple and scarlet but also with gold, jewels, and pearls. She holds a golden cup that symbolizes her sharing of her lifestyle with all who want to feel rich and exotic. "Drink," she seems to say, "and you will share my exuberant triumph."

In John's vision, the harlot is in a wilderness. Wilderness here implies only an uninhabited place, not a bleak sandy desert of burning heat. It could be an oasis with water and vegetation, but it is secure. The woman is there alone and shows a confidence that often charms people. John wrote, "And when I saw her I marvelled with a great marvelling" (Rev. 17:6). Evil can be so attractive that we forget that it is evil. But John could not forget because some of his fellow believers had been martyred by this idolatrous city. Despite this knowledge, he marvelled at how evil could seem so seductively alluring.

B. The Two Prophets Are Rejected
Rev. 11:3-13

In John's vision, two prophets minister powerfully in the last days when God is bringing history to a climax. John saw this climax as occurring in his day or just beyond. God gives authority to prophesy (Rev. 11:3) to the two prophets, called olive trees and lampstands (Rev. 11:4). This image seems to guarantee that the two prophets will have light and enough fuel to keep the light shining.

The authority of the two prophets is validated by their ability to bring down fire, shut off rain, turn the waters into blood, and strike the earth with plagues (Rev. 11:5-6). Only after the prophets finish their ministry is the beast allowed to conquer and kill them (Rev. 11:7). People who had rejected the message of the two prophets show both hostility and joy at their death. They refuse to bury the bodies of the murdered prophets (Rev. 11:9), and they send gifts and presents to each other to celebrate their triumph over the prophets. These acts again reveal the true nature of evil. After killing God's servants, the people celebrate their sin.

But God has the last word. He brought the two prophets to life and lifted them into His presence while their enemies watched. Then He sent more physical upheavals. A great earthquake destroyed a tenth of the city and killed seven thousand people. (If these figures are rough approximations, the population of the city would have been about seventy thousand.) The rest of the inhabitants finally give glory to God; the prophets' ministry and their vindication by God eventually bring many converts.

The people's attitudes and actions show that their hostility was really directed against God. They had rejected the prophets' ministry and rejoiced when they were no longer confronted with the prophets' messages from God. This one aspect of evil is clear: continual evil perpetuates itself and brings further estrangement from God. The people in Revelation 11 killed God's servants and then rejoiced over getting rid of them. Is there another factor here? Did they also rejoice because they felt that they had rid themselves of God? Of course, no one can get rid of God, but their hostile and festive moods suggest that they embraced this ultimate deception of evil—that God can be banished or destroyed. This deception, like all others, is finally swept away by God's own acts.

C. Fresh Water Becomes Blood: A Symbol of What Evil Is
Rev. 16:4-7

In Rev. 16:4-7, when the third angel pours out the third bowl of wrath, the fresh water becomes blood. Here we confront the nature of apocalyptic language. The prophet Joel wrote, "The sun shall be turned to darkness and the moon to blood" (Joel 2:31). These words may describe a blotting out of sunlight and a strange red color in the moon, which is not a scientific statement that the sun will be turned off and blood will cover the surface of the moon. But the language does point to some serious physical changes.

In a similar way, the third bowl of wrath (Rev. 16:4) changes fresh and healthful water into something no longer fit to drink—another potent picture of evil. Evil poisons the very things that are beneficial. It takes away life and causes blood to run freely. Evil boomerangs on the ones who destroy what is precious and valuable. It is destructive, although it often appears attractive. Evil seems to say, "Follow this course and you will get something desirable," but eventually the truth comes out. The person who pursues evil loses the ability to recognize what is wholesome and worthwhile, as well as the ability to act in a wholesome or worthwhile manner.

D. Neutrality Is Not an Option
Rev. 14:6-7

Some people think, "Yes, there is evil in the world, but I have escaped its influence. I don't know what God (if there is a God) might approve or disapprove. So I am neutral about most matters of right and wrong." Such neutrality is a figment of the imagination.

Revelation 14 teaches that: God's people will triumph (14:1-5); people should respond to the one who made all things (14:6-7); the capital city of a world power will fall (14:8); anyone who becomes involved in emperor worship or any deification of the state will suffer eternal punishment (14:9-12); believers who die in Christ (the Lord) will be blessed (14:13); and the harvest at the end of the age will involve God's "crop" that includes judgment (14:14-20).

In this context, John sees in his vision an alternative to evil. An angel flies in the middle of heaven with an eternal gospel to proclaim to every nation, tribe, language, and people. Exactly how the angel proclaims the gospel is not stated. But both Daniel and Revelation picture God's working through angels and His people to bring changes to the human scene. In Revelation what had first appeared to be defeat becomes the first step to transformation. The people who had earlier shown hostility to the two prophets are now confronted with proclamation and witness.

Three commands are given to every nation, tribe, and language: (1) to fear God (show Him reverence); (2) to give glory or praise to Him because the hour of God's judgment (altering the whole course of history) is about to break into the realm where evil had been so powerful; and (3) to worship the one who made the heaven and the earth and the sea and the fountain of waters (Rev. 14:7). Neutrality is not tolerated. People must declare their loyalty. Will they continue to follow evil, or will they follow God?

In Revelation, God is not pictured as some detached Supreme Entity but as the active Lord in heaven and earth. From His throne He sends forth the seven spirits, the eyes of the Lamb, into all the world. From this word picture of God, we recognize that God cannot be avoided or ignored. No one can be neutral.

Some people try to be neutral because they do not face the reality of either moral evil or God, but their neutrality leaves them subject to the power and control of evil. People who decide for God receive a new power to overcome evil.

E. Businesses Are Involved in Moral Evil
Rev. 18:1-24

The first readers understood the harlot city to be Rome, the capital of the world empire. We know this not only because of the seven hills mentioned in Rev. 17:9 but also because of the reference to the city's power in the chapter's close: "And the woman [i.e., the harlot city] which you saw, is the great city which is having the royal rule over the kings of the earth" (Rev. 17:18). Today we understand that God did not choose to complete His program for the human race in the days of the Roman Empire. The final world empire and its capital are yet to appear.

Jesus said it is not for us to know the times or the seasons that the Father has put under His own authority (Acts 1:7). In Scriptures, God's servants usually envisioned the climax of history as being very close to their own times, although it was really much farther away than they thought. Nevertheless, the ancient city of Rome and the future capital city of the final world empire have some of the same characteristics. Their imports, exports, and high productivity indicate a vigorous business community where there is much to buy and sell.

Revelation 18 tells about the business life of and God's judgment on the city of Rome. Rome was called the "harlot city" because it deceived its citizens and others into thinking that the good life came from material possessions. Kings lament (Rev. 18:9-10), merchants from other countries mourn (18:11-17a), and sailors join the outcries of grief about the fallen city. They had prostituted themselves by bringing to Rome imports from other parts of the world (18:17b-19).

The list of imports to Rome (18:12-13) contains twenty-eight items. Only the last one, slaves (human souls), is inherently evil. The rest of the list includes precious metals, precious jewels, cloth and dyes, articles made by craftsmen (wood, bronze, iron, marble), ivory, incense, perfume, oil, fine flour and wheat, cattle, sheep, horses and chariots, and food flavorings. There is nothing morally wrong with these things. Each one could be among the "all things" that God has given us richly for enjoyment (1 Tim. 6:17), but in the context of Revelation 18, these material things become part of sorcery and evil.

John says of the city: "And the fruit for which your soul longed took off from you; and all the bright and costly things and shining radiant things passed away [were ruined] and no longer will they find them" (Rev. 18:14). Most of the citizens of the city longed for, lived for, thought about, and celebrated these attractive possessions at every occasion.

Most of us can identify with the people of the "harlot city." Our possessions appeal to our sight, taste, smell, ease of movement, and sense of beauty. There is nothing inherently wrong with them, but they become wrong in our use of them and in our elevated regard for them. They make us look important, successful, and independent, but they can be the means by which we exclude God from our lives. The more life revolves around ourselves and our possessions, the less room we have for God and for essential spiritual growth.

Revelation 18 surely condemns the wrong use of material things, but in the last part of the chapter, an angel laments the halt of many good occupations and enterprises following God's judgments. The angel takes up a stone that resembles a huge millstone and drops it into the sea (Rev. 18:21). This symbolic act suggests that the harlot city will fall and drop out of sight just as the millstone sinks to the bottom. But many joyful sounds, sights, and activities will disappear with the city. Musicians and their instruments will be silenced. There will no longer be the sounds of craftsmen working with clay, stone, or iron. The happy sounds of a wedding with the excited voices of the bride and the bridegroom will no longer be heard. All the lively, energetic sounds of a healthy city will stop. This picture is awesome and tragic.

The creativity of people in work, in music, in the festivities of a happy evening—these all represent a meaningful contribution to life and culture. Yet obviously worthwhile activities became a part of the idolatrous pursuit of things that took the place of God. Moral evil conceals its true nature by substituting splendid earthly things for the glory, splendor, and radiance of God. Earthly riches are no substitute for the living God, but many people learn too late that moral evil easily deceives.

V. Moral Evil Is Organized and Active in Both Heavenly and Earthly Realms

The writers of Daniel and Revelation explain in detail that moral evil is organized. Its many facets cooperate in a complex strategy. Only the naive can believe that moral evil is accidental or haphazard. When we examine evil, we perceive an intelligent shrewdness much more complicated than a simple irrational force.

Ignorance is a part of evil in the sense that people may overlook God and assume that they are free to do as they please without serious consequences. Irrational stupidity, or ignorance, is sin in the sense that the destructive effects of going one's own way are never fully known to the sinner. But in another sense, evil is purposefully organized to deify the creature and to dethrone the Creator of heaven and earth.

A. Satan Works in Both Heaven and Earth
Rev. 12:1-18

In Revelation 12, Satan appears to know what he is doing, and he proceeds in an organized way. The woman clothed with the sun represents the early messianic community from which Jesus came. The community was gathered together when the Holy Spirit came at Pentecost.

According to this passage, Satan was behind Herod the Great's attempt to put the child Jesus to death (Rev. 12:3-5; Matt. 2:16-18).

Satan no longer had access to heaven where he could constantly bring accusations to God about the believers (Job 1:6-11; 2:1-5). Frustrated in his efforts at the time of Herod and at the end of the Messiah's earthly ministry, Satan could not stop the work of "the one who is to rule all the nations" (Rev. 12:5).

With this Son (Jesus) back in heaven, war broke out there (12:7); Michael and his angels fought the dragon (Satan) and his angels. The expression "war in heaven" is startling. This chapter indicates that Christ's victory on the cross and His resurrection from the dead caused Satan to be cast out of heaven soon after Christ's ascension (12:5, 7-17). The victory of Michael and his angels in heaven was also symbolized as a victory on earth in which believers conquer Satan (12:11). Satan had separate strategies for earth and heaven. The writer describes Satan as "the one deceiving the whole world" (12:9) and the one in heaven accusing the brethren before God day and night (12:10). The gospel enables believers to overcome both this deception and the one who deceives. When Christ ascended to heaven, Satan was banished and could no longer carry out the second phase of his strategy.

God miraculously intervened to protect the early messianic church from being completely decimated by persecution. In the first twelve chapters of Acts, only two martyrs are recorded— Stephen and James, the brother of John (Acts 6—7; 12:1-2). In Revelation, Satan attacked the "rest of her seed," that is, "those who keep the commandments of God and the testimony that Jesus gave [or the testimony about Jesus]" (12:17). Satan turned his attack to the Jewish and Gentile converts to Christianity won by Paul and the other apostles. Most of these converts did not live in Palestine or the eastern end of the Mediterranean. They were spread all across the Roman Empire from Asia Minor to Spain. The last statement about the dragon (Satan) in Rev. 12:18 is ominous: "And he [the dragon] stood on the sand of the sea." Satan paused before his next move.

The titles given to Satan in this chapter reveal something about his identity. He is a dragon, a foe of people; he is the old serpent whose activities extend from the Garden of Eden to John's day and to ours; he is the adversary and the deceiver. We all agree that Satan is not literally a dragon, snake, armed military opponent, or human charlatan. But each figure portrays a being who is strong, powerful, devious, and clever.

116

B. Satan Was Involved with the Synagogue
Rev. 2:9; 3:9

When the Jewish people were exiled in Babylon after the temple was destroyed, they had no place to gather for worship. Apparently during this Babylonian exile, the synagogue developed. The Greek word *sunagogē* means "a gathering together." Jews who were in exile far from Jerusalem began to gather together to hear the reading of the Law and the Prophets, to sing psalms, and to remember their covenant God. The synagogue brought God and His people together.

In a synagogue in Nazareth, Jesus read the opening verses of Isaiah 61 and declared that the prophecies in those verses were being fulfilled on that very day (Luke 4:21). The purpose of the synagogue was to help people know God and to fellowship with Him.

Any institution with such a purpose would naturally be attacked by Satan. When Jesus showed by His life, death, and resurrection that He was the Messiah, the synagogue could have been reborn in purpose and outreach. But the leaders of Judaism, who carefully controlled the synagogues, rejected Jesus as the Messiah, the fuller revelation about the covenant God of Israel. They repudiated the concept of a people of God consisting of both Jews and Gentiles who acknowledged Jesus as Messiah.

In Revelation, John sadly notes that Satan was able to use this great institution that had been the center of Judaism. Christ's messages addressed to the church at Smyrna (Rev. 2:9) and to the church at Philadelphia (3:9) speak of "the synagogue of Satan." Satan became aligned with the synagogue in their mutual opposition to the messiahship of Jesus. On this one point, the synagogue and Satan could agree.

For John, a true Jew could not belong to the synagogue because it would not acknowledge Jesus as Messiah. John referred to the Jews resisting Christians in Smyrna and Philadelphia as belonging to an organization hostile to the church. These synagogues apparently persecuted Christians, but Christ's message to the church at Philadelphia has words of hope: Some of the synagogue of Satan will come and worship (God) "before your feet," and they will know God's love for the church at Philadelphia (3:9). This statement indicates that even in this hostile place some Jews would become "true" Jews, acknowledging Jesus as the Messiah. But such

Jews no longer had a place in their own synagogue. Satan, the deceiver and clever tactician, had maneuvered the synagogue away from serving God. History shows that Satan has similarly deceived the Christian church many times. It is not anti-Semitic to point out that moral evil has deceived Jews as well as Gentiles.

C. Militarism Dominated by Evil Produces Dreadful Effects
Rev. 6:1-8, 9:13-19; 16:12-16; 17:12-13; 19:14-21

Human government, when functioning rightly, praises the good and punishes the wrong (Rom. 13:1-7). However, evil often pushes one group of people or nations against another. War usually occurs because one group or nation violates (or is accused of violating) the rights of another group. The term *militarism* denotes a powerful military machine in which various units work together to intimidate friend or foe. Since militarism demands intensive organization, we should not be surprised that forces of evil try hard to gain control of armies. Evil governments using military might for selfish ends are called "beasts" in Revelation.

The first four seals (Rev. 6:1-8) describe four horsemen and the effects of militarism dominated by evil. The rider on a white horse is a conqueror (6:1-2), and the one on a red horse is war (6:3-4), on a black horse famine (6:5-6), and on a pale horse death and Hades (6:7-8). As Christ breaks the seals and the course of history unfolds under His control, evil moves toward a climax.

The accounts of the sixth trumpet (Rev. 9:13-19) and the sixth bowl of wrath (Rev. 16:12-16) sketch similar pictures of militarism. With the sixth trumpet, a huge demonic army appears with fire, smoke, and sulphur pouring from its horses' mouths. These three elements (fire, smoke, and sulphur) are called "plagues" (9:18).

The depiction of the sixth bowl of wrath reveals more of the same horrors (Rev. 16:12-16). The angel pours the bowl on the Euphrates River, and it dries up, which "prepares the way for the kings of the east." What lies behind these military operations? John saw "issuing from the mouth of the dragon [Satan], and from the mouth of the beast [final Antichrist], and from the mouth of the false prophet [one in charge of emperor worship] three foul spirits like frogs; for they are demonic spirits, performing signs, who go abroad to the kings of the earth to assemble them for battle" (16:13-14).

The demonic powers, with Satan as leader, bring powerful military forces into full operation. The one dominant world power is aligned with the other important countries (Rev. 17:12-13). This unfolding drama reveals evil forces using militarism to push the world into catastrophe.

When Christ comes into the world scene (Rev. 19:11— 20:6), He has three main tasks: (1) He must end the militarism dominated by evil. In this climactic scene, the forces of evil are really focused against Christ (19:11-21); (2) He must deal with Satan who is the mastermind behind militarism (20:1-3); and (3) He must work with all who rise in the first resurrection to establish a new world order that will replace evil militarism (20:4-6). In a few choice words, John tells of Christ's victory over all military forces, the binding of Satan for a long period of time, and the triumph of the saints who live and reign with Christ.

If we look at only the death and destruction brought by militarism, we will have an unbalanced view of the Book of Revelation. If we ignore the power of evil and the way it used militarism, we will not understand why John described Christ as a military leader (Rev. 19:11-16). Military power can be trusted only in the hands of Christ, the one who is without sin and who in His resurrection conquered the power of evil. He is King of Kings and Lord of Lords (Rev. 19:16).

D. People Are Attracted to the Power of Evil
Dan. 12:10; Rev. 9:21; 22:11

Evil attracts us because its proposed course of action often looks and feels desirable. We usually begin by a single questionable act, and when no dire effects follow, we repeat it. Slowly we become habitually involved in a variety of wrong acts and attitudes. To free ourselves from this snare is not easy. Daniel 12:10 contrasts the righteous and the wicked. The righteous purify themselves and make themselves ethically spotless. They are also refined—perhaps by suffering, but this is not clearly stated. Daniel asserts the fact of purification and cleansing; he does not tell us how it occurs.

In the New Testament, we learn that we must become identified with Christ, with His atoning death, and with His power. The wicked or rebellious, on the other hand, continue to act wickedly and fail to understand the paralyzing effects of sin. They do not realize they are becoming enslaved (Rev. 22:11). Instead, they find a kind of exhilaration in their ways as they rush headlong toward certain doom. The righteous (also called the wise) have understanding. The fact that they seek cleansing and ethical purity is evidence of their understanding.

VI. God's Present Judgment Shows the Nature of Moral Evil

Some Christians think of judgment only as the final judgment when each person gives account of his or her life before God. However, the word *judgment*, as used in the Bible, is much broader.

Judgment can mean (1) a final sentence of separation from God; (2) God's final testing of one's deeds or one's faith that could result in eternal fellowship with Him; or (3) God's action during a person's earthly life in which He shows His displeasure at the words, thoughts, or deeds of an individual or members of a group.

The last meaning, involving the continuing present judgment of God, is prominent in the books of Daniel and Revelation. If we are preoccupied with the final judgment, we may pass over this present-day judgment of God as if it had little importance. The daily judgment of God shows that He is involved in His world, constantly seeing the course of our lives.

The following biblical examples of God's present judgment show that God is concerned about evil. Although evil continues, God has so created the world that there is a built-in judgment on evil. Those who practice evil may get what they think they want, but they do not understand that God's judgment is inviolate in this life and in the life to come.

A. Nebuchadnezzar's Good Response
Dan. 4:34-37

Nebuchadnezzar dreamed of a tree that was cut down, but its stump was allowed to remain. The dream, as Daniel interpreted it for Nebuchadnezzar, described the judgment that God would bring upon the king exactly a year later (Dan. 4:31). The king became mentally ill and lived like a grazing ox. Daniel's prophecy said this judgment would last until Nebuchadnezzar learned "that the Most High rules the kingdom of men and gives it to whom He will" (4:32). Nebuchadnezzar learned that God rules and that His present judgment is effective. When Nebuchadnezzar regained his senses and was restored as ruler, he had the same kingly power as before, but his attitude was different. Nebuchadnezzar illustrates how a right response to God's judgment can restore individuals.

B. Belshazzar Has No Chance to Repent
Dan. 5:1-30

The story of Belshazzar illustrates how God's judgment in the present may end a self-centered life. First there was a dramatic confrontation in the midst of a great banquet when he saw the fingers of a man's hand writing on the wall. Terrified, Belshazzar called in his wise men to read and interpret the writing, but none of them could.

Finally, Daniel was called, and when he translated the handwriting (Dan. 5:24-28), he delivered his message prophetically, with a God-given sense of urgency. The words which he translated were Daniel's last words to Belshazzar.

The king had promised that whoever could read and translate the words on the wall would be clothed with purple, receive a chain of gold around his neck, and become the third ruler in the kingdom (Dan. 5:7, 29). Belshazzar kept his promise to Daniel.

But Daniel did not rule. The first six words in Dan. 5:30 are in the Aramaic language: "In that night, Belshazzar, the king, the Chaldean, was slain." Belshazzar's life ended, and his death basically ended the Babylonian Empire. Belshazzar and his kingdom had come under God's judgment.

Belshazzar, of course, was not the only one to be judged by God and die. Daniel's writing, however, focuses on the judgment that befell Belshazzar, not the empire, its soldiers, or himself (the one leader who survived the change in governments). Belshazzar tried to ignore God, the maker of heaven and earth, but he could not avoid God's judgment.

C. Antiochus IV Epiphanes and Titus
Dan. 9:26-27

We tend to emphasize the successes of kings or emperors in building great power structures. Unfortunately, we often fail to note how God brings judgment upon them. Daniel 9:24-27 tells about Daniel's vision of seventy weeks. (We will deal more fully with this section in chapters 6 and 7.) To the Jews exiled in Babylon, this vision must have held both great promise and great terror.

It promised that God would restore the city of Jerusalem, which then lay in ruins, but declared an equally severe judgment against Babylon. The vision foretold a double-dealing oppressor who would bring havoc to the worship of God.

The dark side of this vision showed God's judgment continuing through the course of history after Daniel's time: "And the people of the prince who is to come shall destroy the city and the sanctuary; its end shall come with a flood [of calamities], and until the end there shall be war and strict determinations of desolations" (Dan. 9:26). These statements can certainly be applied to the action of Titus and the Romans from A.D. 66 to 73. The Romans not only destroyed Jerusalem but desecrated Herod's temple. Three years later, when they finally captured Masada, they found 960 of its defenders dead (killed by either their own people or their own hands). Only two older women and five children were alive (Josephus, *Jewish Wars*, VII. 9.1-2).

In Dan. 9:27a we read: "He will confirm a covenant with the many for one week, but in the half of the week he will cause the sacrifice and the offering to cease." These statements describe the action of Antiochus IV Epiphanes, king of Syria from 175 to 164 B.C. Chapter 1 of the Book of 1 Maccabees tells how Antiochus IV made and broke a covenant with the Jewish people. Daniel 11:31 states, "Forces from him shall appear and profane the temple and fortress, and shall take away the continual burnt offering. And they shall set up the abomination that makes desolate." (See also Dan. 8:11-14, 22-26; 11:21-45; 12:7, 11-12.)

Although this is genuine predictive prophecy, God did not reveal all the details to Daniel. The prince about whom Daniel prophesied seems to be a composite of Antiochus IV and Titus. Both men were involved in desecrating the temple, but only Titus destroyed the temple and the city. To his disrepute, only Antiochus IV made a covenant, broke it, offered swine flesh on the altar, and set up another altar to Zeus in the temple area.

God's temporal judgment on Antiochus IV and Titus is concisely given in Dan. 9:27b: "And upon a wing of detestable things will be one causing horror until complete destruction and strict decision pour forth upon the one causing horror." Antiochus IV and Titus reached great heights in their ability to cause horror and desecration. But the final word and action, as always, were God's. Antiochus IV died in 164 B.C. in a campaign against the Parthians.

Titus, who became emperor of Rome in A.D. 79, died two years later at the age of forty or forty-one. The judgment of God in the present is a basic fact of human existence.

D. Final Version of Antichrist
Dan. 7:11-26; Rev. 13:1-18; 19:20

The term *Antichrist* does not appear in either Daniel or Revelation. It is used only in 1 and 2 John where it describes one who denies that Jesus is the Messiah and that He had a real human body (1 John 2:22; 4:1-3; 2 John 7). The term *Antichrist* literally means "one who is against Christ."

Daniel, Revelation, and 2 Thessalonians speak of "the man of sin," "the man of lawlessness," and "the beast" (2 Thess. 2; Dan. 7:11-26; Rev. 13:1-18; 19:20). These terms seem to be nearly synonymous and point to a political leader or a militarist opposed to the covenant God of the Bible, God's people, and a manner of life that glorifies God.

When we see what Antiochus IV did to God's people, we can recognize him as an early version of the final Antichrist. The same can be said of the Roman emperor Nero. Both of these early Antichrists persecuted and killed believers, and they led powerful military organizations. Syria's sphere of influence was not as extensive as Rome's, but Syria under Antiochus IV and Rome under Nero had similar animosity toward the God of the covenant.

Since the earlier Antichrist and the final Antichrist share the same purposes, it is easy to see that God's servants, people like Daniel and the prophets, did not always distinguish between all the different Antichrists. The little horn of the fourth kingdom seems to be this final Antichrist (Dan. 7:19-28), but the ten kings that rise out of this kingdom are not clearly identified. We do not know from Daniel if they arise sequentially, simultaneously, or in some other pattern.

Does the term *ten* refer to an exact number, or does it refer to a group of the most important kings while other kings were also ruling? After these ten will come the "little horn" who defeats three horns. Again, does he defeat them one at a time, or are the three allied together against him? The text offers no clue.

One clear fact is given about this Antichrist: "And as I looked, the beast was slain, and its body destroyed and given over to be burned with fire" (Dan. 7:11). The judgment of God dramatically breaks the power of the Antichrist or beast: "His dominion shall be taken away to be consumed and destroyed to the end" (Dan. 7:26). In Revelation 13, John describes the power of this beast, and Christ's saving and redemptive acts at His second coming which bring the beast to an end (Rev. 19:20).

God's temporal judgments of kings and other powerful world leaders, who often end suddenly and dramatically, easily illustrate the reality of His daily judgment in the course of world history. But not only rulers experience God's wrath during their earthly existence; Christians can experience His judgment during their earthly lives.

E. Warnings to Five Churches in Asia Minor
Rev. 2:5b, 16, 22-23; 3:3-16, 19

In the Book of Revelation, the glorified Christ sent messages to the seven churches of Asia Minor that revealed how intimately He knew each church. In five of the seven messages He issued concise warnings, each having serious implications.

If the Ephesian Christians did not repent of their lack of love for each other and for God, Christ would come and remove their lampstand from its place (Rev. 2:5b). If they did not return to their earlier love, in other words, the church would be destroyed.

Christ said that if the church of Pergamum did not repent, he would come soon and war against believers with the sword of his mouth (Rev. 2:16). The choice of words suggests strong disciplinary action.

In Thyatira a false prophetess taught wrong things. If she and her disciples failed to repent, Christ would cast them into a bed of sickness and send great suffering (including death) to them. They must repent of their sexual immorality or experience the consequences that Christ would pour out (Rev. 2:22-23).

The church at Sardis had a reputation for being alive, but in reality the people were spiritually dead. If they did not repent, the message says, Christ would come to them at an hour when they did not expect him. Because this passage says, "I [Christ] will come like a thief" (Rev. 3:3), some interpreters believe it is a reference to Christ's second coming. But this idea is difficult to support. (The passages about Christ's second coming tell Christians to wait eagerly, with alertness for the joy of His return [1 Thess. 4:16-17].) At any rate, this passage says that if the church at Sardis does not become alive, Christ will come in judgment, a warning of present judgment to a church that stays dull and dead.

Laodicea had a different problem. It was a self-sufficient church that thought it needed nothing. But the church was wrong. It was indifferent and therefore wretched, pitiable, poor, blind, and naked (Rev. 3:17). The text describes the church as lukewarm. Unless it repented and became aware of its own sins, Christ would surely judge it (3:16). Christ reproves and disciplines the ones He loves, but it is still judgment. For this church, the judgment would be one of chastisement that educates, trains, and restores.

No one can read these five warnings to prominent churches of the Roman province of Asia and envision a Savior whose love and kindness forbid Him to use His sword. When He does use His sword, He acts in judgment because He is full of love and concern. True love demands action against those things that destroy loved ones. These five churches are loved but also warned about Christ's judgment against their destructive attitudes and acts.

F. Evil Unmasked: the Supreme Lie
Rev. 2:2; 21:8, 27; 22:15

Evil deceives and lies. Christ commends the church at Ephesus because it examined the claims of persons who said they were apostles. In testing some claims, the church found them to be lies (Rev. 2:2). The word *apostle* means "one sent by God," and it was used of those whom Jesus especially called to carry on His mission. It is not surprising, therefore, that some people falsely claimed to be apostles. People who make similar false claims of being sent by God have appeared in generation after generation.

The last group mentioned in Rev. 21:8 as being eternally separated from God is "all liars." They cannot live with God who is all truth. No one who persistently lies will enter the magnificent Holy City. The true city has no place for that which is false (21:27), but outside the city is another matter (22:15). People not only tell lies; they live lies. Because lies lived are also lies believed, liars become false persons rather than genuine persons—shells that are devoid of what they were or could have been.

Summary

Moral evil is real and can be overcome only through the power

125

of God. Intelligence alone is no defense against moral evil; it can be used for both good and evil purposes. The men who sought to destroy Daniel were highly intelligent and crafty, but they used their intelligence to promote evil.

Because it neutralizes the good influence of the intellect, moral evil is freed to emphasize pride and self-will. King Nebuchadnezzar was proud of his accomplishments and believed that he alone had been responsible for the building up of his kingdom. God brought humility to Nebuchadnezzar through sending him a mental illness. God eventually healed him, and then Nebuchadnezzar glorified God. As a part of moral evil, pride brings jealousy. The jealousy of other officials sent Daniel to the lions' den, but God delivered him, and the ones who plotted against Daniel were themselves destroyed by the lions. Idolatry and self-indulgence are another part of moral evil. Courage and genuine devotion to God enabled Daniel and his three friends to refuse the rich food and drink associated with idolatry and choose a simple diet of vegetables and water.

Moral evil operates both in groups and in individuals. Self-indulgence, prompted by pride, makes people lose their sense of direction and makes fellowship with God and other fellow creatures impossible. God brings judgment on such moral evil, and repentance is the only way out of this predicament.

Moral evil often appears to be good. In Revelation 17, the "harlot city" looks extremely attractive, with a lifestyle given to materialism, pleasure, selfishness, and sensuousness. Yet the people of this city killed the two prophets who came to them (Rev. 11). Their "triumph" over the prophets was short-lived; God raised up the prophets and vindicated them. This episode reveals the true nature of moral evil in that the people of the harlot city grew further and further from God. Perhaps they hoped that getting rid of the prophets would banish God, a foolish and truly evil deception.

In the story of the fresh water becoming blood (Rev. 16:4-7), we see that moral evil poisons the very things that are fresh and healthful. The person who pursues evil loses the ability to recognize what is wholesome and worthwhile.

In both Daniel and Revelation, people are confronted with the need to declare themselves on the side of God or on the side of evil. Neutrality is not tolerated, and anyone who tries to be neutral ends up subject to the power and control of evil. The attitude of the citizens of the harlot city reveals the impossibility of neutrality. They enjoyed the beauty and materialism of their city, but the more life revolved around themselves and their possessions, the less room there was for God and for spiritual growth. Revelation 18 paints the harlot city as a place where people are creative in work, music, and cultural festivities. But all these things become substitutes for God, and the city is finally destroyed in the judgment of God.

Both Daniel and Revelation present an organized evil active in both heavenly and earthly realms. Revelation calls Satan "the old serpent" and a destroying "dragon." These figures of speech show Satan is strong, powerful, devious, and clever. Revelation implies that Satan even gains control of the synagogue, turning it away from acknowledging Jesus as the Messiah.

In several sections, Revelation describes what happens when an evil government unleashes its military might for its own selfish ends. The final Antichrist, the "one against Christ," will lead such a government (called a "beast"). When the evil forces' militarism pushes the world into catastrophe (Rev. 17—19), Christ will return to deliver the world (Rev. 19—20). Christ is the only one in whose hands military power can be trusted.

The term *Antichrist* appears in neither Daniel nor Revelation; it occurs only in 1 and 2 John, where it refers to one who denies that Jesus is the Messiah or that He had a real human body. Certain terms that seem nearly synonymous in their signification of a political leader, such as the Antichrist, opposed to God and His people are found in Daniel, Revelation, and 2 Thessalonians: "the man of sin," "the man of lawlessness," and "the beast."

Several versions of Antichrist, such as Antiochus IV and Nero, have already appeared. Revelation and Daniel seem to indicate that the judgment of God dramatically breaks the evil power of the Antichrist and/or beast once and for all.

The judgment of God involves more than final judgment. It also concerns His continuing present, daily judgment on individuals and groups which shows His perennial involvement in His world and His persistent opposition to moral evil.

Notes for Chapter 4

[1]Edward J. Young, *The Prophecy of Daniel* (Grand Rapids, Mich.: Wm. B. Eerdmans Publishing Company, 1949), p. 44. See also D. S. Russell, *Daniel, The Daily Study Bible Series* (Philadelphia: Westminster Press, 1981), p. 26.

Chapter 5

How Important Is Human Government?

When someone asks "How important is human government?" two passages are often quoted as if they were the only biblical references on human government.

The first, from the Gospels, is Jesus' answer to the Pharisees' question about paying tribute to Caesar (Matt. 22:15-22; Mark 12:13-17; Luke 20:20-26). Because theirs was a trick question, Jesus answered it very carefully: "Give to Caesar what is Caesar's, and to God what is God's."

The other passage comes from Paul's letter to the Romans (Rom. 13:1-7). Paul commands Christians to subject themselves to government, pay taxes, and support the government in its job of punishing the guilty.

But there is much more to the biblical picture of government than these two well-known passages. Not only do Daniel and Revelation speak significantly about government, but these books also depict human government functioning far differently from its God-ordained pattern. How can both God and Satan be active with human government? Why do moral evil and moral good so often clash in human government? To these questions, Daniel and Revelation provide significant insights.

I. God Delegates Authority to Human Government
Dan. 2:20-23; 4:17, 25-27, 32; 5:21-23; 7:18, 26-27; Rev. 17:17

We often see human government as something to which we grudgingly consent because of the moral evil in the world. In twentieth-century democracies we believe that the ones who govern receive their authority from the consent of the people they govern. But to the writers of Daniel and Revelation, God was the source from whom rulers derived their authority and to whom they answered. The monarchs of biblical times rarely acknowledged any accountability to their subjects.

When Nebuchadnezzar dreamed of a large figure made of several metals, he asked his wise men to recount and interpret the dream. When they could not, Nebuchadnezzar threatened to kill them (Dan. 2:1-16). Because Daniel and his friends were included in this group, Daniel requested time to seek help from the God in heaven (the covenant God of Israel) to carry out the king's request.

When God answered his prayer, Daniel was able to tell the king the dream and its meaning. Daniel blessed God (2:19-23): "God changes times and seasons; He removes kings and sets up kings; He gives wisdom to the wise and knowledge to those who have understanding" (2:21). To Daniel the wisdom of the court advisors was a gift from God. His prayer also points to God's constant activity, in that He changes the events of history, and He sets up kings and removes them.

Why is God involved in this constant change? Whether we have absolute monarchs, constitutional monarchs, presidents, prime ministers, or dictators, God appoints sinful people with their imperfections to have authority over others who are also sinful. Change comes because of God's sovereign plan and His control of a sinful world that would quickly reduce itself to absolute chaos without Him. Although there is much chaos in our world of moral evil, with God's presence the chaos is never absolute. God's presence among all people is a basic axiom proclaimed in Daniel. Humanity has not destroyed itself despite its diligent attempts. Because God is involved with the exercise of governmental authority, kings are removed as well as established, and so the changes continue.

The idea of rulers being accountable to God is often brushed aside today, even as it was in Nebuchadnezzar's day. When Nebuchadnezzar tried to deny his accountability, he soon found he could not avoid it forever. In Daniel 4, we read of Daniel's interpreting another of Nebuchadnezzar's dreams, in which a tree was cut down with only its stump left in the ground. The tree had been very important, with all segments of nature coming under its influence and benefiting from it. Daniel said that Nebuchadnezzar was that tree and God would remove the delegated authority He had bestowed on the king: "The sentence is by the decree of watchers, the decision by the word of the holy ones, to the end that the living may know that the Most High rules [is exercising authority over] the kingdom of men, and gives it to whom He will, and sets over it the lowliest of men" (4:17). The watchers and holy ones refer to angels through whom God governs the world; they enforce and carry out His decrees. By this means, Nebuchadnezzar and Daniel were informed of the coming events. All people were to know that the Most High rules eternally.

It was very important that the rulers themselves realized God's eminence. Nebuchadnezzar would be driven from his place of power to live in isolation until he knew that the Most High exercises authority in the kingdom of men (4:25-27, 32). Even after the warning, Nebuchadnezzar could not overcome his habit of pride and independence. Like many rulers, he considered himself to be self-made, autonomous, and free from outside control.

A year later Nebuchadnezzar stood on the roof of his palace, boasting about his building projects. He had built them by his own mighty power, he said, for the glory of his own majesty (4:30). As a result of God's immediate judgment, the king lost his mental equilibrium and lived for a time with the oxen of the field. When Nebuchadnezzar learned that he was accountable to God and that he derived his governing powers from Him, God restored him. Nebuchadnezzar was still aware of his own majesty and splendor, but he recognized who gave him his power: "Now I, Nebuchadnezzar, praise and extol and honor the King of Heaven; for all His works are right and His ways are just; and those who walk in pride He is able to abase" (4:37).

Belshazzar, the last ruler of Babylon, did not have a last chance to repent. He knew what had happened to Nebuchadnezzar, but he did not change his proud lifestyle, independent of God. Before Daniel read to him the meaning of the handwriting on the wall (Dan. 5), Daniel reminded Belshazzar of Nebuchadnezzar's experiences: "And you, his descendant, have not humbled your heart, though you knew all this, but you have lifted up yourself against the Lord of heaven...the God in whose hand is your breath and whose are all your ways, you have not honored" (5:22-23). After the famous banquet, the military forces of Medo-Persia over-whelmed the Babylonian defenders, and Belshazzar was killed (5:30).

All past, present, or future rulers exercise authority under God's jurisdiction, even the final Antichrist. Although Satan, the dragon, gives to this Antichrist his power, his throne, and great authority (Rev. 13:2), God still controls Satan and delineates the sphere in which he may operate (Rev. 12:7-17; 19:19-20:3, 7-10). God controls the Antichrist, the false prophet, and the ten kings (the ten kings of Rev. 17:12-13 represent the important world kingdoms). The ten kings give their power and authority to the beast (the final Antichrist in Rev. 17:13). Why do they do this? "For God has put it into their hearts to carry out his purpose by being of one mind and giving over their royal power to the beast, until the words of God shall be fulfilled" (17:17).

The Christian perspective is that in the past, the present, or the future, God is active in the affairs of people, in the delegation of authority, and in the control of that authority. God overrules, but He does not eradicate the consequences of the moral evil conceived and perpetrated by various rulers. The effects of their monstrous crimes underline responsibility, accountability, and final judgment. The tides of human affairs are much more irregular than the tides of the ocean. God's sovereignty and human freedom are constantly intermingled in the affairs of government. To deny God's sovereignty and His delegation of authority pushes us toward deifying humanity and assuming that secularization and selfishness are the authentic atmosphere in which nations should live. Daniel and Revelation do not support that view.

II. Symbols Emphasize Traits of Human Government

Daniel and Revelation rely heavily on symbols to convey not only important messages but also qualities of human government and human rulers.

A. Metals and Beasts in Daniel
Dan. 2:31-43; 5:24-28; 7:1-28; 8:1-26

Daniel 2 describes a situation in which King Nebuchadnezzar dreamed of an image so startling that it disturbed his sleep. Four metals composed this image: its head was made of gold, the breasts and arms of silver, the belly and thighs of bronze, the legs of iron, and the feet of iron and clay (2:31-35).

Daniel narrated the dream and its meaning, explaining that Nebuchadnezzar and Babylon were the head, thus the gold represented the Babylonian Empire (2:36-38). The silver represented a kingdom that would immediately follow Babylon (2:39a), which we know was Medo-Persia ruled by Cyrus the Great who took over when Babylon fell. The third metal, bronze (2:39b), represents Greece. (Daniel 8 tells about a ram and a he-goat that, respectively, represent the kings of Medo-Persia and the king of Greece [8:20-21].) The legs of iron and the feet of iron and clay represent a fourth world empire. After Greece, no world empire rose until Rome, so the iron and mixture of iron and clay probably refer to Rome (2:40-43).

Why were these metals chosen to represent the four kingdoms? First of all, they were valuable metals, although a pure form of any metal was hard to achieve in ancient times. We should not unduly emphasize the differences between these metals. However, Daniel no doubt complimented Nebuchadnezzar in saying that his kingdom was represented by gold. The kingdom which followed (Medo-Persia) was inferior; hence it was symbolized by silver. The third metal—bronze an alloy of copper and tin[1]—emphasized the third kingdom as a mixture. Chemical analyses show that ancient bronzes possessed two percent to sixteen percent tin.[2] The ancients knew that a larger ratio of tin—approximately up to four per cent—increased the strength and hardness of copper. Hence the largeness of the third kingdom, Greece, and its ability to hold things together (especially under Alexander the Great) are highlighted by the reference to bronze. The last kingdom, described as a mixture of iron and clay, included the sturdy qualities of iron— the ability to break and shatter things—and also the brittle qualities of dried clay. By this description, Daniel suggested that the empire will be such a blend of people that it will lack cohesiveness (2:43). Yet the symbol of iron and its strengths suggests that, in spite of such a mixture, the empire would accomplish a great deal. The symbol adequately fits the Roman Empire throughout its existence. Thus the metals symbolize roughly the quality and cohesiveness of these four empires at their best periods.

The seventh and eighth chapters of Daniel describe world empires in terms of beasts. The vision in Daniel 7 came approximately fifty years after the dream and image described in Daniel 2. Although the similarities between Daniel 2 and 7 are remarkable, the differences are no less significant. In chapter 7, instead of four metals, there are four beasts, each described as a combination of two or more animals.

The first beast was like a lion, but it had eagle's wings. During Daniel's vision, the wings were plucked off, the creature was made to stand on two feet like a man, and the mind of a man was given to it (7:4). This beast, with features part lion, part eagle, part man, describes what happened to Nebuchadnezzar. With the ferocity of a lion, he rose to great heights. But he fell from those heights when God for a short time removed his mental balance. When the humbled king acknowledged that God ruled the kingdoms of people, God gave him the mind of a man more fully than ever before. The beast symbolized the need for a government to become more truly human.

The second beast was like a bear that had three ribs between its teeth. It was commanded to rise and devour much flesh (7:5)—a vivid picture of a government consuming and devouring other nations. The Persians were famous for their organization and their ability to conquer other nations and keep the defeated people paying taxes to Medo-Persia.

The third beast was like a leopard that had four heads and four wings of a bird. Dominion, or sovereignty, was given to this beast (7:6). This language fits the picture of Greece in Daniel 8 and in secular history. The image of the leopard shows its great agility, and the four heads suggest the division of the kingdom under four different successors or rulers. These images are appropriate to Greece under Alexander the Great and his four successors.

Each of the first three beasts is described as a mixture of animals, but the fourth beast is much more complex. It is terrible, dreadful, and exceedingly strong (7:7) with great iron teeth and claws of bronze. After breaking its foes into pieces, this beast stamps the residue with its feet. The beast had ten horns among which a little horn came up and rooted out three of the ten. This little horn had eyes like the man's and a mouth of great speaking ability (7:8).

Who is the fourth beast, and what do its features symbolize? Daniel says this beast is a fourth kingdom that will be present on earth but will differ from the first three and all other kingdoms (7:23). It will devour the whole earth. Ten kings will rise out of this kingdom, and a little horn arising from among the ten will put down three of them. This factor makes nearly impossible the interpretation that the ten kings rise one after the other. One could hardly put down three kings (apparently at the same time) if they did not appear on the earthly scene at the same time (7:24). It seems more likely that the fourth kingdom is a federated world power. The ten kings would be the leaders of the most important nations whose federation makes up this fourth beast. From such a world power would come a leader who would oppose God and His people. According to Dan. 7:25-26, this leader would wear down the saints of the Most High, and he would change the times and the law so that God's people could not serve God in the ways that He commanded. However, this leader would have this power for only a brief time before it would be taken away, and he would be consumed and destroyed.

Earlier world powers fit part of this picture of the fourth kingdom. Syria, under Antiochus IV Epiphanes (175-164 B.C.), produced a leader who was an early version of Antichrist. Later, Rome, a true world power, produced Nero (A.D. 54-68) who certainly was a version of Antichrist. Tyrants usually try to eliminate other kings or rivals to enable their kingdoms to have as wide an influence as possible. The apocalyptic language in this section fits so many tyrants that it could portray all earthly governments opposed to God and His people.

Included in the picture of the four metals in Dan. 2:34-35 is a reference to a great stone that will break the whole image in pieces and become a mountain that fills the whole earth. This stone is said to be God's kingdom that He will set up in the days of those kings (Babylon, Medo-Persia, Greece, and Rome; Dan. 2:44-45). In the period from Babylon to Rome, God did His work in the world through Jesus Christ who became incarnate, lived, died, rose again, and ascended into heaven. These events occurred during the days of Caesar Octavius, later called Augustus (31 B.C.-A.D. 14), and Tiberius (A.D. 14-37). Thus, in the days of the Roman Empire, God set up a kingdom (Christ's) that would not be destroyed. But the final Antichrist did not arise out of the Roman Empire. God did not send His Messiah back to earth in the days of Rome to establish a universal kingdom of righteousness. So the "fourth kingdom" of Daniel that persecutes God's people throughout the whole world has been present and represents a final world empire that will be present again when the final Antichrist arises and is banished by Christ's second coming.

The symbolic beasts of Daniel show how human government controls the people of the world by sheer force. Its beastliness reaches its height when government opposes God and His people. The final Antichrist yet to come crystallizes in one particular ruler all the antagonism of human governments to God and completes a long list of candidates for the dubious honor of being banished by Christ at His return. Many persons in history were clearly qualified to be the final Antichrist if Christ had come during their reigns. But the final Antichrist will demonstrate the same beastly qualities (perhaps in a different combination) that have infected many human governments and made them instruments of Satan's power. Daniel 8 depicts a clash between the ram and the he-goat (Medo-Persia and Greece) that exemplifies the intense hatred possible between governments. Governments are beastly when they scheme to eliminate people who get in the way of their purposes. The greater the number of people affected, the greater the beastliness of the government that participates in such annihilation.

B. Mother of Harlots in Revelation
Rev. 17:1-18

While the beast symbolizes ferociousness, the harlot of Revelation 17 symbolizes deceptive attractiveness. John says that the woman, the harlot that he saw, "is the great city which is having the kingship over the kings of the earth" (17:18). John's original readers in the seven churches knew exactly to what he was referring. Rome, the capital city of the historic Roman Empire, was the harlot. The beast in the same chapter refers to both the empire and certain kings who ruled over that empire. But the symbol that begins and ends the chapter is the woman who is called the great harlot (17:1, 18).

John carefully paints certain features into the woman's portrait. Not only do the kings of the earth commit fornication with her, but the wine, which celebrates the union between Rome, the harlot city, and the kings of the earth, is consumed by all the earth's inhabitants until they are drunk (17:2). The harlot rides a beast, an indication of the close connection between the capital city and the empire (17:3). The woman is clothed with scarlet, gold, jewels, and pearls, and she holds a golden cup filled with abominations (17:4). Upon her forehead is written a name of mystery: "Babylon the great, the mother of harlots and of the abominations that belong to the earth" (17:5).

What does this mean? The woman makes all the nations drink the wine of her harlotry. She herself is drunk with the blood of the saints and the martyrs of Jesus (17:6). Significantly, the harlotry by which she influences the whole world is the idolatry of material things. (That determination becomes apparent in Rev. 18:11-14).

The priorities of the saints and the martyrs of Jesus were diametrically opposed to those of the harlot. They knew they were redeemed from the earth to be a firstfruit to God, and their basic purpose for life was to follow the Lamb wherever He went (14:3-4). They kept themselves from all forms of idolatry, which included the worship of emperors and the pursuit of possessions.

There could be no truce between the harlot city caught up in its vain undertakings and Christians sworn to a God who had redeemed them from such things. So the harlot killed Christians who would not comply with her imperatives. The idolatry of materialism seduced people living in Rome and all peoples who traded with her. They profited by this overwhelming human urge to acquire signs of "the good life," an urge that persists to this day. When John saw that the appearance and lifestyle of the harlot were so deceptive, he marvelled greatly (17:6).

Government often furthers the idolatrous pursuit of things. Great possessions bring us a sense of security and of superiority. Therefore, we vote for officials who promise us more of the good life, things to which we believe we are entitled as part of our national rights. As long as we have plenty, why should we worry about our contemporaries or future generations? In our more honest moments, most of us would have to admit that the idolatry of things is very close to the "god of progress." All such harlotry is a denial of the reality of God.

As we idolize things, we move toward a belief that reality involves only what we can see, feel, and experience. We lump people and things together into one grand mixture. Idolatry of things prevents our serious assessment of the difference between what we need and what we want, and government often encourages our confusion.

III. Right and Wrong Use of Power in Human Government
Rev. 2:26, 27; 6:1-8; 11:15-18; 16:12-16; 17:14; 19:15, 19-21

Throughout history, military strength has been the measure of government's power. People like to be proud of their nation's military machine, and the final Antichrist attracts them for the same reason: "Who is like the beast and who is able to make war against him?" (Rev. 13:4).

Militarism is well described in the first four seals (Rev. 6:1-8). When the first seal is broken, a rider with a bow and crown goes forth on a white horse to conquer. Alone, this figure is ambiguous, but in the context of the other three seals its meaning becomes clear. The figure represents the glamourous side of military preparedness: He is equipped to conquer.

When the second seal is broken, the glamour disappears. A rider and its red horse represent actual war. People kill one another.

When the third seal is broken, we see a rider on a black horse. He represents the famine that comes as a consequence of war. When people use energy and power to destroy rather than to create, tragedy follows.

When the fourth seal is broken, a rider on a pale horse appears. The name of the rider is death who is accompanied by an attendant, Hades, the personification of the realm of the dead. Four agents of death are mentioned: sword, famine, pestilence, and wild beasts.

The power of militarism is a power to destroy. Civilians are expected to support the military by producing food for the armies. Whoever heard of ancient or modern armies growing food for themselves and for the peoples they conquer? Militarism uses the creative energy of people solely to destroy other people, territory, and nature.

How can the versatile creativity of any people be reduced to such a dismal purpose? The Book of Revelation offers some clues (16:12-16). Satanic-demonic powers move governments from a militaristic stance of preparedness to active war. Apocalyptic pictures of nature participating in human struggles appear frequently in Revelation. In this instance, nature cooperates with the invader. When the sixth bowl of wrath is poured out, the great Euphrates River dries up so that the way of the kings of the east will have no barrier. For the first hearers or readers of Revelation, the Euphrates equalled the ideal eastern boundary of the Roman Empire. The phrase, "kings of the east," referred to the Parthians and any war-like people in the Tigris-Euphrates valley that could attack Rome. The rest of the image of the sixth bowl concentrates on the demonic powers that gather together the kings of the whole inhabited world.

What application does the drying up of the Euphrates have to the final world empire? Perhaps it implies the weakening of the outer limits of a world power's defense as a preface to an extensive global war. This application assumes that the Roman Empire becomes a model or symbol to teach about the final world powers just prior to Christ's return. The ability of apocalyptic literature to do this enables us to see the return of Christ as a very realistic, earthly business as well as a masterful intervention of God into human affairs.

But then the vision takes a more sinister turn. From the mouth of the dragon (Satan), from the mouth of the beast (the final Antichrist), and from the mouth of the false prophet (prime minister promoting emperor worship) emerge three unclean, demonic spirits like frogs (16:13). They perform signs (probably like those mentioned in Rev. 13:13-16) and gather all kings and governments to battle (16:14). The place for the final battle—Armageddon — probably means "the mountain of Megiddo," an ancient battle site where the famous King Josiah was killed (2 Kings 23:28-30; 2 Chr. 35:20-27).

Apocalyptic literature often draws upon names of ancient people (people of Sodom, Ezek. 16), places (Sodom and Egypt, Rev. 11:8), and persons of prominence (Elijah, Mal. 4:5) to describe future events. But this usage does not mean that God will turn back the clock and rerun history in the ancient place or with the ancient person. God may utilize other people in that place or the place name itself to depict what will happen elsewhere since associations of the first place may ascribe symbolic meaning to the actual location.

Force in the world is meant to bring stability. Whether stealing is carried out by individuals, groups, or countries, force must be used in a world of moral evil to prevent such thievery. If another nation sought to seize Alaska from the United States, no doubt military action would be necessary. But the right use of power to protect what really belongs to a person or a group can easily move into the wrong use of power. What is not ours becomes what we think ought to be ours. Since it ought to be, force is used to change the "ought" to a reality.

In the second coming of Christ (to be discussed further in chap. 7), we see the right use of force or power. Christ will come as a military conqueror (Rev. 17:14; 19:11, 17-21), which is apparent in John's picture of scavenger birds cleaning up the corpses that are left. In the terrible battle, earthly forces unite against God: "They will make war on the Lamb" (Rev. 17:14). Here apocalyptic symbolism is again ambiguous. How could earthly armies war against heavenly armies or forces? Revelation shows kings allied *with* the beast (the final Antichrist) in a federated world empire, but it never suggests kings allied *against* the beast. Who is fighting whom? Revelation furnishes only scattered snapshots to illuminate the whole panorama. It does seem clear, however, that the goal of moral evil is to dethrone the true God and enthrone people who want to deify themselves.

Christ exercises His power to defeat moral evil not in a temple or church but in "the kingdom of this world": "The kingdom of the world has become the kingdom of our Lord and of His Christ [Messiah], and He will reign forever and ever" (Rev. 11:15). The twenty-four elders give thanks that God has taken His great power and has begun to reign (Rev. 11:17). Such force involves God's wrath, His judgment of the dead, His rewards, and His destruction of the ones who are destroying the earth (Rev. 11:18). True force is both negative and positive. Negatively, true force ends all thoughts, words, and deeds that are contrary to what God has willed. Positively, it provides visible rewards and external recognition of people who live in accordance with His will.

Force (or power) can oppose evil and establish good, or it can oppose good and establish evil. Some Christians assume that when Christ returns, He will wave some magic wand to obliterate moral and physical evil. Then His people, freed from all contact with moral evil, will enjoy perpetual harmony and bliss.

Such scenarios may arise from our longing to have God act for us while we look on and applaud, as if God created us to be a great cheering section! However, Revelation does not teach that. Revelation does state that He will smite the nations and rule them with a rod of iron (12:5; 19:15). Standing alone, these passages suggest the saints are cheering onlookers, not participants. But Revelation also explains that when Christ rules, His people will smite, reign, and rule with Him; for example, the victorious ones in the church at Thyatira are promised that "he who conquers and who keeps my works until the end, I will give him power over the nations, and he shall rule them with a rod of iron, as when earthen pots are broken in pieces, even as I myself have received power from my Father" (2:26-27). Since all the churches were to hear what the Spirit said to each individual church, this promise to a single church is a promise to all other churches as well (5:10; 20:6).

True force involves a rod of iron wielded by Christ and His people. Such delegated authority and distribution of power make us aware of how little we understand God's plan to eradicate moral evil and to make moral righteousness a freely chosen lifestyle. Force that checks but does not eradicate moral evil is temporary and inadequate; Christ's power is permanent and irrevocable.

IV. God's Providence in Human Government Utilizes Good Angels

The phrase "providence of God" means that God not only created but also controls the world. According to Daniel and Revelation (as well as other biblical books), God has not set the world on automatic pilot to run on its own. God is overruling and controlling what is happening in the world, even though the frightful consequences of human decisions are usually left to stand. When persons engage in moral evil, God's laws operate in both the present and the future. The spendthrifts, the gluttons, the sensualists, and the materialists may think they are getting what they want, but the harmful effects of such lifestyles accumulate quietly and relentlessly. This is true of governments as well as individuals.

Daniel and Revelation refer often to God's use of angels and their role in combating moral evil. Angels are created beings. Some fell when Satan revolted against God, and the rest remained loyal to God and carried out His will. They are depicted in Daniel and Revelation as personal, intelligent, and powerful creatures. Their role in regard to people in government interests us here.

A. Angels in Daniel Relating to Government
Dan. 9:21-23; 10:13, 20-21; 11:1; 12:1

At the close of the Babylonian captivity, the elderly Daniel prayed for his people (Dan. 9:1-19). God sent the angel Gabriel to tell Daniel that his prayer was heard and to tell him in part what lay ahead for his people (9:20-23). This angel was God's minister to disclose truth to both an individual—Daniel—and a whole people—Israel. Daniel was not governing Israel, and he was not a statesman in Israel. He was not primarily a prophet but rather a statesman in Babylon. The message he received from the angel Gabriel concerned the people of God under various governments.

The content of the vision that Gabriel revealed to Daniel (9:24-27) centered in God's control of history, but said nothing about Gabriel's tasks in that rule. The same is not true of the heavenly beings involved with history that are mentioned in Daniel 10-12. One of them is described with such grandeur (10:2-9) that some interpreters have identified him with the preincarnate Christ. However, in the story, this heavenly being's activities seem closely linked with those of the angel Michael (10:13, 21). Thus it seems likely that both are God's messengers—angels in charge of God's control in the affairs of people. The text says that the prince of the kingdom of Persia withstood this unnamed heavenly being for twenty-one days, but Michael, one of the chief princes, came to help.

The unnamed heavenly being or angel is described as one who had the appearance of a man (Dan. 10:18). He revived Daniel from the weakening effects of the vision and prepared him to understand it. When Daniel regained strength, he was ready to receive the meaning. The messenger told Daniel that he had been diverted briefly from his main job as God's agent to control nations: "But now I will return to fight against the prince of Persia; and when I am through with him, lo, the prince of Greece will come. But I will tell you what is inscribed in the book of truth; there is none who contends by my side against these except Michael, your prince. And as for me, in the first year of Darius the Mede, I stood up to confirm and strengthen him" (10:20—11:1). The heavenly messenger—probably an angel—was engaged in conflict with the prince of Persia. His next assignment would take him to the prince of Greece. When the Babylonian Empire ended and the Medo-Persian took over, this same angel assisted Darius the Mede (probably another name for Cyrus the Great) in his enormous task of ruling the empire of the Babylonians. Darius made it possible for the exiles from Judah to return to their own land and their capital city of Jerusalem. Thus this angel was in conflict with some nations, but he also provided assistance to nations that were pleasing to God.

The angel assigned to Israel was named Michael. Daniel tells us, "At that time shall arise Michael, the great prince who has charge of your people" (12:1). This suggestion that God runs the world through angels is by no means a full picture of God's providence, for His providence is much more than an angelic corps in charge of the nations of the world. It does indicate, however, that God's providence involves a personal being rather than impersonal forces. God created personal beings; moral evil involves persons with wills who act contrary to what God wills. We all have minds and wills that sort out possibilities and make decisions even in the obscurity and fog that moral evil creates. God's use of angelic beings with intelligence and power shows His respect for His human creatures who live out their days in the dilemmas created by moral evil.

B. Angels in Revelation Relating to Government
Rev. 16:2, 10-14, 16

In the visions in the Book of Revelation, we learn more about angels and their roles in judgments on governments. (Later we will see their function in God's judgments on nature.) When the first angel pours out his bowl of wrath, a foul and evil sore comes upon the persons who carry the mark of the beast (the final Antichrist) and who worship his image (Rev. 16:2). Anyone loyal to the beastly government received God's judgment, poured out by His angel.

Similarly, the fifth angel pours out his bowl of wrath on the throne of the beast, that is, the capital. It becomes darkened, and people bite their tongues in pain (16:10). In response to His judgment, they blaspheme Him because of their pains and sores (16:11), but they do not repent of their evil deeds.

Even today, moral evil has various effects on its practitioners. In the climactic collision of the wrath of God, of Satan, and of the nations at the close of this age, angels play a significant part in bringing about God's judgment.

God is in charge, and His angels supervise for Him a world that

143

seems outwardly chaotic and destined to self-destruction. Angels help us see the personal qualities of human existence. We need this emphasis at a time in human history when so much of our learning and culture tends to depersonalize the universe. We know little about angels, but what we do know points to personal controls on both forces and people.

V. Human Government Becomes Antagonistic to God and His People

When a bad human government looks better to most people than anarchy or no government, people will support oppression and injustice. History has shown that governments usually do not set out to suppress human rights, encourage graft, or start wars. They become evil by the misuse of their powers for the benefit of leaders or their supporters. By the time citizens realize what has happened, the evil government may be thoroughly entrenched and determined to hold its power. The people continue to sustain it in preference to revolution and anarchy.

A. The King Who Tried to Play God for a Month
Dan. 6:3-35

The story of Daniel in the lions' den is usually a favorite with children, but rarely do we seriously consider it as adults.

The story took place at a time of transition in world powers when Medo-Persia took over Babylon. Daniel, emerging from retirement at the close of the Babylonian reign and becoming known for his experience, rose to prominence in the new empire. The king (Cyrus the Great or Darius the Mede) planned to make him supervisor over all the 120 satraps. (A satrap was an official who ruled over a specified area.) A group of prefects, satraps, and counselors that was opposed to a Jewish exile in such a high post devised a plan to eliminate Daniel. They could find no scandal in his life to discredit him, so they concentrated on his religion. They drew up an ordinance that, for all practical purposes, deified the king for one month. No one was to make a petition to any god or person except the king for thirty days. Anyone failing to comply with the order would be thrown into a den of lions (Dan. 6:7).

As far as we know, the Persian government was a good government with many qualified people and a long list of career diplomats. But because of the jealousy of a pressure group, the government began a course hostile to the worship of God. Having no real interest in any gods, the perpetrators of the scheme only wanted to get rid of Daniel. The king, flattered by the suggestion of his exaltation and unaware of the court intrigue, signed the document although he was told in advance that what he signed could not be changed. When Daniel was caught as a transgressor of this law, the king was very much distressed, and he sought—unsuccessfully—to help Daniel. He discovered that even an absolute monarch could not change the absolute law of his own land! Though the decree treated him like a deity, the king was sharply brought back to the reality that he was *not* God. As we know, God saved Daniel's life by closing the mouths of the lions. The plot against him failed, and the schemers suffered the fate they had carefully planned for Daniel.

What is the lesson here? A king who personally made no effort to proclaim his deity became a tool of a government whose acts were antagonistic to God and to His people.

B. Territorial Wars Climax in Conflict with God Himself
Dan. 11:5-39

Conflict between Egypt and Syria over the control of Palestine between 300 and 200 B.C. is discussed in the eleventh chapter of Daniel. The governments of Egypt and Syria possessed both good and bad qualities. Eventually Syria won control of Palestine, and during the first twenty-five years of its rule, the government seemed to be average. Antiochus III (the Great) wanted to expand west as well as east, but Roman pressure kept Syria at the eastern end of the Mediterranean. Antiochus died in 187 B.C., and during the reign of his successor, Seleucus IV (187-175 B.C.), there was constant jostling for territory.

The situation quickly changed. Antiochus IV (175-164 B.C.) wanted greater control of Egypt, but he was stopped by Romans who gave him a swift and final ultimatum. When he became afraid (Dan. 11:29-30), Antiochus withdrew from Egypt and returned to Syria through Palestine, which he ruled. In anger, he acted against the holy covenant. He took away the continual burnt offering in the temple and set up the "abomination that makes desolate" (Dan. 11:30-31). He resolved to eradicate the Jewish religion.

The historian Josephus gives details: "So he left the temple bare;

and took away the golden candlesticks, and the golden altar [of incense], and table [of show-bread], and the altar [of burnt offering]; and did not abstain from even the veils which were made of fine linen and scarlet. He also emptied it of its secret treasures, and left nothing at all remaining."[3]

The "abomination of desolation" was a pagan altar that Antiochus IV built at the site of the great altar of burnt offering in the Jewish temple. On this pagan altar, standing in the pillaged Jewish temple, sacrifices were offered to the Olympian Zeus, the Greek deity whom Antiochus IV worshiped. For three years, Jewish temple worship ceased.

Why did Antiochus do this? He intended to turn Palestine to the worship of Greek gods and to make the Jews accept all aspects of Greek culture (technically called Hellinization). He wanted Syria to be a world power, and he thought Hellenism would be the unifying factor that would hold together diverse peoples in his territory. In this sense, Hellenism was a religion as well as a culture. Most Jews of that time recognized that their very existence as a people was at stake, because of all that Antiochus IV was trying to force upon them. Had Antiochus IV urged only the nonreligious aspects of Hellenism, he might have succeeded. But because he so hated the religious part of Judaism, his deep antagonism to the covenant God of Israel pushed him into this sudden, drastic attempt to root out of Israel its true worship and faith. He failed, despite the Syrian government's mighty force opposed to the God of the covenant. Syria gradually and progressively became an antagonist to the God of the covenant.

C. The Dragon, the Beast, the False Prophet, and Other Allies
Rev. 11:7; 13:1-10; 17:8, 15-17

The New Testament says that what happened in Syria will happen in the world government out of which will come the final Antichrist. This ruler is called the "beast" (Rev. 11:7; 13:1-10; 17:8, 15-17) who ascends from the bottomless pit.

Throughout history, many beastly rulers seem to have come from the very pit of hell. Because of the sinful desire of people for power, evil always threatens to engulf the very process of government. Since we all participate in moral evil, we are tempted to support the particular kind of moral evil that we find attractive. Although Revelation calls such rulers and governments "beasts," the ruler or government may appear at first to be just and pious. A government that once was good, and appears and promises good, can easily become the beast (Rev. 13:1-10; 17:8, 15-17).

D. So-Called "Good Government" May Model and Extol Materialism
Rev. 18:1-24

Revelation 18 is a dirge describing the fall of the harlot city. Various groups of people compose short laments while the smoke of the burning city swirls around them.

The kings, the merchants, and the sailors have similar laments: they all weep over their lost wealth and self-indulgence. In Rev. 18:11-13 is a list of twenty-eight or twenty-nine imports that came into the ancient city of Rome. Except for slaves, all the things could be used in good ways, but all are said to be part of the wine of harlotry (Rev. 17:2). Their very lives revolved around these material things.

> "The fruit for which thy soul longed
> has gone from thee,
> and all thy dainties and thy splendor
> are lost to thee,
> never to be found again!" (Rev. 18:14).

A good government that promises a good life to its citizens may frame that good life only in terms of things, sensations, and luxurious abandonment. When this happens, the government is in the process of becoming antagonistic to God.

VI. Moral Evil Puts Human Government in Constant Tension

We are brought back to the basic question: "How important is human government?" The role of human government is strategic because in its arena occur some of the crucial struggles with moral evil. The rapid rise and fall of governments in every age accentuate the drama of this struggle.

Since government faces tension between the right and wrong use of its power, what is the ultimate solution? How can we make sure that the wrong use of power will not become so dominant that we can scarcely see its right use? Revelation proposes two solutions: (1) The kingdom of the world—all earthly kingdoms, independent or bound together—must become Christ's kingdom (11:15); and (2) Christ must begin and continue to reign forever as King of Kings and Lord of Lords (11:17; 19:16). Christ has both the power and the authority to accomplish all this, which is the reason we pray: "Let your kingdom come; let your will be done [happen or take place] as in heaven, so upon earth" (Matt. 6:10). Peter speaks of "the times of the restoration of all things" (Acts 3:21) and notes that God's holy prophets have spoken of them. The direct reign of God in human affairs will transform human existence. In answer to the question, "How important is human government?" people often quote two passages: "Render to Caesar the things that are Caesar's, and to God the things that are God's" (Mark 12:17), and "Let every person be subject to the governing powers" (Rom. 13:1).

These teachings are important, but there is much more to the biblical picture of government. In Daniel and Revelation, we often see human government functioning far differently from its God-ordained pattern. In both books God and Satan are active in human government.

Many of us grudgingly consent to human government because of the moral evil in the world. In today's democracies, we believe that the persons who govern receive their authority from the consent of the governed. Humanly speaking, this statement is true. But to the writers of Daniel and Revelation, God was the source from whom rulers derive their authority and to whom they are accountable, whether they may realize it or not.

All past, present, or future rulers exercise authority under God's jurisdiction. God appoints sinful people to have authority over others who are also sinful. But He also marks off the sphere in which Satan can operate. Only God's control of this world has kept it from absolute chaos.

While God delegates authority, He does not eliminate the consequences of the moral evil conceived and perpetrated by various rulers. Yet God overrules in the irregular tides of human affairs and brings rulers into judgment.

Summary

Daniel (chaps. 2, 5, and 7) symbolically depicts kingdoms as metals and beasts. The qualities of the metals point to the strengths and weaknesses of the governments with which they are identified. The beastly symbols show human government controlled by sheer force, often characterized by great cruelty. The fourth beast probably represents the final Antichrist, the last in a long list of candidates throughout history who were qualified to bear that title. The Antichrist will demonstrate the same beastly qualities (perhaps in a different combination) that have infected many human governments and made them instruments of Satan's power.

The harlot in Revelation is different from the beast in Daniel and Revelation. The beast symbolizes ferociousness, the harlot deceptive attractiveness. Both get what they want. John says the harlot "is the great city which is having the kingship of the earth" (Rev. 17:18). John's original readers would have recognized that he was writing about the capital city, Rome. The beast in Revelation 17 refers to both the empire and certain of its kings. The symbolism behind the harlot riding the beast signifies the close connection between the capital city and the empire.

The harlotry by which she influences the whole world is the idolatry of materialism that seduced people living in Rome and all people who traded with her. Because the Christians refused both emperor worship and the idolatry of materialism, the harlot persecuted them. Government in our day, like that of the early church, furthers the idolatrous pursuit of things. We vote for officials who promise us more things that belong to the "good life." As long as we have plenty, why should we worry about present or future generations?

People who support the final Antichrist are militarists. The first four seals (Rev. 6:1-8) portray the destructive power of militarism that saps the creative energy of people and destroys them and their lands.

Force or power in the world is meant to bring stability so that people will not wrong or hurt each other. Unfortunately, the right use of power to protect citizens from evil can easily become the wrong use. What is not ours becomes what we think ought to be ours, and we justify the use of force to change the "ought" to reality. In our present world of moral evil, force is both necessary and dangerous, which is why government can so easily become beastly.

Revelation provides only glimpses into what is involved when Christ returns as conqueror to defeat moral evil.

In this battle for the moral ascendancy of Christ, Christ's people will smite, reign, and rule with Him in His permanent and irrevocable power.

Daniel and Revelation set forth a frightening side of human government. Many governments begin with high ideals but become evil through misuse of power by leaders or their supporters. People often consent to support a bad government in preference to revolution or anarchy.

Human government faces tension in the right and wrong use of its power. Tension itself is not bad; in fact, absence of tension may be much worse, for it may indicate apathy and acceptance of wrong use of power as normative. It may indicate acceptance of sensate materialism as the accepted goal of life for a group of people. Where tension exists, protest and renewal are possible. Such a government can carry out its God-given task—opposing evil and promoting good.

How Important Is Human Government?

Notes for Chapter 5

[1]F. V. Winnett, "Bronze," in *Interpreter's Dictionary of the Bible*, I:467.
[2]*Ibid*.
[3]Josephus, *Antiquities*, XII. v. 4.

Chapter 6

What Is Distinctive About The People Of God?

The question of this chapter title could also be phrased: "Who are the people of God, and what should they be doing?" The people of God are called a "covenant" people because this special relationship comes from the agreement or covenant of the people to follow God's ways. God determines the covenant, and the people accept and live by that covenant.

The Bible presents an old first covenant and a new second or eternal one (Jer. 31:31; Luke 22:20; 1 Cor. 11:25; 2 Cor. 3:6, 14; Heb. 8:6-13). The writer of Hebrews says that because of Christ's death, "He is mediator of a new covenant in order that those who have been called might receive the promise of the eternal inheritance, since a death occurred [Christ's death] for redemption [release] from the transgressions under the first covenant" (Heb. 9:15). In other words, the sins committed under the first covenant (Old Testament) were really forgiven on the basis of the atoning death of Christ that inaugurated the new covenant. So there is really only one covenant people.

In the Old Testament, this covenant people consisted primarily of the nation Israel. Although the nation became divided into two parts (northern and southern kingdoms), the division did not release either group from their covenant with God. In the New Testament, the covenant people consist of all persons who acknowledge Jesus as Messiah, call Him Lord, and recognize that He has reconciled them to God by His death as the supreme suffering servant.

Daniel and Revelation magnificently illustrate this oneness of

God's people, even though Daniel deals with God's people under the first covenant and Revelation deals with them under the new one. Daniel emphasizes those who adhere to the holy covenant in contrast to those who forsake it (Dan. 11:30-32). Verse 32 reads: "He shall seduce with flattery those who violate the covenant; but the people who know their God shall stand firm and take action." We see that people who adhere to the covenant are praised. After God's people encounter the final Antichrist, the organized world kingdom will be given to the saints of the Most High (Dan. 7:27). God's people are also called His saints—consecrated, dedicated, holy people.

The Book of Revelation favors two terms for referring to God's people: *servants* and *saints*. Saints are mentioned in 5:8; 8:3-4; 11:18; 13:7, 10; 14:12; 16:6; 17:6; and 18:24. Servants are mentioned in 1:1; 2:20; 7:3; 10:7; 19:2, 5; and 22:3, 6. These saints and servants are covenant people because the Lamb (Christ) purchased them for God by His blood. They come from every tribe, language, people, and nation. These covenant people of the New Testament are made to be both a kingdom and priests (Rev. 5:9-10).

The term, *My people* (Rev. 18:4) reaches its highest significance when God is said to be dwelling (literally, "tenting") with His people: "Behold the dwelling place of God is with His people. He will dwell with them and they will be His people, and God Himself shall be with them, their God" (Rev. 21:3).

A great sense of oneness pervades the holy city where God will dwell with His people. The gates of the city, which are always open, are named for the twelve tribes of Israel (Rev. 21:12-13). The wall of the city has twelve foundations (obviously exposed so their beauty can be seen) on which are the names of the twelve apostles of the Lamb (Rev. 21:14). So the Bride, the wife of the Lamb, consists of God's covenant people (Rev. 21:9).

The concept of conversion is quite similar in Daniel and Revelation. Daniel's prayer (Dan. 9:3-19) is really for the conversion of his people, an action that involves "turning from our iniquities and giving heed to thy truth" (9:13) and admitting the shortcomings of all who had "not obeyed His [God's] voice" (9:14). There is no righteousness or merit by works: "We do not present our supplications before thee on the ground of our righteousness, but on the ground of thy great mercy" (9:18).

153

In the Book of Revelation, repentance and faith are central factors. People repent to give God glory (Rev. 16:9); they exercise faith in God (2:13) and Jesus (14:12). Conversion in Revelation involves a break with the past: "To the one who is loving us and who loosed us from our sins by His own blood" (1:5). Conversion means victory over moral evil: "Blessed is the one who is alert and is keeping his garments" (16:15).

To ask, "What is distinctive about the people of God?" and to recognize answers from Daniel and Revelation will yield many valuable truths. These two apocalyptic books focus on conveying how God's people can overcome moral evil and explaining what this means in both the present and the future.

I. The People of God Participate in a Growing Relationship with God

A covenant people are to be vitally related to God. How do they get into that relationship, and how do they maintain it?

A. Repentance

One Greek word for our word *repentance* means "a change of mind"; another means "to feel regret afterwards." These words involve both intellect and emotions. A common Hebrew word for *repent* means "to return," or "to turn around." Repentance, therefore, indicates coming into a vital relationship with God. Although Hebrew people in the Old Testament believed they were part of God's people by birth, they needed more than that. They needed to repent. Christians, too, needed to repent if they were to become truly God's people.

1. Repentance for non-believers. Dan. 4:25-27, 34-37; Rev. 1:7; 9:20-21; 11:13b; 14:6-7; 16:8-11

Many people today think repentance is needed only by those outside any covenant relationship with God. Such people do need to repent, but so does everyone else!

After Daniel told Nebuchadnezzar about the coming judgment (Dan. 4:4-27), he advised the king: "Therefore, O king, let my counsel be acceptable to you; break off your sins by practicing righteousness, and your iniquities by showing mercy to the oppressed, that there may perhaps be a lengthening of your tranquility" (4:27). Daniel suggested specific ways for the king to express his repentance, but Nebuchadnezzar refused to take his advice. God's judgment fell on him, and he became mentally unbalanced for a brief period, just as Daniel foretold.

When Nebuchadnezzar's reason returned, he blessed, praised, and honored the Most High (Dan. 4:34). He proclaimed that God's works were truth and His ways justice, that God was able to put down anyone who walked in pride (4:37). These were the sincere words of a person who had made radical changes in his life. Now God was more important than self to Nebuchadnezzar.

In the first chapter of Revelation, one verse (1:7) pertaining to Christ's second coming says that Christ will come with clouds; every eye will see Him, even those who pierced Him will see Him. The last phrase declares: "And all the tribes of the earth will mourn for Him." This mourning has two possible meanings: (1) the tribes of the earth can mourn because of what will come upon them, or (2) the tribes of the earth can mourn in the sense of genuine repentance.

Since the army of the beast will be slain (Rev. 19:17-21), some scholars conclude that only the first meaning is possible. But there is no evidence that every person in the world will join the army of the Antichrist. More likely this mourning represents genuine repentance. The mourning of Israel mentioned in Zech. 12:1-14 (from which the language of Rev. 1:7 is taken) is surely that of true repentance. If the mourning in Rev. 1:7 does express genuine repentance, then the book's apocalyptic pictures dealing with both judgment and conversion are evenly balanced. The book begins and closes on a note of victory. The last words in 1:7 seem to point in this direction: "Even so. Amen."[1]

The seven trumpets in Revelation are trumpets of judgment. As they sound, God changes the function of nature and uses even demonic forces to judge those who seek to destroy the earth, everyone around them, and eventually the demons themselves. After the fifth and sixth trumpets, John shows how firmly attached people are to moral evil. The people without the seal of God upon their foreheads maintain their stubborn ways. They will not repent of their idolatry, murders, sorceries, sexual immorality, or thefts (Rev. 9:20-21). People do not abandon such practices unless something decisive occurs to turn them in another direction. Even after the fourth and fifth bowls of wrath are poured out, the people refuse to repent (Rev. 16:8-11).

As noted in chapter 5, Daniel and Revelation teach that God runs the world through angels, which applies equally to controlling nations and preaching the gospel. Revelation 14:6 describes an angel flying in the middle of the heaven with the everlasting gospel to preach to every nation, tribe, language, and people. We do not know how the angel does this. Perhaps God's people are involved, as was John, the writer of Revelation (10:11). At any rate, the angel's message states: "Fear God and give Him glory, for the hour of His judgment has come; and worship Him who made heaven and earth, the sea and the fountains of water" (Rev. 14:6-7). People who respond will fear God and give Him glory; they will worship Him as creator of heaven and earth. They will repent and acknowledge who God is and what He has done.

Such revival is part of one bright scene in the Book of Revelation. In Revelation 11, two prophets bear witness, are killed, raised up, and brought to heaven. This event is followed by a great earthquake (11:13a) in which a tenth part of the city falls; seven thousand people die. Numbers in apocalyptic literature should not be forced into precise mathematics. Hence, these figures do not necessarily mean that the city had seventy thousand people or that one-tenth perished. But it does point to the vast majority (nine-tenths) who survived, about which the text says, "The rest were terrified and gave glory to the God of heaven" (11:13b). The two prophets' witness and death were not in vain. Repentance came, and the survivors gave glory to God.

2. Repentance for the people of Israel. Dan. 9:3-16

Daniel's prayer was really for the conversion of his people. As Daniel depicts the sins of his people and their departure from God, he eloquently expresses repentance for them: "To us belongs confusion of face, as at this day, to the men of Judah, to the inhabitants of Jerusalem, and to all Israel, those that are near, and those that are far away in all the lands to which thou hast driven them" (9:7). To clear up such confusion, Daniel made full confession for his people and himself (9:20).

Although the Hebrew people were both chosen and judged by God, they needed desperately to repent. Their repentance was not an option that they should choose because they were loyal Israelites. Repentance was necessary because they were rebellious and had to acknowledge the seriousness of their revolt against God.

3. Repentance for Christians. Rev. 2:4-5, 16, 21-23; 3:3, 18-20

The glorified Christ called five of the seven churches in Revelation to repent. In the seven churches, Christ found many things to commend, but He did not treat lightly the things that were wrong. Our tendency today is to play up the good points of churches and to play down things that are wrong. Not so Christ. As He walked in the midst of the seven churches of Roman Asia (present-day Turkey), He is walking today in the midst of His churches throughout the world. Many churches today combine some or all of these needs for repentance, but they rarely emphasize group or individual repentance. Yet repentance is essential to a growing relationship with God. When we repent and turn away from acts that displease God, we receive new joy, peace, and understanding. Without repentance, we live complacently and insensitively.

B. Mercy and Forgiveness
Dan. 9:9, 18-19

Repentance involves the mind, words, and deeds of people; God responds with mercy and forgiveness. Daniel writes, "To the Lord our God belongs compassions [mercy] and abundant forgivenesses" (9:9). The plurals in the Hebrew text emphasize the numerous acts of God's mercy. Daniel reminds us that we are to present our supplications on the grounds of God's great compassions (mercies). The plural is an intensive form to indicate that compassion is an emotion that involves God's whole being. But like sheep, we get into many difficulties. We are lost and cannot find our way, but we refuse to admit it. Yet God's intense compassion takes our sin into account and God responds with "tough love."

God forgives the sin and the sinner, the deed and the doer, the thought and the thinker. God hears and acts (Dan. 9:19). Daniel's picture of forgiveness is not that of some private legal decision. Rather, forgiveness is God's announcement that He has blotted out the sin. The sin is put away from both God and the sinner, enabling the two to have a closer relationship that has no place for psychological gimmicks where the sinner says, "Lord, forgive me," and then returns to practice the same sin. Forgiveness is in the daily arena of life where God meets with His people and pushes forward into a growing relationship.

C. Faith
Dan. 4:25, 34-37; 6:4, 23;
Rev. 2:10, 13, 19; 13:10; 14:12; 17:14

The Hebrew verb *aman* (basic form) and the nouns under the root are not found in the Hebrew part of Daniel. *Aman* means "to be faithful, reliable, trustworthy, to trust, believe." The nouns from this root mean "firmness, faithfulness, steadfastness, fidelity."[2] The Aramaic verb (used in Daniel) is identical with the Hebrew word except for a shorter vowel. In the Aramaic part of Daniel, the verb meaning "to trust" and the participle meaning "trustworthy" are found only three times (6:4, 23; 2:45).[3] The Greek noun *pistis* (used in Revelation) means "faith" or "trust," and the adjective *pistos* means "trustworthy, faithful, dependable, trusting, believing, full of faith."[4]

The biblical words for faith do not imply mere intellectual assent. A person exercises faith (trust) while at the same time she or he is faithful and reliable (trustworthy). A growing relationship between God and His people demands commitment, reliability, and trustworthiness. The commitment to God is fundamental. Just as we are faithful and dependable to God, we ought to be equally faithful to others. Our identification with God makes us substantial persons and solid citizens in His kingdom.

Daniel 4 recounts Nebuchadnezzar's mental illness and his full recovery brought by God. Daniel declared that Nebuchadnezzar would be separated from men until the king acknowledged the rule of the Most High. Daniel urged Nebuchadnezzar to practice righteousness and show mercy to the oppressed—to turn from his old way of thinking, to seek new knowledge, and to act in new ways. That is what faith involves.

After God restored Nebuchadnezzar, the king changed dramatically. He "blessed the Most High, and praised and glorified Him who lives forever and ever" (Dan. 4:34). These words express the true worship demanded by faith. The last recorded word from

Nebuchadnezzar is about the King of heaven: "All his works are right and his ways are just; and those who walk in pride he is able to abase" (4:37).

From youth to old age, Daniel fellowshiped with the covenant God of Israel. He prayed faithfully and had a growing relationship with God. As a result, God protected Daniel from the lions. The king happily ordered that Daniel be taken out of the den and "no kind of hurt was found upon him because he had trusted in his God" (6:23). Whenever anyone faces the crisis of death—as Daniel did—trust and a vital relationship with God are indispensable.

Faith is commitment, trust, and reliability; it is not simply stating, "I believe." The Book of Revelation, like the rest of the New Testament, emphasizes Christ as the object of faith. Christ commends the church at Pergamum: "You...have not denied faith *in me*" (Rev. 2:13). The term *saints* is important in Revelation. They are "those who are observing [keeping, practicing] the commands of God and the faith in Jesus" (14:12). They uphold their faith in Jesus Christ, the Lamb and the Lord of His church.

The Book of Revelation centers in Christology—who Christ is. Because He died, was resurrected, and ascended to heaven, Christ has earned the right to control history. Our faith is in a unique Christ who sits with His Father on His Father's throne (3:21). Therefore our relationship with God is through Jesus Christ His Son. We must hear what the Spirit is saying in Revelation to us as participants in this growing relationship.

In the message to the church in Thyatira, faith is mentioned with works and endurance (2:19). (This word is also coupled with endurance in Rev. 13:10.) Throughout the New Testament faith does not exist in isolation but is evidenced by works. Since we trust Christ, we endure in all situations because the one we trust is also our guide. We are God's covenant people who follow the Lamb wherever He leads (Rev. 14:4).

The exhortation first given to the church at Smyrna is for all Christians: "Become faithful unto death and I will give you the crown of life" (2:10). In the pressures of life we are always in the process of becoming faithful. God calls us to be faithful (reliable, trustworthy) in doing His work. The ones who will be with Christ when He returns share the title—the called, the chosen, the faithful (Rev. 17:14).

D. Holiness
Dan. 7:18, 21-22, 25, 27; 12:7, 10; Rev. 22:11

The English terms *holy* and *holiness* convey many ideas. One is that of being set apart, implying superiority. The Hebrew word can mean "apartness" or "sacredness,"[5] but it usually refers to sacred places, sacred things, or sacred priests. It sometimes refers to God and people. The Greek verb means "to consecrate, dedicate, sanctify, keep oneself holy."[6] The Greek adjective *holy* referring to people, means "consecrated to God."[7] Thus the term holy basically means "consecrated and dedicated to all that God is"—His love, compassion, mercy, and truth.

Saints are consecrated or dedicated persons in the sense that they are in the process of conforming their lives to what God desires. As they achieve more dedication to Him, they will exhibit more of His qualities of loving concern for others. In Dan. 7:18-27, the word *saints* occurs six times. In Revelation, the term *saints* and the adjective *holy* (referring to saints) occur fifteen times. Thus holiness, in the sense of dedication or consecration to God, is a central relational term in both Daniel and Revelation. The commands and warnings in the two books indicate that saints have not achieved full dedication or consecration.

People must exert themselves to achieve dedication or consecration. Daniel describes times of pressure for God's people, and of such times, he says, "Many shall purify themselves, and make themselves clean, and be refined" (Dan. 12:10). Such acts bring wisdom and understanding, but only through God's power and their own initiative may people purify themselves. "Be refined" in this context implies suffering, which may serve to purify people just as the refining process purifies metals. Thus genuine holiness may be costly. Our life experiences can either refine us (provided we are in a growing relationship with God) or embitter us.

The Book of Revelation ends with a call for growing holiness: "The righteous person, let him do righteousness even more; the consecrated, let him be consecrated even more" (22:11). Most of us have vast untapped capacity for growth. When God renews us and we come into vital relationship with Him, we are called to "the even more." We do not know the potential capacity of our consecration. Growing holiness provides the atmosphere in which we can attune ourselves to God.

II. The Genuine Commitment of God's People Is Seen in Their Daily Living

The life of the people of God is not idealized in the Bible, especially in Daniel and Revelation. They have so many needs and complex problems to solve that being in difficult places is apparently normative for God's people.

A. Commitment in the Book of Daniel: Selected Leaders in Exile
Dan. 1:8-16; 2:23; 3:16-18; 6:21-23

When the Book of Daniel opens, four young Hebrew men had been carried by Nebuchadnezzar into exile a long way from their homes. They were chosen to be a part of an elite, selected group; others in the group came from the royal family and the nobility (Dan. 1:3). The Hebrew names of the four were Daniel, Hananiah, Mishael, and Azariah, but they were given the Babylonian names of Belteshazzar (Daniel), Shadrach (Hananiah), Meshach (Mishael), and Abednego (Azariah) (Dan. 1:7). As part of their new careers, they pursued an intensive, three-year course of training in the book learning and language of the Chaldeans (3:5).

These four young men and the Chaldean youths who were being educated were to eat the king's food and drink. But because idolatry touched all aspects of the Babylonians' lives, Daniel requested a vegetarian diet for himself and his three companions. After a test period of ten days, the Hebrews were "better in appearance and fatter in flesh" (1:15), and their simple diet was permitted to become their standard fare during their training period.

More was involved than dietary laws. At stake for Daniel and his friends was their commitment to the covenant God of Israel. They began with elementary matters of food and drink, but they were also serious about their education and even more serious in their commitment to the covenant God of Israel.

Daniel's ability to interpret Nebuchadnezzar's perplexing dream (Dan. 2) catapulted him into prominence. After Nebuchadnezzar's wise men failed to tell him both the dream and its meaning (2:5), the king threatened them with death. Daniel asked for an appointment with the king. Then he prayed, and God revealed all aspects of the dream to Daniel. As a result, Daniel blessed God and ended his burst of praise with thanksgiving: "To thee, O God of my fathers, I give thanks and praise, for thou hast given me wisdom and strength, and has now made known to me what we asked of thee" (2:23).

Self-centered people rarely give thanks, whereas thanksgiving often indicates spiritual commitment. If we are involved in what we are getting, we tend to pay little attention to the giver. That was not true of Daniel. He knew that this special revelation and all his wisdom had come from God. His commitment, therefore, is apparent in his thanksgiving. He did not thank God for removing the death threat from him and all the other wise men. He was thankful that the God of his fathers was living and active in his life.

In Daniel 3 we learn what really counted for Daniel's three friends. Nebuchadnezzar had prepared a great golden image so that all people would gather at a mass rally to worship it. The dedication of the image, the ceremonies, and the mass rally were probably planned to bring a spirit of unity in a vast empire of contrasting ideas and cultures. Daniel is not mentioned in this chapter (perhaps he was away on some diplomatic mission); this incident belongs to his three friends who refused to worship Nebuchadnezzar's image.

After some Chaldeans informed the king of the disobedience of the three friends, Nebuchadnezzar called in the Jewish exiles. He told them they would have one more chance to comply. If they refused, they would be thrown into a fiery furnace. Their answer is a classic statement of true commitment to God: "If it be so, our God whom we serve is able to deliver us from the burning fiery furnace; and He will deliver us out of your hand, O king. But if not, be it known to you, O king, that we will not serve your gods or worship the golden image which you have set up" (Dan. 3:17-18). Their statement is a humble, unequivocable confession of loyalty. They did not know what God's response would be, but they knew that they must put their lives on the line and leave the outcome to the covenant God of Israel. God demonstrated His power in delivering them from death in the furnace. Their commitment was genuine, and they registered an unbroken loyalty to the God of their fathers, the God of Abraham, Isaac, and Jacob. The three young men are never mentioned again in the Book of Daniel.

Daniel's experience of being thrown into a lions' den was a similar test of loyalty. Would he observe his regular times of prayer despite an edict that forbade such activity and promised lethal punishment? Daniel continued his daily prayer habits and clashed with the scheming officials of Medo-Persia. When the king (Cyrus the Great or Darius the Mede) found that Daniel was safe, Daniel explained that God had delivered him from harm "because I was found blameless before him; and also before you, O king, I have done no wrong" (6:22). Daniel's commitment to God affected his conduct before both God and the king. Daniel's faithfulness to God resulted in his being faithful to the king as long as the king made no demands that would cause him to be disloyal to God. The pressures of life provided the backdrop for testing how loyal to God Daniel and his friends actually were. They had to make a clear choice and they chose rightly.

B. Commitment in the Book of Revelation: Selected Churches in Roman Asia Evaluated by Christ

The glorified Christ walked among the seven churches to examine their commitment to Him. In the letters in the Book of Revelation, we see their needs, their difficult problems, and their strengths. What they did and how they lived revealed the nature and degree of their commitment.

1. All the churches. Rev. 1:3; 22:7, 9

The Book of Revelation begins with a blessing on the one who reads aloud the whole book to each church. People who both hear and keep (observe and practice) the things written in the book will also be blessed (1:3). John repeats this promise at the close of the book: "Blessed is the one keeping the words of the prophecy of this book" (22:7). Thus obedience to the book's content brings a blessing. *Any Christian who wants to use the Book of Revelation primarily to chart out a version of future events has missed its point.* Even if such a future timetable were correct—a highly dubious assumption—the purpose of the book is to tell Christians how to live. They are to practice the words of the prophecy.

The seven churches to which John wrote were part of the Roman province of Asia. Ephesus and Smyrna were on the Aegean Sea, while the other five were inland cities located on the same road. Pergamum was ten miles inland from the sea. South and east of Pergamum was Thyatira, then came Sardis, Philadelphia, and finally Laodicea. The road continued south and east through Perga and reached the Mediterranean at Attalia. The distance from

Pergamum to Laodicea was approximately one hundred and fifty miles.

To appreciate the victories and failures of commitment in these churches, we should know something of their historical and cultural situation. (What follows are only highlights; a good commentary will give a more comprehensive picture.[8])

2. Ephesus.

Historical situation: Ephesus was located on the Cayster River on a gulf of the Aegean Sea. The silt carried down by the Cayster eventually filled in the bay and brought an end to Ephesus as a port city, but in New Testament times it was large—more than a quarter of a million people lived there. The cult of emperor worship was evident, but the main attraction was the temple of the goddess Artemis. Paul spent at least three years ministering in Ephesus (Acts 20:31).

Degree of commitment: As recorded in Rev. 2:2-7a the glorified Christ commends this church for its (1) works, (2) toil, (3) endurance, (4) intolerance of evil persons, (5) testing of false apostles, (6) tirelessness, and (7) hatred of the Nicolaitans' works. Christ reproves the church because it had abandoned its first love—both its love for people and its love for God. The remedy was to do the first works (2:5). Although Ephesus was an effective and committed church, it needed more Christian love that provides the energy for committed Christians to do their work.

3. Smyrna.

Historical situation: Located thirty-five miles north of Ephesus, this city on the Aegean Sea is now called Izmir. Ancient Smyrna had a better harbor than Ephesus, and its cultural advantages included a library, theater, and stadium. It was also reputed to be the birthplace of Homer. Although Smyrna showed signs of literary vitality, it was certainly an idolatrous city. Smyrna had a temple in honor of the goddess of Rome as well as a temple to Emperor Tiberius. The most famous boulevard in town—the Street of Gold—had a temple at each end: one to a goddess cult figure called Sipylene Mother, the other to the Greek deity Zeus. A large Jewish population there was hostile to the Christians. The church father Polycarp died a martyr's death in the city in A.D. 156.

Degree of commitment: The church at Smyrna experienced both

tribulation and poverty, but Christ knew that this church was still spiritually rich. Although the believers lived in adversity, the church had genuine commitment. There was apparent conflict with the Jewish synagogue in the city, and Christ tells them that even more tribulation is at hand, but they are not to fear it. This church receives no rebuke. Instead, Christ encourages the people to "be faithful until death" and promises "I will give you the crown [a life freed from the surroundings of moral evil]" (2:10). The narrative exudes confidence that this church will continue faithful and will receive the crown—life in the presence of Christ.

4. Pergamum.

Historical situation: Pergamum, a cultural city, had a library of more than 200,000 volumes. The use of parchment for scrolls was developed there when war cut off the supply of papyrus from Egypt. Among the sacred and royal buildings on this mountainlike citadel (from which it derived its Greek name) was the great altar of Zeus. Other deities worshiped in Pergamum included Athene, Dionysus, and Asklepios, the god of healing (hence his title, "Savior"). Pergamum was also the official center in the Roman province of Asia for the imperial cult of emperor worship.

Degree of commitment: In this center of emperor worship, one church member, Antipas, was put to death for Christ, probably because he came into conflict with the imperial cult (2:13). The angel said about this church, "And you are holding fast my name" (that is, you have really laid hold of my person). This statement shows the commitment of the church. But some church members were eating food offered to idols and engaging in sexual immorality. So within this church were those deeply committed to Christ and others whose way of life resembled that of their pagan neighbors.

5. Thyatira.

Historical situation: Although Thyatira, forty miles inland from Pergamum, was not a major city, there were many trade guilds. Lydia, a seller of purple dye (Acts 16:14-15, 40), came from Thyatira. The city's protector god, Tyrimnos, was just another name for the Greek sun god, Apollo. Consequently, Apollo was the cult deity of these guilds.

Degree of commitment: This church is commended by Christ

for (1) the works they have done, (2) their love, (3) their faith, (4) their service or ministry, (5) their endurance, and (6) their present works, which exceed their earlier works (Rev. 2:19-25, 29).

But the church was faced with one obvious problem. Some church members followed the teachings of a false prophetess called Jezebel who advocated eating meat offered to idols and engaging in sexual immorality. Apparently she taught a mixture of Christian and non-Christian ideas. Possibly she followed some teachings of the Gnostics who believed they had secret knowledge that made them superior. Jezebel may have taught something like this: "As Christians you received grace so that you can overcome any kind of sin. All matter is evil, and since we have a material body, we are predisposed especially to sexual sins. But if we confine our sexual activities to Christians, and if we avail ourselves of God's grace, we will be immune from any effects of sexual sins. In fact, they will not be sins at all but just part of Christian fellowship."

Christ said, however, that if the disciples of Jezebel's teaching did not repent, they might be punished with death. Christ asked the faithful ones to hold fast to what they had. The gospel does not teach that matter is evil, and therefore we do not sin because we have a material body. The followers of Jezebel's false precepts had much to learn, because we are not to use grace that sin might abound. If they repented, we can assume that this church became victorious and kept Christ's work until the end (2:26).

6. Sardis.

Historical situation: Sardis had a rich history as the capital of the ancient kingdom of Lydia, which was captured by Cyrus the Great in 546 B.C. The city later fell successively to Syria, then Pergamum, and finally Rome. The goddess of the city was Cybele, whose Greek name was Artemis. The first gold and silver coins were minted and circulated in this prosperous city of much wealth, fame, and gold.

Degree of commitment: This church was reputed to be alive, but when Christ tested the works of the vast majority, the church proved to be dead (Rev. 3:1-4, 6). The lively reputation of the church was based only on superficial, external works. Commitment must be connected with deeds that leave no doubt about loyalty and allegiance to Christ. But such deeds were largely missing in Sardis.

A few in Sardis had been faithful, those who had "not defiled their garments." Christ promised that these persons would walk with Him in white clothing because they were worthy (3:4). Thus even in a church that was mostly dead, there were some worthy followers of the Lamb.

7. Philadelphia.

Historical situation: Philadelphia lies on the same road as Sardis, but further south and east. Its location almost due east from Smyrna and Sardis gave it the title "gateway to the East" and enough trade to become a commercial city. The land north of Philadelphia was right for growing grapes, so the area had a balance of agriculture and industry. Like many other cities, Philadelphia was located in an earthquake area, and although it was the youngest of the seven cities addressed by John, it was still two hundred and fifty years old when he wrote. After the Lydian tongue was replaced by Greek, the city promoted Greek culture and various idolatrous cults, with many temples and religious festivals. Situated in a wine-producing district, Philadelphia participated in the worship of Dionysus, the god of wine. A little more than a century after John wrote to the church, the city became the provincial home for a temple to the imperial cult.

Degree of commitment: Christ commended this church for (1) its works, (2) its practice of His message, and (3) its faithfulness to His person (Rev. 3:8-13). Philadelphia experienced some hostility between the synagogue and the church. Because this church had kept Christ's message, Christ said He would preserve them in a coming hour of testing. Apparently this church showed a firm commitment to Christ in its whole manner of living.

8. Laodicea.

Historical situation: Laodicea was a commercial center forty miles southeast of Philadelphia, six miles south of Hierapolis, and ten miles northwest of Colosse (to whom Paul wrote a letter). At the time John wrote to Laodicea, this wealthy city was about three hundred and fifty years old. Because many sheep were raised in the nearby Lycus valley, Laodicea became a textile and banking center. Destroyed by an earthquake in A.D. 60, Laodicea arranged its own finances and rebuilt itself without help from Rome. Laodicea had a medical school famous for producing healing salves and ointments. The city's water came by stone pipes from a spring six miles away; thus, it was militarily vulnerable and always interested in maintaining friendly relations with its neighbors.

Degree of commitment: The church in this city had the outward trappings of worldly success. The church thought it was self-sufficient, but Christ revealed its true nature (Rev. 3:15-22). Although it considered itself wealthy, Laodicea really needed to procure true gold from Christ. It thought it had fine clothing, but only Christ could dress them in true clothing. The members presumed they could see, but they needed a healing eyesalve. The church believed it was in fellowship with Christ, but their "lukewarm" actions evidenced only a half-hearted commitment that would not last. Christ pleaded with the people to open the door to Him so that He could transform their half-hearted allegiance into a full commitment and have true fellowship with them. Because Christ promised that the spiritual victor would sit with Him on His throne (3:21), many people in Laodicea probably repented and became zealous for God (3:19).

The Book of Revelation teaches that actions establish true commitment to God. Whenever we turn aside from this loyalty, or when sin breaks our fellowship with Christ, we need to read the last "blessed" in Revelation: "Blessed are those who are washing their robes, that their right to the tree of life will be a reality, and that they may enter into the city by means of its gates" (22:14). This is what it means to be victorious.

III. The People of God Are a Unique Group

The people of God in the Book of Daniel are the nation Israel. Although most people from both the northern and southern kingdoms remained dispersed after 586 B.C., some returned to Israel when Cyrus the Great made this possible in 539 B.C. The Old Testament people of God were not unique because of their rebuilt temple, their synagogues inside or outside Palestine, or even their physical descent from Abraham and Sarah. They were unique because of their obedience to God and His covenant.

In the Book of Revelation, the people of God are all persons who acknowledge Jesus as the Messiah. They come from every tribe, language, nation, and people, but despite language and cultural differences they remain one unique group in that all confess Jesus as Messiah and Lord.

Ever since the Reformation, Christians have adopted certain names to differentiate themselves from other Christians. If these appellations serve only to identify what the various groups emphasize, nothing need be lost. However, if we as Christians accentuate our differences, cast aspersions on the integrity of other Christian groups, and fail to learn from each other or to cooperate with each other, then we are losing one of our distinctives as the people of God. We make an impact because we obey God and keep His covenant.

A. Daniel's People Were God's People
Dan. 10:14; 11:28-30

When the unnamed heavenly messenger came to Daniel in a vision, he conversed with Daniel about important things that lay ahead for his people. The messenger told Daniel that he had come "to make you understand what is to befall your people in the end of the days" (Dan. 10:14). When Daniel closed his prayer (recorded in Daniel 9), he pleaded with God not to delay "because your name is called upon your city and upon your people" (9:19). This claim was significant. God called Abraham and judged His people, but He never abandoned them.

The people of Israel were unique in the Old Testament because they possessed a holy covenant. God laid down the terms, and the Israelites announced publicly that they would live according to them. Succeeding generations were obligated to reaffirm this covenant given to Abraham and his descendants (Gen. 12:7; 15:15; 17:7; 24:7; Gal. 3:29).

Antiochus IV Epiphanes knew how central this covenant was for the people of Israel. Daniel 11:28-30 says: "His heart shall be set against the holy covenant...he shall turn back and be enraged and take action against the holy covenant...he will give heed to those who forsake the holy covenant." Even though Antiochus IV in his rage profaned the temple and caused the sacrifices to cease for three years, he could not nullify this holy covenant that continued and was fulfilled in the new covenant which Jesus inaugurated (Luke 22:20; 1 Cor. 11:25).

The covenant relationship distinguishes God's people. No matter how far they are scattered or how great are their differences, they have pledged to carry out God's commands. In neither the old nor the new covenant was this transaction merely intellectual. The covenant established a relationship with God as a base for moral transformation in the life of the covenant people. Further, the relationship also involved action toward fellow members of the covenant and toward those outside it. Where such action does not occur, the covenant is only a matter of words. The new covenant must be written on the heart (Jer. 31:33; Heb. 8:10; 10:16), so that it is more than just words. Unfortunately, some in Israel and in the church assumed that since they knew the language of the covenant, they also knew the Lord of the covenant. Obedience to the covenant's demands is the only test of true knowledge.

B. Christ's People Are a Kingdom and Priests
Rev. 1:6, 20; 5:9-10; 20:6

The terms *kingdom* and *priests* have distinct meanings in the political and religious worlds of the Old and New Testaments. A kingdom encompassed people in a specific area living under one rule; priests, whether in Israel or in the surrounding nations, were intermediaries between deity and human beings. Priests offered sacrifices, carried out rituals, led worship, read from sacred scriptures or oracles, and were in charge of music. (In reference to the Israelites, we are using the term *priest* to cover both sons of Aaron and the Levites.)

What did John mean when he wrote, "He made us to be a kingdom, priests to God and His Father" (Rev. 1:6), and "He made them [people from every tribe, language, people, and nation] a kingdom and priests to our God, and they shall reign on earth" (Rev. 5:10)? A valuable key to the meaning comes from Ex. 19:5-6 where God promises three things to His people Israel if they obey His voice and keep His covenant: (1) they will be God's own possession among all peoples; (2) they will be a kingdom of priests; and (3) they will be a holy nation. Revelation also teaches that God expects obedience. In Rev. 1:6 a blessing is promised to those who keep the words of this prophecy. For John, a kingdom designates God's people as the group over whom God rules. God's people, spread throughout the world, are His realm or kingdom (Rev. 1:6; 5:10).

In Rev. 1:6 and 5:10, the kingdom is associated with priests. George R. Beaseley-Murray suggests that the abstract word *kingdom* is used for the concrete term *kings*,[9] which would mean that God's people are both kings and priests. This interpretation certainly has merit, but we prefer to maintain the idea of a kingdom, a sphere of rule by God in which each subject in the future is to become a king. Revelation 5:10 declares that those who are a kingdom and priests for God will reign upon the earth. We think this means we have a kingdom of potential kings and right now these same people are actual priests.

God now reigns over His people, and His people respond by being priests (or mediators)—representing God to all people in the world and representing the people in the world to God. This priesthood, of course, involves both men and women. The people of God are now a kingdom but can expect an even greater function in the future: "Let thy kingdom come, let thy will be done as in heaven, so upon earth" (Matt. 6:10; Rev. 2:26-27; 5:10, 12; 20:6).

When John describes the second coming of Christ (Rev. 19:11—20:6), Christ is central. Those who take part in the first resurrection will be priests of God and of Christ, and they will reign with Him for a thousand years (meaning a long period of time). Christ's people are meant to reign with Him to remove every vestige of moral evil and to bring all who do not know God into vital relationship with Him. *Kingdom, priests,* and *kings* are terms that indicate what God expects of His people right now and what He plans for them in the future. If we carried out all the elements of being a kingdom, priests, and kings, we would certainly be distinctive people. Perhaps our lack of distinctiveness indicates we have forgotten to what God has called us.

C. Prayer Is Important for People Who Are Priests

The books of Daniel and Revelation set forth the essential nature of prayer for the people of God.

1. Importance of prayer in the life of Daniel.
Dan. 6:10-11; 9:3-23

High officials in the Medo-Persian government who were jealous of Daniel persuaded Darius to sign an order designating that no one could petition any god or man except the king for one month. As an old man, Daniel would be dispatched to the lions, and the jealous officials would be rid of their rival. The scheme seemed foolproof.

Although the intrigue was devilish, it revealed what kind of prayer life Daniel had. When everything was signed and the trap was fully laid, Daniel continued his prayers. Three times a day when he went to his house with its windows opened toward Jerusalem, he knelt and prayed. Four Aramaic verbs are used to describe the prayers he made: (1) he bowed in prayer, (2) he praised, (3) he asked or requested, and (4) he implored favor. Both his posture and words show Daniel's intensity when he came before the Lord in prayer. Although he was a busy statesman, he set aside three specific prayer periods that even his enemies could anticipate. Prayer was obviously central to Daniel's life.

In Daniel's prayer of confession for his people and himself (Dan. 9:3-23), we see similar qualities in his prayer life. What appears to be repetition reveals the intensity of his confession. Using eight Hebrew words, he described the disobedience of his people. Their revolt against God and the judgment that followed were great national tragedies to Daniel. He grieved that so few had returned to God in their period of exile. His language is saturated with terms showing his right communication with God: "While I was speaking and praying, confessing my sin and the sin of my people Israel, and presenting my supplications before the Lord my God for the holy hill of my God; while I was speaking in prayer..." (9:20-21).

Daniel prayed this prayer shortly before Cyrus decreed that Jewish exiles could return to their homeland. Perhaps Cyrus' decree was part of the answer to Daniel's prayer. It might have been first a private prayer and later a public one at some Jewish religious gathering. Daniel's prayer centered on God's people and on God's city, Jerusalem: "Thy name is called upon thy city and upon thy people" (9:19). Possibly many of Daniel's contemporaries sincerely joined him in this prayer, which helped prepare them for a long hazardous journey from Babylon to Jerusalem.

2. Importance of prayer in the description of heaven.
Rev. 5:8; 8:3-4

In Revelation 4—5 is a complicated vision of God's throne. Around the throne are twenty-four elders who represent the people of God and four living creatures who represent nature. The Lamb is Christ who, by virtue of His death and resurrection, became worthy to break the seals and open the scroll. Seven spirits are there, representing the Spirit of God in His fullness (the same Spirit who speaks to the churches).

In this section, there are several references to prayer. When

Christ takes the scroll, the four living creatures and the twenty-four elders fall down before the Lamb. Heavenly worship and prayers are directed toward the throne. Each elder has a harp and a golden bowl full of incense; the bowls contain the prayers of the saints (5:8).

Just before the seven angels with the seven trumpets blow their trumpets of judgment, there is a pause that emphasizes the central place of prayer in heaven. An angel comes and stands before the altar of incense. "He was given much incense to mingle with the prayers of all the saints upon the golden altar which is before the throne" (8:3). John re-emphasizes the centrality of prayer when he adds: "And the smoke of the incense rose with the prayers of the saints from the hand of the angel before God" (8:4). Before God and His throne the prayers of the saints ascend.

The half-hour silence in Rev. 8:1 may have something to do with these prayers. George R. Beasley-Murray comments: "That the silence is for the solemn hearing of the prayers is thoroughly plausible."[10] The people of God make an impact because they pray both individually and collectively. When God's people do not talk to Him, something is wrong with their relationship.

God does not communicate with us like an authoritarian parent who demands that His offspring do exactly as He desires. In the Scriptures God has told us a great deal about what He wills. Now God communicates with us by His Spirit who reminds us of what He has taught and helps us apply these truths. As we pray for more enlightenment, God grants it and communes with us on the highest plane. As we talk reverently, openly, and simply to God, He responds in similar fashion. After all, He has asked us to pray.

D. Worship Is Important for People Who Are Priests
Rev. 4:10-11; 5:11-14

The Book of Revelation oscillates between visions of heaven and earth. In one section God's people will be sealed upon earth (7:1-8), and in the next a great multitude stands before the throne of God. This vast multitude comes from every nation, tribe, people, and language (7:9-17).

In our thinking, boundaries between heaven and earth are fixed. Visions of things in the heavenly realm must be described in earthly language or else we cannot understand anything about it.

Most of this language comes from the Old Testament rituals involving altars, incense, the ark of the covenant, and walled cities.

The extent of this language problem becomes evident in the picture of worship in Revelation which features the twenty-four angelic representatives of God's people—Israel and the church (12+12). The four living creatures (who represent nature) give glory, honor, and thanksgiving to God (4:9). Similarly, the twenty-four elders worship the one who lives forever. They cast their crowns before His throne because He is Creator: "You created all things and because of your will they existed and were created" (4:10-11).

In Rev. 5:11 we are told of the sounds of worship. We hear living creatures and the sounds of the elders as they celebrate the worthiness of the Lamb who was slain. He is worthy to receive all that is connected with worship (5:11-12). Then every creature in God's immense creation acclaims blessing, honor, glory, and power to God and to the Lamb. Here the atonement is the reason for the worship and praise. The four living creatures say "Amen," and the twenty-four elders fall down and worship (5:13-14).

These two visions show the importance of worship. God's people and all His creatures worship Him. They anticipate God's victory and the final, total harmony of His creation.

What do these passages say about worship to us today? We learn to worship now because this will be a central activity of the people of God in heaven. All God's people who have ever lived have moved generation by generation into the heavenly realm. The twenty-four elders—angelic representatives—have been joined by millions of those whom they represent. There are infinitely more of God's people in heaven than there are on earth. But the Book of Revelation emphasizes God's people who are in the earthly setting struggling with the many forms of moral evil that beset them. At the same time, the worship in heaven, led by the twenty-four angelic representatives, is growing in volume.

Perhaps these heavenly models are given to us so that we can "tune" our worship to acknowledge God's worth. Revelation's pictures of the eternal realm illuminate God's worth in terms of His being Creator and of His providing atonement for His people. As the book progresses, we see why the boundary between the earthly and the eternal realms needs to be eradicated (Rev. 21:1—22:5). Until that time, worship is necessary in both realms.

E. Endurance and Faithfulness Characterize the People of God

The people of God do not surrender in the face of opposition. The Book of Revelation helped the first readers and continues to help present-day readers understand why there is such opposition to the gospel and who is responsible for it.

1. War in heaven sets stage for satanic pressure on God's people. Rev. 12:1-18

The twelfth chapter of Revelation depicts both God and Satan active in events in history. The chapter opens with the representation of a pregnant woman clothed with the sun, the moon under her feet, and a crown of twelve stars on her head. The woman signifies the messianic community of humble believers into which Jesus was born. Jesus is the Man-Child she bears, the one whom Satan wants to devour. In actual history, Herod the Great killed all male children two years and younger in the Bethlehem area in his effort to kill the baby Jesus (Matt. 2:13-15).

The messianic community is promised protection in 12:6, 13-16, but from whom or what? The rest of Revelation 12 provides the answer.

The war in heaven (12:7-9) is seen to occur at the time of Christ's ascension to heaven (12:5b). Thus Christ's victory on earth removed Satan's access to God so that he had no opportunity to "accuse the brethren" before Him. Heaven rejoiced over Satan's removal, but the earth and the sea were warned: "The devil has come down to you in great wrath, because he knows that his time is short" (12:12). The messianic community needed protection from the intense wrath of Satan, portrayed in pursuit of the woman who bore the male child (12:13).

God protected the "woman" for a short time. The Book of Acts, which records the beginning of the church, tells of only two martyrs: Stephen (Acts 7) and James, the brother of John (Acts 12:2). When Satan found that he could not defeat the messianic community—now spread from Jerusalem to Antioch of Syria—he went after "the rest of her seed." These were believers won to Christ by Paul and his companions on the missionary journeys. These believers are "those who keep the commandments of God and bear testimony to Jesus" (Rev. 12:17). The death, resurrection, and ascension of Christ were acts of God that will eventually defeat moral evil. Immediately Satan's sphere of influence was reduced, but he now exercises greater activity in the earthly sphere where he is still allowed to function. If God's people are to be victorious, they must endure and be faithful.

2. God promises to protect His people under pressure.
Rev. 3:10-11; 7:1-8; 9:4; 11:1-2; 14:1-5; 13:9, 10; 16:2, 10, 11

The Book of Revelation speaks of the wrath of: (1) the nations (11:18); (2) Satan (12:12, 17); and (3) God (6:16-17; 11:18; 15:1, 7; 19:15).

Christ promised to protect the church at Philadelphia from the trial that would come to all those who dwell on the earth (3:10). Since this testing was for those who were satisfied with their self-centered lifestyle, the church at Philadelphia would not be exposed to God's wrath.

All Christians will be sealed with God's seal (7:3). The number 144,000, followed by 12,000 from each tribe, is a symbolic number designating God's faithful covenant people, the true Israel, who acknowledge Jesus as the Messiah. Interpreters who would like to consider this as an exact literal group must face the fact that these are 144,000 Jewish males (14:4). Since the seal is for protection from God's wrathful judgments on people who do not belong to Him, a literal interpretation of the 144,000 males is incomprehensible. Instructions to the demonic locusts are specific: "They were told not to harm the grass of the earth or any green growth on any tree, but only those of mankind who have not the seal of God upon their foreheads" (9:4). The 144,000 stands for Jews or Gentiles who acknowledge Jesus as the Messiah and therefore belong to Christ. They are His body, His covenant people; they are His believing, trusting, and loyal servants. The tribe symbolism points to the diversity within a truly unified people, something that the literal twelve tribes of Israel will never really achieve. The unity is highlighted by intensive dedication (Rev. 14:1-5); the diversity is apparent in that all were purchased for God from the earth (Rev. 14:3), from every tribe, language, people, and nation (5:9). If only 144,000 male Jews have the seal, Christian Jewish women, as well as men, women, and children who were Gentile believers, would all be doomed. God would be pouring His wrath on them, which He promises He will not do (9:4).

In Rev. 11:1-2, the verb "to measure" means "to preserve." No one would measure the worshipers to see how tall they were! Rather, the language here describes God's people and their earthly worship. The symbols come from the Jewish temple with its altar, inner courts, and outer court. It means that God's people will be protected while those who are not God's people will be running rampant and destroying.

The words *keeping, sealing* (several times), and *measuring* (or *preserving*) indicate that God will take care of His people. But such words do not promise that Christians, facing the wrath of either Satan or the nations, will escape the threat of death. They may even die, as did Antipas from the church at Pergamum (2:13). Protection from God's wrath is total, but protection from Satan's wrath is partial even as the limits to which he can torment are partial. He can slay the body, but he is powerless to separate the Christian from God.

When Christ breaks the fifth seal (6:9-11), we learn of additional martyrs. They are praying that God will vindicate their cause, the gospel for which they gave their lives (6:10). These martyrs are described as being "under the altar." This odd expression actually affirms their security and closeness to God Himself. "Then they were each given a white robe and told to rest a little longer, until the number of their fellow servants and their brethren should be complete, who were to be killed as they themselves had been" (6:11). The number of martyrs will be enlarged, and there will be loss of life for a respected minority. But all will be vindicated, especially those who loved not their lives unto death (12:11). In the conflict with moral evil, many of God's people stand firm under pressure and will be protected.

F. Conviction About God's Control
Rev. 13:10; 14:12

Christians endure many pressures and resolutely move forward. One reason is their belief in God's sovereign reign in the affairs of people. Revelation 13:10 says that captivity and death come to those who kill and take others captive. Anyone who is loyal to the beast—the final Antichrist—will experience God's undiluted wrath (14:9-10). John concisely comments: "Here is the endurance of the saints" (14:12). The saints have ample reason to endure.

G. Prospects for the Future Are as Bright as the Person of Christ
Rev. 11:16

The people of God are faithful because Jesus is communicating with His people. Jesus sent His messenger to communicate with

John, through him to the seven churches, and through them to all the churches. Christ, who was from the root of David, is now the "bright and morning star" (22:16) and the herald of a new day. The night is almost gone; a new epoch is dawning. Jesus the Messiah and the leader is the morning star of hope. With such a leader, the people of God can endure and remain faithful.

IV. God Promises and Demands Decisive Action

God not only promises but also carries out His promises and expects His people to respond decisively. In a world of moral evil, failure to act can have sad consequences.

A. God Promises to Deal with Sin and Moral Evil
Dan. 9:24

"Seventy heptads [weeks]," Daniel says, "are decreed for your people and your holy city" (9:24). Such apocalyptic numbers are symbolic, designed to arrest our attention and to infer shorter or longer periods of time. They show God is in control. They do not tell us exact, precise time periods.

Daniel says that the heptads have six purposes: (1) to make an end of the transgression, (2) to seal up sins, (3) to atone for iniquity, (4) to usher in everlasting righteousness, (5) to seal up the vision and the prophet, and (6) to anoint the sacredness of the holy things (9:24). All six things were fulfilled by Christ when He cried out on the cross: "It has been completed" (John 19:30). All things that had been completed concerned the redemptive work of the incarnate Son. Jesus' return will make effective in the human sphere and beyond what He has already completed in His life, death, and resurrection.

If any person rejects God's provided remedy for sin, then God's decisive action is of no avail for that person. But in the total plan of God, His acts transform lives.

B. God Promises that True Works Will Abide
Rev. 14:13

A voice from heaven told John to write: "Blessed are the dead, those who are dying in the Lord from this point on [in the clash between loyalty to God and a false god, Antichrist]. They are blessed indeed, says that Spirit, that they may rest from their toils; certainly their works will follow them" (Rev. 14:13).

The ones who die begin their new life resting from the toil essential in being loyal to God. Our most creative acts are those we do for the Lord. When we move on, they move on with us.

C. God and His People Promise Life to Persons Who Respond
Rev. 22:17

This invitation in Rev. 22:17 is one of the most interesting in the Bible: "The Spirit and the Bride say, 'Come.' And let him who hears say, 'Come.' And let him who is thirsty come, let him who desires take the water of life without price."

The invitation is extended by the Spirit (the Spirit of God) and by the Bride (God's people from both covenants). The individual Christian hears the Spirit and the Bride offer the invitation, and to this Christian, John says, "Let him join in the invitation."

The person who is thirsting for reality must be willing to come. He must take the water of life as a gift. Here is another interesting quality in the people of God. They can join with God, and together God and His people extend an invitation that brings the Water of Life to those persons thirsting in the parched desert of the soul.

Summary

Who are the people of God, and what should they be doing? They are in a special, vital covenant relationship with God. The covenant is an agreement, determined by God, by which the people of God agree to live.

In the Old Testament, the covenant people were the nation Israel. In the New Testament, the covenant people are all those who acknowledge Jesus as Messiah. Daniel and Revelation both communicate the oneness of the people of God, although each uses different terms. Daniel contrasts those who keep the covenant with those who forsake it, while the Book of Revelation employs the terms *servants* and *saints* to designate God's people. Nevertheless, there is only one covenant people.

Because the people of God are prominent in Daniel and Revelation, both books stress repentance and faith. They also have similar concepts of conversion. Daniel's prayer, recorded in Dan. 9:3-19, reveals how deeply he felt the Hebrew people needed to repent. In Revelation, the glorified Christ calls on the believers in five of the seven churches to repent of their sinful lifestyle, their abandonment of their first love, their false teachings, their indifference, and their self-sufficiency. Repentance involves the mind, words, and deeds of people, to which God responds with mercy and forgiveness.

A growing relationship of God with His covenant people demands faith. The biblical words for faith imply more than intellectual assent. Where faith is present, there are commitment, reliability, and trustworthiness. Daniel is a good example of a man with such true faith. In Revelation, people observing God's commands and having faith in Jesus are called saints.

Holiness is also a quality of the people of God. They are dedicated to doing what God desires, though such dedication requires effort. Revelation ends with a call for growing holiness: "The righteous person, let him do righteousness even more; the consecrated, let him be consecrated even more" (22:11).

The life of the people of God is not idealized in the Bible. They face very difficult problems. Three young friends of Daniel had to endure a fiery furnace because they put their lives on the line and left the outcome to the covenant God of Israel. That is commitment. In Revelation, the glorified Christ walked among the seven churches to examine their true commitment to Him. The purpose of Revelation is to tell Christians how to live in situations of great stress. (Its primary purpose is not to chart future events.)

The people of God are unique. In the Old Testament, the people of God are those who are obedient to God and to His covenant. In Revelation, they are the ones from every tribe, language, and nation who acknowledge Jesus as Messiah. Although scattered around the world, they are one group because of their common loyalty to Christ.

In Revelation, Christ's people are called a kingdom and priests. In the Old Testament, a kingdom meant people in a specific area living under one rule, and priests were intermediaries between God and humans. When John writes, "He made us to be a kingdom, priests to His [Christ's] God and Father" (Rev. 1:6), the kingdom designates God's royal rule. God's people, spread throughout the world, are His realm or kingdom.

At present, God reigns over His people, and they respond by being priests—representing God to all people and representing the people of the world to God. These priests, both men and women, are mediators. Partakers in the first resurrection (Rev. 20:5-6) will be priests of God and of Christ and will reign with Him for a long period of time. As kings, they will still be priests.

Worship is equally important for these priests. The Book of Revelation oscillates between visions of heaven and earth. Visions of eternal things must be described in earthly language, or we understand nothing. Thus most of the language regarding worship in heaven comes from Old Testament rituals involving altars, incense, the ark, and crowns. Worship will be a central activity of the people of God in heaven.

Endurance and faithfulness must characterize the people of God if they are to be victorious. Revelation pictures a heavenly war which cast out Satan and sent him to the earth where he instigates persecution of the church.

All Christians will be sealed with God's seal (Rev. 7:3). The number 144,000 is a *symbolic* number designating God's faithful, covenant people. While God protects His people from His own wrath, His protection from Satan's wrath is only partial, as the many martyrs for Christ testify.

God promises to deal with sin and moral evil. Jesus' life, death, and resurrection effectively deal with sin and its punishment. When Christ returns, the defeat of moral evil will be complete.

The last picture in Revelation is that of the Spirit of God and the Bride (God's people from both covenants) extending an invitation to "Come...let him who desires, take the water of life without price" (Rev. 22:17). The people of God join with Him in extending the invitation.

[1]Bauer, "nai," in *Greek-English Lexicon*, p. 533. Bauer classifies this as a solemn assurance.
[2]Brown, Driver, and Briggs, pp. 52-54.
[3]*Ibid.*, p. 1081
[4]Bauer, "pistis," and "pistos," pp. 662-665
[5]Brown, Driver, and Briggs, pp. 871-872.
[6]Bauer, pp. 8-9.
[7]*Ibid.*, pp. 9-10.
[8]George R. Beasley-Murray, *The Book of Revelation, The New Century Bible* (Grand Rapids, Mich.: Wm. B. Eerdmans, 1981), pp. 57-58.
[9]*Ibid.*, p. 150.
[10]Robert Mounce, *The Book of Revelation, The New International Commentary on the New Testament* (Grand Rapids, Mich.: Wm. B. Eerdmans Publishing Co., 1977), pp. 85-86, 91-92, 95-96, 101-102, 108-109, 114-115, 122-124.

Chapter 7

How Much Does God Want Us To Know About The End Of History?

Earlier, we discussed the two elements of prophecy—forthtelling and foretelling. Forthtelling involves telling people truths about God, their need for Him, and their need to worship Him. Foretelling involves telling what God wants His people to know about His plans. If they obey God's commands, blessing will come; if they disobey, judgment will come. God's actions toward all people, His ultimate removal of moral evil, and His establishment of everlasting harmony are also themes that appear in foretelling.

When we examine biblical materials about the future, we must ask, "How much does God really want us to know?" This question is basic to all study of prophecy, especially that in Daniel and Revelation. If we are convinced that God has revealed much of His blueprints for the future, we will read our ideas into the text. On the other hand, if we conclude that God does not intend for us to have detailed foreknowledge, we will be influenced in our openness toward what God wants us to know today.

I. One Teaching of the Risen Christ Should Affect All Our Interpretation
Acts 1:6-8

Between Jesus' resurrection and His ascension to heaven, He appeared to His disciples and taught them. His last words to them concerned the total change that was to come in their lives when He would no longer be visibly present with them in the same way He had been with them during His earthly ministry and the brief period after the resurrection.

At one of Christ's post resurrection appearances, the disciples questioned Him just as they had done when they traveled together. They asked, "Are you at this time restoring the kingdom to Israel?" (Acts 1:6). If Jesus had wanted to continue the Olivet discourse (where He spoke about the destruction of the temple, false Messiahs, and His second coming, Matt. 24-25; Mark 13; Luke 21), this question would have provided the ideal starting point. Jesus then could have given them the enlarged blueprint for the future, but He did otherwise.

He said, "To know times or seasons does not belong to you [plural]; these times which the Father has fixed [arranged, established] under His own authority. But you shall receive power after the Holy Spirit has come upon you and you shall be witnesses of me" (Acts 1:7-8a). Here Jesus flatly stated that knowing times and seasons is not for Christ's disciples—neither the ones He addressed orally then nor the ones today. It is not ours to know the future that belongs to physical Israel, to the true Israel (Jews and Gentiles who acknowledge Jesus as the Messiah), or to the kingdom of Christ. God has arranged this under His own authority.

The Book of Acts and the epistles of Paul reveal some things about physical Israel (1 Thess. 2:14-16), the true Israel (Gal. 3:26-29; Phil. 3:3), and the kingdom, or reign, of God (Acts 28:23, 31; Rom. 14:17; 1 Cor. 15:24, 50; 2 Thess. 1:5). But when we examine these passages, we must remember the words of Christ cited in Acts 1:7. God, in His grace, has told us certain things about the future, but we still do not know the times and the seasons—we have no sure pattern that shows future events.

If this is true, how shall we read Daniel and Revelation? Might not such study lead us to think we know more about the future than we really do? Sadly enough, that can happen. But it need not happen if we examine Daniel and Revelation in light of Jesus' words (Acts 1:7). Some things that God disclosed through Daniel and John can be known. But because both books are characterized by dreams, visions, and a rich variety of apocalyptic symbols, we must not allow our imaginations to fill in what God left ambiguous. Even Daniel was perplexed about many things that were revealed to him (Dan. 12). John warned strongly against anyone's adding to or subtracting from the Book of Revelation (Rev. 22:18-19), which implicates many modern "prophets."

What God does want us to know is important for us. But we

dare not claim that we can pull back the curtains of the future and give our little group of Christians a peek into what no one knows except us. We should be wary of those who brush aside Jesus' declaration in Acts 1:7. We know little about God's program, but we do know His promise to us: "Now the promise is to you, and to your children, and to all that are far off, as many as the Lord our God called" (Acts 2:39). His promise is of salvation in this life and in the life to come. What God tells us enables us to live, to serve, and to persevere.

II. Biblical Language About Physical Upheavals and Time Periods

Apocalyptic literature often delineates cosmological upheavals: "The sun shall be turned to darkness, and the moon to blood, before the great and terrible day of the Lord comes" (Joel 2:31). In the Olivet discourse, Jesus spoke of many false Messiahs who would come in His name and declare, "The time of crisis [the last times] has come near" (Luke 21:8). Because of this, Jesus warned, "Do not go out after them" (Luke 21:8). Natural catastrophes and unusual time periods confront the readers of most apocalyptic literature, including the books of Daniel and Revelation.

A. Nonscientific Language Describes These Physical Changes
Rev. 6:12-17

Many people who read Daniel and Revelation are unaware that the two books are part of a large body of similar Jewish literature identified by the term *apocalyptic*. Although unscientific, the language does designate real occurrences in the world of nature.

The sixth seal (Rev. 6:12-17) describes certain physical changes in the earth while God is judging people who live idolatrous and wicked lives. Various aspects of nature are affected: (1) a great earthquake occurs; (2) the sun becomes black as sackcloth; (3) the full moon becomes like blood; (4) the stars of heaven fall to earth; (5) the heaven is separated like a scroll rolled up; (6) every mountain and island is removed from its place; and (7) leaders and ordinary people hide themselves in the caves and rocks of the mountains.

These things are part of the wrath of God, according to Rev. 6:16-17. The language of physical change is dramatic and hyperbolic—it is consciously exaggerated. Scientifically, if the sun actually became dark for even a short time, everything would freeze. The text also says the stars of heaven fall to earth. If the sun, our nearest star, came even slightly closer to us, we would all roast. Interpreters who want to keep this apocalyptic language more attuned to our scientific knowledge suggest that the word *star* here refers to a meteor or meteorite. Therefore, the falling stars are a shower of meteorites. But the simile that follows (rolling up heaven like a scroll) does not favor this interpretation. The Revised Standard Version translates 6:14a as: "The sky vanished like a scroll that is rolled up," which is hardly scientific language. The next phrase is "Every mountain and island was removed from its place" (Rev. 6:14b). If all mountains and islands were actually rooted up, everyone would be killed, and no one would be alive to pray that the mountains and rocks shield them from the wrath of God. There is no way to push this language into literal, scientific statements.

The first readers understood these images as apocalyptic language. As such, the images may have implied something like this: A great earthquake will herald other physical changes. The sun and moon will change in ways that will affect all who live on the earth. The stars' falling to earth and heaven's being rolled up may indicate the loss of all points in navigation. The movement of every mountain and island means that these physical upheavals will be felt in every part of the world.

When we interpret this in apocalyptic rather than scientific terms, we retain some of the mystery that was intended—suggestive, but imprecise. It indicated to past and present readers that nature will go on the rampage. Because nature is and always has been unbalanced, when this age closes, nature will become even less stable, perhaps making people more aware that they are not masters of their own fate nor are they in control of the forces of nature.

B. God Controls and Uses Nature in Judging Sinful People
Rev. 8:2-13; 15:1; 16:1-21

The first four trumpets and the seven bowls of wrath in Revelation offer additional apocalyptic pictures of how God will use nature to judge those persons loyal only to their own sinful ways. However, these people will not be the only people on earth at that time. Interpreters who see these judgments taking place in the real world must admit that Christians will be here, too. (The first bowl of wrath [Rev. 16:2] is poured only on persons bearing the mark of the beast, which indicates that sinners are not the only people on earth.)

The rest of Revelation, however, shows people on earth, so there must be other meanings to these four trumpets and seven bowls of wrath. When the first angel blows his trumpet (Rev. 8:7), hail and fire mixed with blood fall on the earth. A third part of the vegetation on earth is burned up. Again, this must be considered an apocalyptic picture rather than a factual one in which one-third of all the oxygen and carbon dioxide will be eliminated.

How are we to understand the word *earth*? The Greek word *gē* has several meanings: "1. soil, 2. ground, 3. bottom (of the sea), 4. land (as opposed to sea), region, country, 5. earth, a. in contrast to heaven, b. as the inhabited globe."[1] The meaning in Rev. 8:7 can be a mixture of ground, land, region, or country. The Greek word *(gē) used here is not the usual word for the inhabited earth, or the world (oikoumene).*[2] Since the second and third trumpets involve the sea, followed by the rivers and fountains of waters, *gē* here probably refers to the land in contrast to the sea.

When the second angel blows his trumpet (Rev. 8:8-9), a great mountain, burning with fire, strikes the sea (salt water) and it becomes blood. When apocalyptic literature speaks of the moon's becoming blood and the sea's becoming blood, it apparently means a bloody color. The water in the sea becomes unfit to support life, and a third of the sea creatures die. The fact that a third part of the ships were destroyed in the sea suggests that the cause is more than pollution.

The word *sea* can mean the sea in general, as contrasted with earth, or it can refer to specific seas, such as the Red Sea or the Mediterranean Sea. It can be used of a fresh water lake, like the sea of Galilee.[3] Since the beast and his capital city are mentioned so often in Revelation, probably John was thinking of the Mediterranean Sea or possibly the sea in contrast to land.

The second bowl of wrath (Rev. 16:3) involves the sea's becoming like the blood of a dead man, so that every living creature in it dies. The second trumpet and the second bowl of wrath have similar effects on nature. They probably do not involve two separate judgments, although that is possible. It seems more likely that the first judgment had restricted effects that were later broadened. The sea now becomes hostile to people in a new way.

The third angel blows his trumpet (Rev. 8:10-11), and a great star called Wormwood strikes the waters. A third of the waters become bitter, and many people die. The effects of the third bowl of wrath (16:4-7) reflect those of the third trumpet with one exception. The angel of the waters celebrates the justice of God's judgments and says that those who shed the blood of the saints and prophets must themselves drink bloody water. However, this description of the third bowl of wrath mentions nothing about deaths caused by what people drink, only that the fresh water supply is affected by God's judgment.

Because of the nature of apocalyptic language and its influence on our imaginations, we all tend to picture differently and dramatically what may happen. The temptation is to imagine something like a secret weapon that causes all nuclear-powered ships to explode and contaminate the seas, but this is imagination run amok. Apocalyptic language does portray real physical happenings as part of God's judgments, but beyond that, all is conjecture. Whatever the judgments on the salt water and the fresh water mean, multitudes of people will survive and join the hostile armies of the final Antichrist. They will be defeated and judged by Christ when He returns (Rev. 19:17-21). We also know that Christ's followers will be present in the world (Rev. 16:15; 18:4; 21:7a; 22:7, 12, 20).

When the fourth angel blows his trumpet (Rev. 8:12), a third part of the sun, the moon, and the stars, as well as a third of the day and the night, will be darkened. Again, it is obvious that this is apocalyptic language, not scientific language that records what happens and seeks to explain the how. Apocalyptic language shows that God the Creator will use heavenly bodies—sun, moon, stars—to bring judgment, but we know very little of the circumstances. Scientifically, we ask, "Would anyone survive on earth if the amount of heat reaching the earth was reduced by one-third? Would that not produce an ice age so that our planet would resemble other planets farther out in our solar system?" We dare not try to make apocalyptic language become a kind of crystal ball to see into the future—the very thing that Jesus said the Father has put under His own authority (Acts 1:7).

The fourth bowl of wrath (Rev. 16:8-9) has quite the opposite influence on the sun. Instead of ceasing to shine, the sun is allowed to scorch people with fire and intense heat. The apocalyptic language does not divulge how. What might bring intense heat in California—forceful winds from the desert—would not happen in Hawaii. If the actual combustion rate of the sun was increased, most people would die. There would be no one left to experience the fifth, sixth, and seventh bowls of wrath. Again, we must not consider apocalyptic language to be scientific.

The fifth bowl of wrath is felt only in the capital city of the beast (Rev. 16:10-11). Like the first bowl of wrath (which affects only those who have the mark of the beast, Rev. 16:2), the fifth bowl has a limited influence. While the fourth bowl brought too much heat, the fifth bowl brings darkness that is not ordinary night. Rather it actually penetrates and causes pain to the people enveloped by it. They gnaw their tongues, hoping that one pain will counterbalance the other. They blaspheme God because of these pains and because of the sores (perhaps skin ulcers) that came with the first bowl of wrath. But still they do not repent from their evil deeds.

This judgment upon moral evil involves a complex symbol. The people who lived in the darkness of evil thought they enjoyed it. The darkness seemed attractive, and it gave them a convenient anonymity. Now these same people are experiencing totally their favorite atmosphere. But this time they feel not only the pain of moral evil but also the judgment of God. The apocalyptic symbol reveals some of the features of judgment, but we know very little about the "how."

The sixth bowl of wrath dries up the Euphrates River (Rev. 16:12-16), a terrifying prospect to the first readers. The Euphrates River formed the eastern boundary of the Roman Empire. Rome had few stable allies in this region and feared that powerful foes would come from this area to destroy its empire. The apocalyptic picture of demonic forces gathering people for war suggests that the days of the powerful world empire were numbered.

What might the apocalyptic picture of the Euphrates' drying up say to modern readers? The Euphrates no longer provides some Maginot line of defense. Now nations in the area align themselves on the basis of common fears and common needs such as oil, food, and weapons. This was also true in ancient times—except for the modern demand for oil. But Rome was the world power exuding an aura of overwhelming self-confidence, having inherited previous civilizations and empires. The sixth bowl of wrath reminds us that natural defenses can no longer protect any world power. Oceans and other physical barriers can easily be overcome by nuclear weapons. When God pours out judgments on people because of their attachment to moral evil, "natural" defenses are useless because God controls everything, even the complex mutual dependence of nations.

In Rev. 16:17-21, the seventh angel pours out his bowl of wrath into the air, bringing lightning flashes, loud noises, peals of thunder, and a great earthquake. These signs appear often in Revelation to warn of unusual events about to begin. In conjunction with this image, the earthquake commands more attention than the other events, and it is apparently more severe than previous ones in history. The great city—unnamed but probably referring to Rome—is split into three parts. God remembers Babylon (Rome), which suffers from the earthquake and more catastrophes.

The apocalyptic language depicts more violent physical upheavals: "Every island fled away and no mountains were to be found" (Rev. 16:20). Then fall horrendous-sized hail stones, weighing as much as a talent (approximately one hundred and twenty pounds).[4] Even in our limited experience, we have seen nature rampage with terrible consequences. Is this not a picture of people who go their own way, forget God and everyone else, and seem to care nothing about the consequences of their acts? The physical chaos of the seventh bowl is a reflection of moral chaos. Yet in all physical chaos, God remains in control, regulating exactly what is happening.

C. Time Measurements in Daniel and Revelation: Common Arithmetic and Apocalyptic Arithmetic

Apocalyptic literature focuses on cosmology—physical upheavals, such as islands and mountains moved from their places. The language refers to genuine physical happenings, but if God suddenly rearranged the earth's geography so that every island flew away and no mountain could be found (Rev. 16:20), humans would not be found either. In a similar way, the figurative expressions designate time but not in a way that permits us "to know times and seasons" (Acts 1:7). Some people have concocted elaborate schemes to establish precise times in Daniel and Revelation. For every such scheme, we must ask: "Is the time period common arithmetic or apocalyptic arithmetic?"

1. Ordinary time expressions are used literally.
Dan. 6:7, 10, 12-13; 9:2; 10:2; 12:13a; Rev. 2:21; 9:5; 11:9-11

The immediate context, as well as the context of the whole book, indicates when a time expression refers to either ordinary or apocalyptic time. Where the context demands a precise period—hour, week, month, or year—then the meaning is usually literal.

For example, in the third year of the reign of Cyrus Daniel had a vision about an important matter, which involved great distress for him and his people. Daniel only partially understood the vision and the words of the unnamed messenger who came to him (Dan. 10—12). Before this vision took place, he had been mourning and fasting: "In those days, I, Daniel, was mourning for three weeks of days; the bread or food of desirable things, I did not eat; meat and wine did not come unto my mouth until the accomplishment of three weeks of days" (Dan. 10:2-3). Daniel knew that his writing was rich in apocalyptic symbolism, so he emphasized that here he used common, not apocalyptic, arithmetic. For three weeks of days (three literal weeks), Daniel mourned and lived on a Spartan diet.

Ordinary time expressions are quite common in Daniel. In the episode of Daniel in the den of lions, the satraps and presidents of Medo-Persia drew up an ordinance that no one should petition any god or man except the king for thirty days (Dan. 6:7, 12). Daniel had three definite prayer times every day (Dan. 6:10, 13). In the first year when Cyrus was king over Medo-Persia (Dan. 9:1 uses the name Darius the Mede), Daniel learned through words given by Jeremiah (Jer. 25:11-12; 29:1-14) that the desolations of Jerusalem would be for seventy years. If the first year of Cyrus was 539 B.C., and if the city with its walls was destroyed in 586 B.C., then forty-seven years had already passed, and approximately twenty years were left. A small temple in Jerusalem was dedicated in 516 B.C. Thus God's word through Jeremiah was carried out during a literal seventy-year period.

The Book of Revelation also incorporates many literal time expressions. The glorified Christ said about Jezebel, the prophetess at Thyatira, "I gave her a period of time [ordinary time] to repent, but she refuses to repent of her immorality" (Rev. 2:21). Because she did not repent, Christ would bring judgment upon her and her followers.

When the fifth trumpet blows, locusts coming out of the pit of the abyss represent a demonic host (Rev. 9:1-3). They attack "only those of mankind who have not the seal of God upon their foreheads" (Rev. 9:4), and "they were allowed to torture them [people] for five months, but not to kill" (Rev. 9:5). John uses the five-month life cycle of locusts as a measure of the time that this demonic horde attacks those who follow the final Antichrist. Hence it is possible that the five months are figurative, representing a comparatively short time.

Although the tormentors are called locusts (Rev. 9:3), they are described by other similes: "like the torment of scorpions" (Rev. 9:5); "like horses prepared for war" (Rev. 9:7); "what looked like crowns" on their heads (Rev. 9:7); "faces like human faces" (Rev. 9:7); "hair like women's hair" (Rev. 9:8); "their teeth were like lions' teeth" (Rev. 9:8). Typically, apocalyptic imagery combines many animals' and people's characteristics. The locust is the predominant image here, and its life cycle is approximately five months, apparently the extent of time of the fifth trumpet.

In Rev. 11:3-6, two prophets or witnesses are martyred when they finish their testimony (Rev. 11:7). The rulers, aligned with the final Antichrist, refuse to permit the two prophets to be buried. Instead, the rulers and their supporters celebrate their apparent victory over these two servants of God who had "tormented" them by their witness to God. After three and one-half days, God raised up the prophets, and they ascended to heaven (Rev. 11:11-12). Although three and one-half in other contexts often has a figurative meaning of a short period of time, perhaps here it designates a literal time period between the death and resurrection of the prophets.

2. Ordinary time expressions are sometimes used figuratively.
Dan. 4:16, 23, 25, 32; Rev. 2:10; 3:10; 10:6-7; 11:6; 12:12; 16:14

God spoke to Nebuchadnezzar through a dream involving a powerful tree that was cut down, with only its stump remaining. Daniel interpreted the dream and indicated that Nebuchadnezzar would be forced to relinquish his throne, although he would be restored if he acknowledged the rule of the Most High. Nebuchadnezzar was told four times about the length of his ordeal: "And seven times shall pass upon you" (Dan. 4:16, 23, 25, 32).

The Aramaic word *iddan* is a common word for "time." The

word sometimes means a point of time, but more often it means duration of time. Does this mean seven days, seven weeks, seven months, or seven years? Interpreters have preferred a period of seven years because of the growth of Nebuchadnezzar's hair and nails. His hair grew as long as eagles' feathers, and his nails grew like birds' claws (Dan. 4:33).

However, the word *times* in this instance refers only to a specified period. The number seven signifies completeness so that here "seven times" designates a complete period to bring the changes God wanted to see in Nebuchadnezzar. Of course, even seven months would have made some radical changes in Nebuchadnezzar since he lived like the beasts and ate grass like an ox. Seven times may refer to a specific time period, but its main purpose is not to explain exactly how long the period was, but rather how complete in terms of results. We do not know the exact length of time, but we do know the results: God achieved what He wanted to achieve in Nebuchadnezzar.

Another example of the figurative use of ordinary time expressions occurs in Christ's message to the church at Smyrna. This church would have tribulation for "ten days" (Rev. 2:10), when Satan would cast some members of the church into prison to test them. The Greek form of the word used for "ten days" stresses the *quality* of time rather than the length or point of time. In this apocalyptic arithmetic, "ten days" designates a short but important period of time. Church history does not reveal exactly the duration of the tribulation. But however long, the church was told to become faithful unto death during this period (Rev. 2:10).

Christ promised to protect the church of Philadelphia from the "hour" of testing intended for all who "dwell on the earth" (Rev. 3:10). Other passages in Revelation about God's wrath and judgments indicate that "the hour of testing" is a comparatively short period of time but certainly longer than sixty minutes. It is a time when God would test persons devoted to the world and its pleasures rather than to Him.

Holding a little scroll, an angel makes a key announcement as he stands with his right foot on the sea and his left foot on the land. He declares that there will be "no more delay" in the days of the trumpet call to be sounded by the seventh angel. Then the mystery of God becomes fulfilled or complete (Rev. 10:6-7). We often use the phrase, "in the days of," in a figurative sense. We speak of the "days of the depression" and the "days of World War II," although each event lasted several years. Though we are using ordinary language for a specific time period, the expression indicates a prescribed boundary of time that may involve few or many hundreds of literal twenty-four-hour periods.

This use of the word *days* is found in the narrative about the two prophets in Rev. 11:6. Like Moses and Elijah, these two prophets do miracles "during the days of their prophesying." Here the word covers the active ministry of two prophets during the time of the final Antichrist.

When John wrote Revelation and used figurative time expressions, he may not have fully realized the "unliteralness" of his language. For example, in Rev. 12:7-13, John recorded Satan's being thrown out of heaven by the angels of God. The context makes clear that this occurs shortly after the ascension of Jesus to heaven (Rev. 12:1-6). Then John heard a loud voice from heaven warning the earth to beware: "The devil has come to you in great wrath, because he knows that his time is short" (Rev. 12:12). Yet we know that Satan's "short time" has extended to almost two thousand years. God did not grant the knowledge of times or seasons to the original seven churches addressed by John's letter. They lived in an atmosphere of belief that Christ's return and the end of time were soon. (This will be discussed further at the end of this chapter.)

God's last judgment upon militarism (which is part of Christ's coming) takes place "on the great day of God, the Almighty" (Rev. 16:14). Here John adapts the phrase "day of the Lord" to describe a larger period when the final war of this age will occur. Neither idiom implies that events happen in a single twenty-four-hour period.

3. Apocalyptic time expressions are connected with the future.

Both Daniel and Revelation have many expressions that speak of "the end" or "the end of the age" (see Appendix II, p. 245). Yet we learn from a study of such expressions that God did not enable Daniel or John to know times or seasons. From where we now stand in history, we realize that some of these apocalyptic time expressions referred to severe crises in the future while others referred to the final future crisis. This does not mean that Daniel and John intended to describe two different future events. They intended to describe one future event, but because history tends to repeat itself, the language could illuminate several such events that, owing to certain features, anticipate events in the final days at the end of the age. We dare not devise rigid or fixed classifications. We must remember the axiom of Jesus: "it is not for God's servants to know the times or the seasons that the Father has put under His own authority" (Acts 1:7).

The "end of the days" that Daniel wrote about in Daniel 2 referred to the empires of Babylon, Medo-Persia, Greece, and Rome. Daniel 2:44 clearly states that "in the days of those kings, the God of heaven will set up a kingdom which will never be destroyed." The fourth beast of Dan. 7:7-11 seems to correspond to the iron and clay part of the image of Dan. 2:40-43 (Rome). But the little horn in 7:20-26 seems to be the final Antichrist, who did not appear under the Roman Empire. In Daniel 8 a little horn coming out of Greece (the he-goat) seems to foretell Alexander's empire that would be broken up into four divisions. Out of one division comes a little horn who takes away the Jews' sacred continual burnt offering and profanes their sanctuary (Dan. 8:11-14). According to the story in 1 Maccabees, Antiochus IV Ephiphanes did exactly that from 167 to 164 B.C. Thus the apparent references in Daniel 8 that reached completion with Antiochus IV Ephipanes surely seem to picture a man who was an early version of the final Antichrist.

Some of the visions recorded in Daniel 10—12 also refer to Antiochus IV Epiphanes. But Dan. 12:2 discusses the broad sweep of the resurrection of the dead: "Many sleepers of the land of dust will awake, these to everlasting life and those to reproach and everlasting abhorrence." The word *many* is a Hebraism that really means "all."[5] Daniel included himself and his people in the first group, "these to everlasting life." He would not identify his covenant people with the people who would awake to reproach and everlasting abhorrence. But Daniel 12 ends with Antiochus' desecrations: "From the time that the continual burnt offering is taken away and the abomination that makes desolate is set up" (Dan. 12:11; 11:31). Thus in Daniel there are time expressions that concern both severe crises in the future and the final resurrection of the dead.

The opening chapters of Revelation picture the coming of Christ as very near and refer to happenings connected with that coming (1:1, 3; 3:11). The book ends on the same note (22:6-7, 10, 12, 20). But between the opening and the closing of the book we find time expressions for very short to very long periods of time. One hour and one day seem to refer to a very short period of time. The phrase, "a thousand years," means a very long period of time, but we do not know exactly how long. Where Satan is said to know that he has "little time," the expression means Satan knew that God would later sharply curtail his activities: "For the devil has come down to you in great wrath, because he knows that his time is short" (Rev. 12:12b). The word for "little" (translated "short" in the RSV) fits the overwhelming sense in Revelation of the nearness of the end times. While such conviction is also important to us, we must be aware that earlier generations of Christians also thought the end of the age was imminent. We must remember God intends for us always to be prepared, but He does not intend for us to know times or seasons.

D. A Prophecy Concerning the Desecration of Jerusalem
Dan. 9:24-27

Interpretations of these few verses have given rise to elaborate prophetic charts and dogmatic agendas about the future. Yet in this passage, apocalyptic time measurements (highly symbolic) simply provide a framework for important truths for Daniel and his people, and they are not meant to convey exact time periods.

Some interpreters have tried to work out exact time periods for what the vision conveys, usually ending one time period with Christ's death. They leave a short period (usually the seventieth week) for the future. But apocalyptic numbers were never meant to be treated with such precision.

Because this passage deserves careful study, we may be able to understand it better if we put it in outline form:

I. God's redemptive purpose for the apocalyptic seventy heptads (weeks): "to finish the transgression, to put an end to sin, and to atone for iniquity, to bring in everlasting righteousness, to seal both vision and prophet, and to anoint a most holy place" (9:24).

II. The seventy weeks—an enigmatic picture of key events from Daniel's day to the second destruction of Jerusalem (A.D. 73) (9:25-27).

A. Cyrus' decree to restore and rebuild Jerusalem (9:25a).

  B. Seven weeks to the coming of an anointed one, a prince—probably Nehemiah (9:25b).
  C. Sixty-two weeks for the continued rebuilding of Jerusalem (9:25c).
  D. Death of an anointed one (Christ) "after sixty-two weeks, an anointed one will be cut off and shall have nothing" (9:26a).
  E. One week of intensive activity produces drastic effects on the city of Jerusalem (9:26b-27).
     1. People of a coming prince (Titus and the Romans) destroy the city and the sanctuary (9:26b).
     2. Until the final end, war and desolations will characterize human history (9:26c).
     3. A coming prince makes and breaks a covenant, causes sacrifice and offerings to cease, causes general horror (Antiochus IV Epiphanes) (9:27a).
     4. Destruction of the horror causer or desolator (9:27b).

1. Key elements in the passage about the seventy weeks.

Central to the passage is the redemptive purpose of these weeks. Verse 24 is the key. It has six infinitives, and the first three summarize God's acts in providing atonement: (1)"to make an end of transgression," (2) "to seal up sins," and (3) "to atone for iniquity." The next three show the consequences of God's atonement: (1) "to bring in everlasting righteousness," (2) "to seal the vision and the prophet" (to authenticate), and (3) "to anoint the sacredness of the holy things" (to consecrate what is truly holy).

Daniel 4 points out God's decisive action in dealing with moral evil. Daniel 9 also shows God's action in judgment, but in this chapter the seventy weeks are considered as a complete unit involving God's redemptive purposes. From our vantage point on this side of Calvary, Christians can be more specific: God provided redemption by the incarnation of His Son—by Christ's life, death, resurrection, and ascension.

2. Cyrus the Great (ruled 550 to 529 B.C.) commanded the rebuilding and restoring of Jerusalem.

Several Old Testament passages show the importance of Cyrus: Ezra 1:1-11; 5:1—6:15; 2 Chr. 36:22-23; Isa. 44:24—45:6, 13; Dan.

9:1-2; 10:1. Many Jews returned to Jerusalem as the result of Cyrus' decree, and they built a small temple that was dedicated in 516 B.C. But the rebuilding of the city proved slow and difficult (Zech. 1—8; Hag. 1—2). During the time of Ezra (458 B.C.), the Jews who were rebuilding were harassed by neighbors fearful of a growing, vibrant Jewish state. Some kings of Persia were asked to check the historical records (Ezra 5:17—6:5). After they found Cyrus' decree, they supported the Jews' reconstruction work in Jerusalem and allowed them to continue. Thanks to Cyrus' decree, the building process continued long after his own time.

The Lord calls Cyrus "my shepherd" and declares that "He [Cyrus] will complete or perform all my purpose" (Isa. 44:28). Isaiah 45:1 speaks of him as God's anointed. Cyrus' words indicate he was performing God's purpose; he said of Jerusalem, "She shall be built," and of the temple, "Your foundations shall be laid" (Isa. 44:28). God says of Cyrus: "He shall build my city and set my exiles free" (Isa. 45:13).

3. Time periods in Dan. 9:24-27.

Daniel 9:24-27 refers to seventy weeks (heptads), seven weeks, sixty-two weeks, and one week. The one week is discussed less frequently than the seven weeks or the sixty-two weeks. The Hebrew word *shavu'a* could refer to "seven days, years, or a heptad week" [6](Ex. 34:22; Deut. 16:10, 16; 2 Chr. 8:13; Num. 28:26), but it usually refers to one week (Dan. 10:2-3). Only in Dan. 9:24-25 does Brown, Driver, and Briggs (the standard Hebrew lexicon) suggest years as a possible meaning. Interpreters who consider apocalyptic numbers to be like common arithmetic calculate that one week = seven years; seventy weeks = four hundred and ninety years; sixty-nine weeks = four hundred and eighty-three years. Even if this was correct (which is by no means certain), we must still ask: "Do these apocalyptic numbers mean actual years, precisely measured off in common arithmetic, or are they "epochal" years—approximate periods of time from which we gain only a rough idea?"

Scholars supporting the precise mathematical interpretation assume that apocalyptic numbers are like common arithmetic. To achieve their desired ends, however, they must disregard the eight or so chapters (part or in whole) devoted to Cyrus the Great as the one who approved and ordered the rebuilding of Jerusalem and begin instead with the time of Artaxerxes I (464-424 B.C.). Nehemiah 2:1 states that in the twentieth year of Artaxerxes (445 B.C.), Nehemiah was sent to rebuild the walls of Jerusalem. The only part Artaxerxes played, however, was to send letters to some officials telling them to cooperate with Nehemiah in his work. The Old Testament never suggests that Artaxerxes was the one who commanded the rebuilding and restoring of Jerusalem and its temple. It portrays Cyrus as the one who gave the order.

Why, then, do some interpreters direct so much attention to Artaxerxes I? The answer lies in their assumption that apocalyptic numbers are precise mathematical numbers. In 539 B.C. Cyrus gave his decree to rebuild and restore Jerusalem with its temple. According to Dan. 9:26a, "After the sixty-two weeks, an anointed one [usually thought to refer to Christ] shall be cut off and shall have nothing." Assuming that one week = seven years, then Daniel's seventy weeks = four hundred and ninety years. If we subtract 490 years from 539 (the decree of Cyrus), we get 49 B.C. as the year for the death of Christ (the time when the anointed one shall be cut off and have nothing.) Obviously, 49 B.C. is too early for the death of Christ. Furthermore, most people who use this common arithmetic approach want to have seven years some place in the future to fit their prophetic time chart. For this reason they can subtract only 483 years from 539, which marks 56 B.C. as the time of the death of Christ—even further removed from historical facts. But if they begin with Artaxerxes in 445 B.C. and subtract 483, they get A.D. 38—close to the actual date of Christ's death.

The problem lies in the fact that Cyrus the Great in 539 B.C. (not Artaxerxes I) was the one who was the Lord's anointed and His shepherd, and the one who sent the Jews back to their own land. Isaiah 45:13 says of Cyrus, "I will make straight all his ways; he shall build my city and set my exiles free." There is no biblical basis for starting any computation with Artaxerxes. Rather, it is the desire to make the figures come out a certain way. This kind of manipulation is unnecessary when we recognize that the Old Testament was dealing with apocalyptic numbers rather than common arithmetic. The chart below compares actual years with years that are epochal—representing periods rather than exact years.

CYRUS' DECREE (539 B.C.)

Periods of time (heptads) in Daniel	Epochal Years	Actual Years
7 *weeks*, Cyrus to Nehemiah (539-445 B.C.) (persons' names not mentioned in Dan. 9:25)	49	94
62 *weeks*, Nehemiah to Christ's death (445 B.C.-A.D. 29) (persons' names not mentioned in Dan. 9:25c-26a)	434	474
1 *week of intense activity* pertaining to Jerusalem—its city and temple (Dan. 9:26b-27)	7	44

This week describes the action of a prince who is a composite. Two different men carried out and fulfilled Daniel's prophecy.
1. Antiochus IV, 174-164 B.C. (Dan. 9:27a, b).
   He was active in Israel from 171 to 164 B.C.
   a. For 5 1/2 years he was known as King Antiochus
   b. For the next 5 1/2 years he took the titles "God manifested" (Epiphanes) and "Victorious" (Nicephorus)
2. Titus and the Romans, A.D. 66-73 (Dan. 9:26-27)
   a. Beginning of war and Roman victory in Galilee, A.D. 66-67
   b. Roman attack on Jerusalem, A.D.67-70
   c. Roman attack on Masada, A.D. 70-73

Daniel's language about this one week applies to both Antiochus' desecration of the temple and Titus' destruction of the city, the sanctuary, and Masada. If the sixty-two weeks end with the death of Christ,

then this one week included Jerusalem's
desecration by Antiochus IV and the destruction wrought by the Romans from
Christ's death until the fall of Masada
(A.D. 29-73).
70 weeks   490   612

The seven weeks begin with Cyrus' decree and continue to the
time of an anointed one, a prince (Dan. 9:25b). This seven-week
language is ambiguous. It is only one-tenth of the seventy weeks.
If we view these years as epochal years, then Nehemiah, who was
a prince, governor, and acknowledged leader of the rebuilding of
the walls of Jerusalem, would be a likely candidate on which to an-
chor the end of the first period.

The sixty-two weeks portray the continued rebuilding of Jerusalem. Herod the Great, who came to power in 37 B.C., played a
prominent part in rebuilding Jerusalem. He ordered the materials
brought to the site of the temple and initiated the building of the
temple that existed during Jesus' life. Jesus taught in the courts of
Herod's temple.

In Daniel's prophecy about this period appears the statement:
"An anointed one, a prince will be cut off and there will be nothing
to him" (literal translation of Dan. 9:26a). Despite its ambiguity,
the language surely fits the death of Christ. There was "nothing to
him" in terms of material wealth or political power.

The one week gets little attention in the passage. Daniel 9:26b-27
reads: "And the people of the prince who is to come shall destroy
the city and the sanctuary. Its end shall come with a flood, and to
the end there shall be war; desolations are decreed. And he shall
make a strong covenant with many for one week; and for half of
the week he shall cause sacrifice and offering to cease; and upon
the wing of abominations shall come one who makes desolate, until the decreed end is poured out on the desolator."

Daniel's vision about the seventy weeks, beginning in Dan.
9:24, reveals the good news that God will deal with moral evil. Cyrus' command to restore and rebuild Jerusalem will be continued
for a long period. But the death of an anointed one, a prince, is
ominous. The prophecy declared that the temple would be profaned; sacrifice and offerings would cease. Then the prophecy
spoke of another complete destruction of Jerusalem and its sanctu-

ary (Nebuchadnezzar had destroyed it in 586 B.C.). This announced catastrophe would be hard to bear by people who had not been able to restore the city to what it was before Nebuchadnezzar's assaults.

The statements of Dan. 9:26-27 are at the same time clear and obscure. Tracing through the history of what actually happened during the following five hundred years, we see that the "prince who is coming" probably was a composite. Antiochus IV Epiphanes profaned the temple (171-164 B.C.). The Roman army of Titus destroyed the city, the sanctuary, and Masada between A.D.66-73, some forty years after Jesus' death. Daniel's words in 9:26-27 simply portray the adversity and tragedy of Jerusalem's rise and fall.

4. Message of the seventy weeks in the center of apocalyptic arithmetic.

The basic message of the seventy weeks is that God will bring about a redemption from sin and He will usher in everlasting righteousness accompanied by true worship. Jerusalem with its temple would be rebuilt, but it would be profaned and destroyed again.

One phrase in this section became clear only after the death of Christ: "An anointed one shall be cut off and there will be nothing to him" (Dan. 9:26a, literal translation). The rest of the verse says, "And the people of the prince who is to come shall destroy the city and the sanctuary." From our historical perspective, we can see that 9:26a described Christ's death and that 9:26b described the Romans' destruction of Jerusalem and the end of all temple worship. The great temple of Herod the Great lay in total ruin after A.D. 70.

The apocalyptic language of "weeks" was useful not only to the first hearers and readers of Daniel but also to us. Although the seventy weeks do not offer precise time calculations, they symbolically showed the readers of Daniel's time—and show us—that God is concerned with moral evil. When the passage in Daniel speaks of an anointed one who would be cut off, we know from the New Testament that this one was a unique servant. We also know that the future of God's people does not depend on the city of Jerusalem or on a sanctuary in that city. War and desolations will characterize human history until God pours out His final judgment. Apocalyptic arithmetic gives us a framework from which we learn truths God wants us to know. But we do not know times or seasons that the Father has put under His own authority (Acts 1:7).

III. How Moral Evil Functions as History Moves Toward Its Climax

Revelation has several apocalyptic pictures of moral evil that reveal its operation, organization, defeat, and banishment. History as we know it is a conflict between moral evil and moral good, between sin (revolt against God) and righteousness (obedience to God). The conflict will sharpen as this age, dominated by moral evil, moves toward its close.

A. Satan's Kingdom Is Subject to God's Control

The Book of Revelation persistently declares that Satan's kingdom and the ones loyal to Satan are subject to God's control. This control is often implied in the use of the passive of the Greek verb such as "to give" or "it was given." Sometimes it is translated "he was allowed to...." Who gave? Who allowed? The meaning obviously is that God allows or gives—God is in control (Rev. 6:2, 4, 11; 9:3, 5; 11:2; 13:5, 7, 14-15).

1. God controls the demonic locusts of the fifth trumpet.

Apocalyptic imagery is often complex. John sees a star that has fallen to the earth (Rev. 9:1-11). The key of the shaft of the abyss is given to it or to him (the star). This probably means an angel in conjunction with the star (see "angel of the waters" in Rev. 16:5). When this star angel opens the shaft of the abyss, smoke and locusts come out. But verses 7 to 11 show that these are not ordinary locusts. They are described in a series of similes: like horses...like crowns...like human faces...like women's hair...like lions' teeth...like iron breastplates...like the noise of many chariots...like scorpions. Apocalyptic symbolism depicts demonic creatures who torment those who do not have the seal of God upon their foreheads. The Greek name of the leader of the creatures is Apollyon, meaning "destroyer." These tormentors do not kill the people without God's seal; they simply hurt them.

This language provides little information about how these demonic hosts operate. We know they are demonic from their source, the pit of the abyss. They torment the opponents of God who will not die but will feel the effects of the demonic tormentors. These people loyal to the self-centered life of moral evil will be harassed by the very moral evil to which they have been devoted. This should not surprise us. At the heart of moral evil is its capacity to deceive and destroy. This apocalyptic picture illustrates God's control of moral evil so that those who are committed to it reap the adverse effects of their commitment. The demonic force appears as a terrifying animal-human monstrosity to magnify its hideous nature. God sovereignly controls a world that is chaotic because of moral evil, but in this apocalyptic representation people are damaged by the forces that contribute to revolt and chaos.

2. God controls the demonic horses (and horsemen) of the sixth trumpet.
Rev. 9:13-19

All the angels who blow the trumpets are under God's control (see Rev. 8:2, 6), but the sixth trumpet brings a demonic host more lethal than the demonic locusts of the fifth trumpet. Death comes with the sixth trumpet. Four angels who are bound at the Euphrates River are released at a specified time, and they are said to kill a third of humankind. The number of the armies of their horsemen is twice ten thousand times ten thousand—an incalculably large number. Nothing is said about the riders of these horses, but the horses are said to have heads like lions and tails like snakes. Fire, smoke, and sulphur come from the horses' mouths. This demonic host carries hell's fire, smoke, and sulphur into the earthly scene and brings death to people.

Some interpreters see this infinitely large demonic host as standing behind some future collision of huge military forces, with the angels and demonic horses spurring humans on to the hatred that brings mutual annihilation. The sixth bowl of wrath might support this interpretation. The text, however, emphasizes God's control of the forces that bring about this great destruction: "The angels had been prepared for the hour and day and month and year" (Rev. 9:15). Moral evil so deceives people that they seek to get what they want by killing anyone who stands in their way. But God so controls moral evil that He utilizes demonic hosts to bring back upon such people the very destruction that they intend to afflict upon others. As in all periods of human history, both good and evil people become involved in wars and in the right and wrong use of power. Even when evil forces relentlessly pursue their lawless course, God can use the forces of righteousness and wickedness to show the destructiveness of idolatry and immorality (Rev. 9:20-21).

3. God's judgment in the sixth bowl of wrath divulges more about the organized kingdom of moral evil.
Rev. 16:13-16

The sixth bowl of wrath is poured out on and dries up the Euphrates River so that the kings on the eastern side of the river could move west. This would be very important in ancient warfare. The rest of the account of the sixth bowl of wrath describes a satanic trinity, consisting of Satan (the dragon), the final Antichrist (the beast), and the false prophet who ascribes godlike qualities to the final Antichrist.

Unclean spirits like frogs come from the mouths of these three beings. With our mouths we speak truth, falsehood, or a mixture of the two. Revelation 22:14-15 mentions that one quality of persons ultimately banished from the presence of God is that they "love and practice falsehood." The three unclean spirits, who possess and control Satan and his two cohorts, deceive those people who want to ignore God and actively fight against Him. Thus with eloquent but false words and powerful signs these spirits of demons gather the kings of the earth for final battle at a place called Armageddon (Rev. 16:16).

Armageddon means the "mountain or hill of Megiddo" and probably refers to the place where King Josiah was killed (2 Chr. 35:10-27). However, reference to this name does not mean that the final battle of the world will occur at that exact location. Many place names in Revelation, such as Sodom and Egypt, have meanings quite different from their usual literal meanings. Here Armageddon may designate a future battle whose place God has not made known to us. The well-known battle site in Israel may be only a convenient expression to designate this place. We know neither times nor seasons, nor, we might add, the precise geography of future wars, including the final war of this age.

4. God's angel binds Satan.
Rev. 20:1-3

In Revelation God is portrayed as deity active in the arena of moral evil. When Christ ascended to heaven, a war broke out there, and Satan was thrown down so that his sphere of influence was limited to the earth (Rev. 12:7-17). When Christ returns to earth—His second coming (Rev. 19:11—20:6)—God's angel will confine "the dragon, that ancient serpent, who is the devil or Satan" in the abyss from which the demonic hosts came in Revelation 9.

For a long period of time—a thousand years—Satan, the leader of moral evil, will not be able to work in the earthly sphere. "A thousand years," an apocalyptic number, does not designate a precise period of time but rather a period of perhaps 750, 1500, 2100, or 3600 years. We will not know how long it actually is until God's plan for this period has been carried out.

Thus when Satan is operative in the world, so is God. In God's plan, Satan will eventually be curbed and finally banished. Why does God permit Satan to operate at all? Why doesn't He just get rid of Satan and his followers? This question implies that God has chosen eventually to banish moral evil by His power alone and by His decree. However, in Revelation, both the saints and Christ rule with a rod of iron (Rev. 2:26-27; 12:5; 19:15). God has chosen to banish moral evil by a process—through Christ and His people. By God's grace, the final victory over moral evil will be a shared victory.

5. God's final test of loyalty and Satan's last deception.
Rev. 20:7-10

Most readers of Revelation are puzzled by the statement: "After these things it is necessary for him [Satan] to be loosed for a short time" (20:3b). Why should Satan be loosed for a short time during the period when Christ and His people are ruling together in the earthly and heavenly spheres (Rev. 20:4-6)?

The rod of iron wielded by Christ and His people symbolizes organizing the world for righteousness instead of for the selfishness that brings wars, strife, and conflict. A world organized for righteousness, using power only for the advancement of good, will be a new epoch, totally different from anything we have experienced. The rod of iron suggests, however, that even with Satan bound some people will prefer to serve self rather than God. During this time, "the earth will be filled with the knowledge of the glory of the Lord as the waters cover the sea" (Hab. 2:14; Isa. 11:9). There will be no atheists or agnostics. The knowledge of God will be universal. But obedience could still come only by conformity rather than by conviction. Satan's being loosed for a short time would differentiate between the ones who serve God out of conviction and the ones who serve Him out of compliance.

Many interpreters of Revelation identify "Gog" and "Magog" with the twentieth-century countries of Russia and China. In Revelation, Gog and Magog simply represent people in distant places (20:8). Likewise the phrases, "camp of the saints" and "the beloved city," are biblical expressions for an earthly dwelling place of God's people. Revelation 20:9 says, "But fire came down from heaven and devoured them" [those who were marching against the people of God], ending their brief revolt. This fire from heaven against the enemies of God is reminiscent of the story of Elijah's deliverance from the men sent by King Ahaziah (2 Kings 1:10-12).

John chose similar language to describe the last outburst of moral evil and its defeat. Revelation 20:10 notes that Satan will then be cast into the lake of fire, a representation of eternal separation from God. The triune God and His people thus eliminate the cause of the curse of sin. Moral evil will forever disappear.

B. Antichrists Appear in Successive Versions

The term *Antichrist* appears only in the epistles of John (1 John 2:18, 22; 4:3; 2 John 7). Of his own lifetime, John wrote, "many Antichrists have come" (1 John 2:18) who denied that Jesus was the Messiah (1 John 2:22). Any spirit or false prophet who did not confess that Jesus had come in the flesh, or denied He had come from God, had the spirit of Antichrist (1 John 4:3). John repeats this in 2 John and calls such people deceivers (2 John 7). Thus the term *Antichrist* is synonymous with one who is against the covenant God of Israel and applies, therefore, to many more people than a single future opponent of God. The final future opponent is an Antichrist, but only the last one in a long succession. Both the Old and New Testaments refer to several versions of Antichrist.

1. Antiochus IV Epiphanes is described in Daniel as being against the covenant God—an Antichrist.
Dan. 8:9-14, 23-26; 11:21-39

The language describing this Syrian king, who reigned from 175 to 164 B.C., is colorful but imprecise. In Dan. 8:9, he is called "a little horn" who comes from the breakup of the empire of Alexander the Great (the "he-goat"). In this passage, the "little horn" (Antiochus IV Epiphanes) may not be the same little horn who came out of the fourth beast or world kingdom of Dan. 7:8. Both could be early versions of Antichrist, or Antiochus may be an earlier version and the other a final version.

The little horn (Antiochus IV Epiphanes) of Daniel 8 grows great against God, His hosts, and His creation. The little horn opposes the Prince of the host (Dan. 8:11) and removes all outward forms of worship of God. Deceit or treachery prosper in his hand, and He rises up against the Prince of princes (Dan. 8:25). He is presented as an arrogant, tyrannical leader, skilled in double-dealing (Dan. 8:23).

In Daniel 11, a similar picture unfolds. The anti-God leader makes alliances or covenants but then acts deceitfully (Dan. 11:23; cf. 9:27a). He scatters plunder, spoils, and goods to make friends. He despises the holy covenant and all religious observances that pertain to that covenant (Dan. 11:28-32). He is a supreme egotist who magnifies himself and speaks against the God of gods (Dan. 11:36). Antiochus IV certainly fits this description.

2. Daniel's composites of leaders who oppose the covenant God. Dan. 9:26b-27; 11:40—12:13

Daniel 9:26-27 describes a coming prince—a composite of Antiochus IV Epiphanes, who caused the sacrifices and offerings to cease (Dan. 9:27a), and Titus and the Romans, who destroyed both the city and the sanctuary (Dan. 9:26b-27). Both Antiochus IV and Titus were hostile toward almost everything Jewish, especially toward the Jewish claims that their God was the only God.

The statements in Dan. 11:40-45 do not fit any one leader. The language about the king of the south and the king of the north is used throughout Daniel 11, but verses 5-20 seem to describe the wars between Egypt (king of the south) and Syria (king of the north) from 300 to 175 B.C. Verses 21-39 of the narrative concentrate on Antiochus IV Epiphanes who wars against Egypt (king of the south) and Israel.

However, Dan. 11:40-44 seems less appropriate to Antiochus IV Epiphanes than to the Roman ruler Titus who invaded the area in A.D. 66-73. The king of the south will wage war with the king of the north by thrusting out his forces (Dan. 11:40). According to the text, the king of the north comes with ships, then he enters the lands, overflows, and passes through. Antiochus IV would not have to pass through countries to reach the "glorious" land, or Israel (Dan. 11:41), because his kingdom adjoined it.

These verses better illustrate the coming of the Romans into Palestine under Titus. In that case, the king of the south would not be Egypt. From the Roman perspective, it would have been the Jewish nation because of their treatment of Roman officials. The Jews (especially the Zealots) attacked Roman troops and initiated the tragic war of A.D. 66-73. When the Romans decided to insure their full control of the eastern Mediterranean, they cared nothing about the areas occupied in past times by the Edomites, Moabites, and Ammonites on the east side of the Jordan River (Dan. 11:41). Instead, their primary concerns were the land of Egypt, the upper Nile, and the northern coast of Africa (Dan. 11:43). The tidings from the east (Dan. 11:44) allude to events that enticed Antiochus into the battle in which he was killed, while Dan. 11:45 describes the approach of the Romans to Jerusalem after their victorious campaign in Galilee.

Thus, as is typical of prophetic apocalyptic literature, the language is not precise as to time or place. There are missing pieces and some parts that can be applied to more than one person or to no known persons. The language is fluid, which would be appropriate to the shifting perspective of a vision.

3. Is the little horn of Daniel 7 the final Antichrist?
Dan. 7:7-8, 19-26

This little horn comes out of the fourth beast. He is an evil ruler described at length in Dan. 7:24-26. After he is judged and his power removed, the series of apocalyptic sketches turns to a world kingdom in the hands of God's people, His saints, whose kingdom will be everlasting and whose dominion will be universal (Dan. 7:27). This prospect favors the conclusion that the leader described as the little horn of Daniel 7 is the final Antichrist. He is said to have the eyes of a man and a mouth that spoke great things (7:8, 11). He wears out the saints (7:25), makes war with them, and prevails over them as long as God allows him to do so (7:21-22). He will speak words against the Most High (7:25), but God's judgment will end his activity (7:9-10, 26). This final Antichrist resembles earlier Antichrists: great powers of speech, hostility to God's people and to God, and a brief period of dominion followed by judgment.

Candidates for the final opponent of God seem to emerge persistently, and each generation must consider the possibility that the final opponent of God could come from its midst.

4. Career of Antichrist in Revelation completes the picture of Daniel.
Rev. 11:7; 13:1-8; 19:20

The term *beast* in Revelation can refer to the government, or world power, or to one of its rulers. In Rev. 11:7 we learn of a ruler who puts to death God's two prophets. This ruler is called "the beast who is arising from the abyss." This language hints at why there are earlier versions of Antichrist as well as a final one. Moral evil is always seeking to break out of the abyss and take over the earth. However, God so controls our world that Antichrists do not last long. This will be true also of the final Antichrist.

In Revelation 13, the beast from the sea (moral chaos, sea of cosmic evil) emerges. The dragon (Satan) gives to this evil leader power, a throne, and great authority (Rev. 13:2).

The passive verb form *edothe* ("it was given") appears six times in this chapter. Twice the Revised Standard Version translates *edothe* with "was given" (Rev. 13:5, 7) and four times with "was allowed to" (Rev. 13:5, 7, 14, 15). Revelation 13:2 suggests a hierarchical organization of moral evil. Satan gives to the final Antichrist his capacity and energy to rule and also the authority that causes people to respond to that rule. But all expressions in Revelation 13, such as "the beast was given" and "he was allowed to," show what God permitted him to do. This same idiom is used of the martyrs: "A white robe was given to each of them" (Rev. 6:11). It is also used of the Bride and saints of the Lamb: "It was granted her to be clothed with fine linen, bright and pure," (Rev. 19:8), "and judgment was given to them" (Rev. 20:4). In each case, God rewards or gives.

Since *beast* in Revelation can mean both the beastly government and its beastly ruler, the final Antichrist seems to be the last in a series of tyrants. In Revelation people worship both the beast and the dragon (13:4). Emperor worship is suggested by the false prophet or beast from the earth (Rev. 13:12; 19:20) who makes an image of the final Antichrist. Anyone who refuses to worship this image will be slain (Rev. 13:15).

At the end of Revelation 13 is the famous riddle "its [the beast's] number is 666." This riddle is based upon the fact that the people of the first century had no arabic numerals (1, 2, 3, 4, 5, etc.). For mathematical purposes, they gave a numerical value to the letters of their alphabet (*alpha* = 1; *beta* = 2; *gamma* = 3; *delta* = 4; etc.) Hence, the letters in any name could be added up to equal a certain number. The numerical value of the Greek letters in Jesus' name add up to 888. If the final Antichrist had come in John's day, John said that the numerical sum of all the letters in his name would be 666. Since he did not come in that day, and since Greek is no longer the international language, that part of the riddle is now quite meaningless. Some commentators have tried to read foreign names from our own times back into Greek. But the Greek alphabet is quite different from the alphabets of many other languages. It does not have the same vowels, combinations of vowels, or consonants as other Western languages. And of course, the alphabets of Eastern languages such as Japanese, Chinese, Hindu, and Urdu have vastly different alphabets. Efforts to translate names from other languages into Greek letters and then figure numerical values to total 666 can be so manipulated as to be worthless. For example, one could choose short or long vowels, or combinations of vowels, to get almost any numerical results desired.

Some people do not believe that the riddle should be confined to the first century A.D. when Greek was a universal language. They argue that 666 shows how Satan's agent falls short of 777—the number of perfection. Since the numerical value of Jesus' name came to 888, He would be as much beyond perfection as Satan is below it. All this may be true, but it had nothing to do with the first century riddle!

Just as Paul declares that Christ will destroy the man of sin by His second coming (2 Thess. 2:8), so John emphasizes that the beast and the false prophet will be seized and cast into the lake of fire when Christ returns (Rev. 19:19-20). Satan, with the final Antichrist and the false prophet, will be cast into the lake of fire (Rev. 20:10). This trinity of evil will be forever banished from God's presence. Within this trinity, Satan tries to assume the role of God, the Antichrist plays the role of Christ, and the false prophet or beast from the earth mimics the work of the Holy Spirit.

The successive versions of Antichrist remind us that moral evil perpetually attempts to dethrone God and replace Him with some other person or persons or selfish desires. Satan deludes his followers by making them believe they are independent and self-existing. Yet all God's creatures are dependent upon Him. New Testament writers wisely considered the Antichrist in terms of many and of one. Both Old and New Testaments perceive the Antichrist (or the one hostile to God) appearing in successive versions, ranging from Pharaoh to Antiochus IV Epiphanes to Herod the Great and to Nero. Some New Testament writers believed that the final version was near at hand. The last two thousand years have revealed other candidates. But too much speculation about the future or about possible candidates for the final Antichrist may blind us to the spirit of Antichrist now present in our world.

C. God's Judgments in History Show God's Conflict with Moral Evil

Although both Old and New Testaments illustrate God's conflict with moral evil, the apocalyptic books of Daniel and Revelation underscore this conflict. The fact that God does not blot out the people who practice and support moral evil signifies His mercy, kindness, and desire to heal and restore. The fact that He has judged, continues to judge, and will hold a final judgment shows Him to be in active conflict with moral evil.

1. God has determined moral evil to have immediate and recurring effects.
Dan. 9:26-27

The composite prince—the Syrian Antiochus IV Ephiphanes and the Roman Titus—wreaks havoc upon both the city of Jerusalem and the temple. The desolator has his day "until complete destruction and *strict decision* [that which is strictly determined] pour forth on the desolator" (Dan. 9:27). The same word is found in verse 26: "Until the end there will be war and *strict determining* of desolations." Literally the word means "to cut, sharpen, decide"[7]; in other words, God has so cut and sharpened the world that moral evil brings back certain results on the perpetrators. In verse 26 the results come upon groups or nations and in verse 27 upon individuals.

There are many secondary causes of wars and desolations, but the basic cause lies in God's strict determination that the ones who use force to accomplish their desires will find force and desolations coming back upon themselves. Jesus spoke of wars and reports of wars (Matt. 24:6; Mark 13:7; Luke 21:9) but said the end is not yet. Jesus further declared: "Those who have taken the sword will perish by the sword" (Matt. 26:52). Regardless of the sophistication of our weapons, how and why we employ force are moral issues. The wrong use will eventually bring desolation to the user.

2. God will accomplish judgment for His people against Babylon.
Rev. 14:8; 18:20; cf. 18:1-24

In Revelation 17, "the woman" and "the harlot city" are clearly Rome. In Revelation 18, the imagery and name of Babylon are also applied to Rome. The imports listed in 18:12-13—gold, silver, jewels, pearls, fine linen, and more—all came into the city of Rome. The words *the woman, harlot city,* and *Babylon* all describe the worldly arrogance and independence from God of a capital city of a prominent world empire. Probably the final Antichrist will also have an empire and a capital city that serve his end. The symbolic Babylon has risen many times in history and will no doubt rise again.

In Rev. 14:8, an angel announces the fall of the city and enunciates her crimes. She (the great capital city) has made all nations drink of the wine of her passionate immorality. This language is symbolic of a life caught up in the abundance of things. Just as people are addicted to wine, so they often become addicted to a more and more aggressive materialism (Rev. 18:3). The eighteenth chapter of Revelation is one long lament of kings, merchants, ship-masters, and sailors who profited from Babylon's ability to make glamorous things the purpose of life. Who could resist the dainties and splendor, the fine clothing, the gold and jewels and pearls? Babylon provided everything to make the good life better, creating the illusion of self-sufficiency.

But then God acted: "In one hour all this wealth has been laid waste...God has given judgment for you against her" (Rev. 18:17, 20). When things become gods, the true and living God brings judgment.

3. The final battle is the great day of God.
Rev. 14:17-20; 16:14, 16; 19:17-21

The Hebrew name *Armageddon* does not really tell us where the

213

final battle will be fought. We do not witness the battle itself, only the corpses that the vultures devour (Rev. 19:17-21). The picture in Rev. 14:19-20 also highlights the battle's destructiveness—blood flowing as high as the horses' bridles. This battle marks Christ's victory over all His foes on the great day of God when He begins to reign (Rev. 11:15-16). God's conflict with moral evil comes to an end. God and His anointed will receive the blessing, honor, glory, and power (Rev. 5:13).

But is such drastic judgment the only way to end the reign of moral evil? Is there no better way? Just before the angel announces the fall of Babylon (Rev. 14:8), another way is presented: "Fear God and give Him glory, for the hour of His judgment has come; and worship Him who made heaven and earth, the sea and the fountains of water" (Rev. 14:7). This, of course, is the better way. Those who are loosed from their sins by Christ's blood (Rev. 1:5) can truly fear God and give Him glory. But for those who will not repent from their idolatry and other immoralities, God's judgment is an awesome reality.

D. God's Final Judgment Shows People's Ultimate Accountability

God's judgments have been apparent throughout history, but the final judgment is the last chapter in the conflict with moral evil. People try vainly to get rid of God because they want to be accountable only to themselves, not realizing the chaos that would follow. People would create their own hell of eternal anarchy. Daniel and Revelation disclose that every person is accountable to God.

1. Any picture of final judgment is inadequate.

Both Daniel and Revelation describe God's taking His seat on the throne. Multitudes of people stand around the throne while scrolls are opened. Revelation specifies a scroll of life and the scrolls from which the dead are judged (20:12). Daniel describes the throne of God as being a throne of fire (7:9-10), while Revelation calls it a "great white throne" (20:11). So great is the one who sits upon the throne that the earth and the heaven flee away (Rev. 20:11). Revelation states that every person who ever lived will appear to be judged; the sea, death, and Hades are all personified as captors who will deliver up all whom they have imprisoned (20:12-13).

This is an impressive apocalyptic picture—the best we have—but it is still inadequate. A judgment of billions of persons boggles our imaginations, and it is a personal judgment. To give that sense of personal attention, the apocalyptic imagery is of an oriental court where God sits like a king, opening scrolls of writing. Surely God does not need to read a trillion scrolls to know what we have done! Since God is not like us, He does not require written records. The symbolism of the written scrolls points out our accountability rather than the mechanics of how God will judge each one of us.

2. Any picture of final punishment is inadequate.
Rev. 14:9-11; 20:14-15; 21:8; 22:15

In the Book of Jude, false teachers are punished in "the nether gloom of darkness" (Jude 13), implying absolute cold and darkness. In the Book of Revelation, final punishment is called the "second death" and is described as the "lake of fire" (Rev. 20:14-15; 21:8), implying intense heat and light. Why such different, opposing symbols?

We were created to have fellowship with God. Salvation (redemption) makes possible such a fellowship in this life and forever, but God does not force it on anyone. Those who will not repent and return to Him are permitted to have their chosen destiny, but they are separated from God. The Book of Revelation dramatically sets forth why people should choose to have their names on God's roll of citizens of His heavenly city.

The lake of fire and everlasting darkness are inadequate representations of eternal separation from God. Human language cannot adequately describe the tragedy of rejecting God: "The one who is thirsting, let him come; the one who is willing, let him take the water of life as a gift" (Rev. 22:17). The ones who do not come, are unwilling, and refuse to take the Water of Life choose their own destiny. Their chosen separation will take them further and further from God, a more terrifying prospect than any apocalyptic writer could describe. The passage closes with the solemn statement: "Since some individual was not found written in the scroll of life, that someone was cast into the lake of fire" (Rev. 20:15). Since the individual chose to continue moving away from God, God made that separation fixed and final. This wretched condition transcends all apocalyptic attempts to depict it.

The picture of eternal punishment in Revelation has some minor variations. Revelation 14:9-11 refers to fire and sulphur (brimstone) but mentions no lake of fire. This passage states that anyone who revolts against God will be tormented in the presence of angels and the Lamb. Moral evil changes its devotees. God leaves them in their changed condition because of their commitment to what is false. Although they are still aware of the reality of God, they continue to live apart from any fellowship with the God who created them.

These people are described in Rev. 21:8. Their life patterns conform to those of persons who are (1) cowardly—failing to stand for justice or righteousness; (2) faithless—exhibiting infidelity; (3) polluted—practicing what is detestable; (4) murderers—disregarding the right of others to live; (5) sexually immoral—feigning love but really loving only themselves; (6) sorcerers or magicians—claiming imaginary or actual connections with evil powers; (7) idolaters—giving loyalty and worship to false deities; and (8) liars—having no respect for the truth or for telling the truth. These same kinds of people are mentioned in Rev. 22:15 where another strange phrase occurs: "Outside are the dogs." Wild dogs outside ancient cities preyed upon other animals. Therefore, this phrase designates persons who prey upon the helpless and the weak.

The kingdom of moral evil will finally be defeated and dispersed. Those who refuse to let Christ deliver them from the authority of darkness will find their dispersion permanent, painful, purposeless—except the peculiar purpose of getting away from God.

IV. The Second Coming of Christ Inaugurates the Visible Worldwide Kingdom of God

Both Daniel and Revelation have much to say about earthly kingdoms and God's kingdom. They speak of God's leader—"one like a Son of man" and "His Messiah"—and how God's people work with this leader. Although the return of Christ is a New Testament theme, it builds upon the concern of Daniel and other Old Testament writers for a world where right will reign through God's chosen servant. The concept of a universal king and kingdom is harmonious with Old and New Testament writers, and Daniel and Revelation contribute significantly to this theme.

216

A. Christ's Return, Like His Incarnation, Will Be an Unparalleled Event in Human History

The most important aspect of Christ's second coming will be the enlargement of our view of creation. Throughout the twentieth century, we have become increasingly aware of the vastness of the physical creation. Christ's return will demonstrate the reality of heaven and the eternal realm. When Christ returns, heaven will open and stay open (Rev. 19:11). (See accompanying chart, Appendix, pp. 242-243).

The return of Christ will reveal a great deal about the meaning of existence and about God's plans to change human affairs from chaos to harmony, from the corruption of moral evil to the complete harmony of moral good.

1. God's gifts to one like a son of man.
Dan. 7:13-14

Daniel 7 describes a vision of one like a Son of man who came with the clouds of heaven. The man, with human shape and figure, came not to earth but to God. There he was presented to God in lofty language appropriate to an important person's appearing before a ruling monarch. God granted to this person (1) dominion or sovereignty, (2) the organized world kingdom, and (3) the honor that comes with sovereignty. All peoples, nations, and languages serve him. His dominion or sovereignty is everlasting, and his kingdom will not be destroyed.

In verse 27 of this same chapter, the kingdom and the dominion and the greatness of the kingdoms under the whole heaven are given to the saints of the Most High. Because of this, some interpreters believe that the "one like a son of man" is another expression for "the saints." All dominions shall serve and obey them. There are similarities, but there are also differences. In Dan. 7:14, the people serve *him*; in 7:27, dominions serve *them*. Daniel 7:14 takes place in heaven; 7:27 takes place on earth.

The New Testament also encompasses both ideas. The one like a Son of man is Jesus Christ, the true man. All who believe in Him become part of Him; we have been baptized into Christ Jesus (Rom. 6:3). Dominion, the organized world kingdom, honor, and obedience are also given to His people. The close relationship between Christ and His people is clear. Exactly how they both will function awaits fulfillment, however.

2. Believers must prepare for Christ's return.
Rev. 16:15; 22:7, 10, 12-13, 20

The sixth bowl of wrath involves the trinity of evil—Satan, the final Antichrist, and the false prophet—and the unclean spirits who gather the kings of the earth for a final battle. But in the midst of this picture of God's judgment, Christ speaks an urgent word to His people: "Lo, I am coming as a thief. Blessed is the one who is alert and is keeping his garments, lest he should walk naked and they should see his shame" (Rev. 16:15). In many societies, when a soldier is captured, he is disrobed so that he cannot carry concealed weapons. This is the image here. If moral evil conquers us, we become defenseless. Believers are to be alert in keeping themselves free from the defilements of moral evil.

Preparation is a central theme in Revelation. In 22:7, believers are told to "keep the words of the prophecy of this book" (Revelation). In 22:10-12, they are instructed to do right because Christ is coming soon to repay each one for what he has done. The close of the book (22:20) reminds us that the same Christ who testifies to the things in this book is coming back soon.

The word *rapture*, widely used to describe the return of Christ, does not appear in most English language translations of the Bible. It means "caught up" and comes from 1 Thess. 4:17: "Then we who are alive, who are left, shall be caught up together with them in the clouds to meet the Lord in the air." The saints who are living will be transformed and join Christ and those with Him. The rapture is the same as Christ's second coming, which involves saints who are living upon earth and the ones who have died and are with Christ in heaven. Those living on earth at that time are warned to be well prepared: "Be alert..." (Rev. 16:15).

The phrase "the great tribulation" occurs only once in the entire Bible, in Rev. 7:14 (see 7:9-14). There it describes a numberless throng that comes from every nation, tribe, people, and language. They have come out of the great tribulation, which will be the experience of Christians until Christ comes. When the adjective *great* is attached to the word *tribulation*, the combination refers to any tribulation in which Christians are put to death for their faith in Christ. This has happened in every generation of Christians since the time of Stephen (Acts 6—7). Because we all suffer when fellow Christians suffer, we all come out of the great tribulation. Like the

218

Antichrist who was present in New Testament times and in every generation since then, so it is with the great tribulation. Further, there will be a final Antichrist and a final tribulation. (See the chart on pp. 242-243.)

If we combine Rev. 7:9-17 and 15:2-4, we sense the tremendous note of victory that all Christians share. From the first Antichrist to the final one, Christians, like the three Hebrews of Daniel 3, have replied: "Our God whom we serve is able to deliver us...but if not...we will not serve your gods or worship the golden image which you have set up" (Dan. 3:17-18). When Christ returns, the agony of the contest will be past. Christians can sing the song of Moses, the servant of God, and the song of the Lamb:

Great and marvelous are your works
   Lord, God, the Almighty.
Righteous and true are your ways
   The king of the nations (Rev. 15:3).

3. Christ's return brings worldwide reaction.
Rev. 1:7

When Christ returns, all people will know who is coming: "Behold He comes with clouds, and every eye shall see Him; and whoever pierced Him. And all tribes of the earth will mourn for Him" (Rev. 1:7). This apocalyptic language about Christ does not mean that if the weather is clear, Christ will not come!

Clouds, in apocalyptic literature, usually depict the mysterious movement between the heavenly and the earthly realms. When Jesus ascended, "a cloud received Him out of their sight" (Acts 1:9). In the Old Testament, God is often associated with clouds, as in Psa. 18:9-12 and 104:3. But in some other cases, such as Dan. 7:13 and Rev. 1:7, the clouds could refer to the normal, atmospheric type. Whatever their meaning, the clouds depict Christ's return as mysterious a phenomenon as was His ascension to heaven.

"Every eye will see Him." Some people suggest that this will involve worldwide television, which implies that Christ could not have come until our generation got its communication satellites into space! Rather, John envisioned that when Christ returns, everyone will be aware that something has begun an entirely new epoch.

"Those who pierced Him" (Jesus) is a quotation from Zech.

12:10, where Zechariah delivers God's word about a leader for whom the house of David will mourn. But in Rev. 1:7, John applies the Zechariah passage to all the tribes of the earth. Thus "those who pierced Him" applies to more than the Roman soldiers who crucified Him; it apparently refers to all who have been hostile toward Christ. At His first coming, some Jews and Romans were hostile, but others responded in love and faithfulness. John broadens and extends the mourning of grief and repentance in the passage in Zechariah. In other parts of Revelation we see armies fighting against Christ, but in Rev. 1:7, we see only a universal awareness of wrong.

4. Christ's return is described as a harvest.

Revelation 14:14-20 describes "one like a Son of man" (an expression from Dan. 7:13) sitting on the cloud with a golden crown on His head and a sharp sickle in His hand. An angel of God announces to Christ ("one like a Son of man") that the harvest is ripe. Christ puts in His sickle and reaps not crops, but people. When Christ reaps the harvest of His people, it will be immense.

The symbolic harvest of grain is followed by a harvest of grapes in which wine and blood symbolize judgment on those arrayed against Christ (Rev. 14:17-20). Such agricultural figures stimulate our imaginations and suggest judgment.

During His earthly ministry, Jesus said that the harvest is the end of the age and the angels are the reapers (Matt. 13:39). Furthermore, the Son of man would send out His angels with a loud trumpet call, and they would gather His elect from one end of heaven to the other (Matt. 24:31). Christ's return is part of a glorious, joyous harvest (Matt. 13:43) that, sadly, also includes the removal of the tares from the wheat (Matt. 13:40-42). John's visions of harvest in the Book of Revelation correspond to Jesus' words on the same subject because Jesus, the risen and exalted Lord, is the source of John's visions.

5. Christ's second coming as a military commander indicates that the kingdom of God will become visible.
Rev. 19:11-20:6

"The kingdom of God is not food and drink but righteousness and peace and joy in the Holy Spirit" (Rom. 14:17). But Paul also recognized that there were future aspects to the kingdom. He boasted about the endurance and faith of the Thessalonians in their persecutions, normal experiences for Christians in a world of moral evil. They were being made worthy of the future kingdom of God for which they were suffering (2 Thess. 1:4-5). Jesus taught us to pray: "Let your kingdom come, let your will occur also upon earth as in heaven" (Matt. 6:10). The kingdom is coming as well as the king.

The flow of thought at the close of Revelation points to Christ's coming as an integral part of His kingdom. The kingdom emphasis is evident when the seventh trumpet sounds (Rev. 11:15-18). "But in the days of the sound of the seventh angel, when he is about to blow his trumpet, the secret of God will be completed in the manner as He announced it as good tidings to His prophets" (Rev. 10:7). The king and the kingdom fulfill the promises that God made known to His servants, the prophets of both the Old and New Testaments.

Perhaps the most important New Testament passage about Christ's second coming is Rev. 19:11-20:6. "I saw that the heaven has been opened and stays open" (Rev. 19:11). The Greek perfect tense of the word *open* indicates that the action is permanent. Greek verb tenses are more concerned with *kind* of action than with *time* (past, present, or future). "The heaven has been opened" (and stays open, implied in the perfect tense) indicates an event at Christ's second coming that will happen and will have continuing effects.

Heaven, the eternal heavenly realm, is where Christ has been since His ascension. Paul spoke of death as a "departing and being with Christ which is far better" (Phil. 1:23). One by one the saints of each generation have joined their Savior. But the way to this eternal heavenly realm has been a one-way street for all of history thus far.

Recent books on death and dying have reported the experiences of many people who were "clinically dead" but came back to life. Many described their experiences as going down a long dark tunnel with a brilliant light at the other end. But those who report this were only a little way down the tunnel; they were allowed to return. When Christ comes as a military conqueror, the way to and from heaven will be opened and will remain open. However, persons who go in either direction will be fully under Christ's control.

As a military commander, Christ will judge and make war in

righteousness with His people and angelic forces (Rev. 19:11, 14). The sword in His mouth is symbolic of His power (Rev. 19:15). His title demonstrates that His kingdom is visible: "King over kings and Lord over lords" (Rev. 19:16). He defeats all earthly forces of the final Antichrist and the false prophet who will be seized and thrown into the lake of fire (Rev. 19:17-21). Satan himself will be bound for a long period of time (Rev. 20:1-3).

But His work is much more profound than defeating His foes. He opens the eternal heavenly realm for His people. Revelation 20:5-6 describes it thus: "This is the first resurrection. Blessed and holy is the one having part in the first resurrection." Resurrection means standing up in this material earthly realm victorious over both sin and death.

Paul says that when Christians die, they lose their bodies but receive a better dwelling place: "If our earthly house, the tent, collapses, we have a building from God, a house not made with hands, eternal in the heavens" (2 Cor. 5:1). We can identify with Paul's picturesque language. Presently all of us have only a tent— our present earthly bodies. But the tent's collapse—our death— will mean for each of us "a building, a house not made with hands." Paul contrasts a tent that collapses easily with an edifice or building that is permanent. It functions first in the eternal heavenly realm, "eternal in the heavens" but it is a permanent dwelling place.

When Christ comes and heaven is opened to stay open (Rev. 19:11), His people come with Him. For the first time, the permanent dwelling place (body) that saints received in place of their tent (earthly body) will show its versatility. It will function normally and naturally in the material earthly realm as well as it does in the heavenly sphere. This is what Christ's "spiritual body" did during the forty days after His resurrection when He appeared to His disciples.

The idea of Christ's coming back with His saints is a difficult concept for all interpreters. When Christ comes back to this world, "every eye shall see Him" (Rev. 1:7), and if the saints come with Him, every eye will see them too. The people on earth who identified themselves with the beast will be destroyed (Rev. 19:17-21; 2 Thess. 1:7-10). Those who did not identify themselves with either the followers of the beast or the believers will be left on earth with mortal bodies that function only in this earthly realm. The saints from heaven and the believers on earth (who have been transformed at Christ's coming) will have "heavenly bodies" that can function either in the eternal heavenly realm or in the material earthly realm. How can these two groups function together?

The picture in Revelation seems to indicate that the eternal heavenly realm opens and stays open, so Christ allows His saints to come and go as He pleases. Their presence on earth shows their victory over death, and they will function wherever Christ assigns them. "For the earth will be filled with the knowledge of the glory of the Lord as the waters cover the sea" (Hab. 2:14; Isa. 11:9). The earth will not be crowded, for the eternal heavenly realm stays open. But those with earthly bodies must stay in the earthly realm. Christ's kingdom on earth will be visible as will the eternal heavenly realm. When moral evil has been forever banished, then all God's people can move freely between the eternal heavenly realm and the material earthly realm as they choose. Until that time, Christ's people move under His commands.

B. The Complete Removal of Moral Evil from Creation
Dan. 7:15-18, 22, 25, 27; Rev. 2:26-28; 12:5; 19:15; 20:4-6

We must not pretend that we can comprehend God's great plan. History indicates that when we have made the universe and the world too small, we have made God and His plans too small. Whatever God has revealed must be perceived against the background of a huge panorama having only a few of its scenes sharply delineated. Sometimes we want to picture Christ as a wizard returning with a kind of magic wand that will cause all evil to disappear; He will do it all while we applaud and celebrate His victory.

But this is not the picture presented in Daniel and Revelation. In Daniel 7, dominion, sovereignty, and the organized world kingdom are given to Christ *and* to His people. People may choose to obey or disobey, but Daniel indicates that the vast majority will show respect and obedience to Christ and His people (Dan. 7:27).

But what of those who do not show respect or obedience? Three times Revelation applies Psa. 2:9 to either Christ or His people. The Hebrew text of Psa. 2:9 reads, "You shall *break* them with a rod of iron." The Greek version of Revelation, as well as the Greek version of the Old Testament [the Septuagint] says instead "...shall *rule* them with a rod of iron." Revelation 2:26-27 reads: "I will give *him* authority over the nations and he will rule them with a rod of iron." The word *him* refers to the Christian who is victorious and practices Christ's works. In Rev. 12:5 and 19:15, the one who rules with a rod of iron is clearly Christ. Apparently moral evil will not be dismissed by mere decree or the waving of a magic wand. Instead, Christ and His people will lead a campaign against moral evil and for moral good.

Those who take part in the first resurrection and reign with Christ for a thousand years (meaning a long period of time) will sit upon thrones and judge (Rev. 20:4). This large group of believers includes a small group of martyrs who gave their lives for their testimony of Jesus and the word of God. They did not compromise with the final Antichrist (or any earlier versions) or show loyalty to the false leader. The thrones symbolize not only their rule but also their roles as judges (Rev. 20:4-6). The same is said of the saints in other parts of the New Testament (Matt. 19:28; 1 Cor. 6:2-3). They will be priests of God and of Christ, and they will reign with Him (Rev. 3:21; 5:9-10; 20:6) for a thousand years (a long period of time).

This kind of authority is different from any government we have known. Because Christ is the leader, some might call it a theocracy, but that would overlook the role of Christ's people. If we paraphrase Lincoln's definition of democracy to read "a government of God's people, by God's people, for all of God's creatures," we leave out Christ. This is instead a new theocratic, democratic, participatory rule by people who are united because they died and rose together with Christ. They have returned together to achieve the full effects of their union in Christ. This union and rule will continue until the final battle (Rev. 20:7-10). After Satan is cast into the lake of fire, moral evil will be gone and life will be centered in God, freed from all the chaos of selfish and self-centered living.

V. New Heaven, New Earth, and New Harmony
Rev. 21:1-22:5

When moral evil is eradicated, free movement will be possible throughout the material earthly realm and the eternal heavenly realm. Before Christ's second coming, these two realms could not be transversed except by God and His messengers or angels. When Christ returns and makes His kingdom visible, the two realms become two divisions of one realm, but movement from one to the other is possible only under Christ's orders. When moral evil is banished and all creation is unified, the new possibilities are beyond our imaginations. John's apocalyptic imagery can only give us clues about all that is largely beyond our comprehension.

A. Contrast Between the New and the Old
Rev. 21:1-8

John mentions three things from the old order: (1) first heaven, (2) first earth, and (3) first (former) things (Rev. 21:1, 4). The former things include (a) the sea (Rev. 21:1), (b) death, (c) mourning, (d) crying, (e) pain (Rev. 21:4), (f) the curse (Rev. 22:3), and (g) night (Rev. 22:5). The first earth was filled with these things, and even the first heaven was affected by them. For example, there is war in heaven (Rev. 12:7-8). The effects of moral evil are all-pervading.

Three parallel realities characterize the new order: (1) new heaven, (2) new earth, and (3) new things (Rev. 21:1, 5). The holy city (mentioned briefly in verses 1-8 and developed more extensively in the rest of chap. 21) comes down out of heaven from God, prepared as a bride for her husband (Rev. 21:2). The holy city belongs to both the new heaven and the new earth. Christ's second coming made visible His kingdom and caused heaven to be opened and stay open. God will dwell (the Greek word means "tent" or "camp") with His people. The camping metaphor suggests that God again tents with His people, even as He had done in the wilderness after the Exodus, only now all have access to Him! We will be His people, and He will be our God (Rev. 21:3).

God, who created people to have fellowship with Him, has planned a gigantic future transformation in that fellowship. In fact, this transformation has already begun: "Lo, I am making all things new" (Rev. 21:5). As we are experiencing renewal now, we are becoming samples of the new things to come. But these verses point beyond the "sample period" in history to the fulfilled reality of the new heaven and new earth. Everyone who is not part of this new reality will be separated from God (Rev. 21:8). Self-centered people cannot fellowship with God because they have made an idol of themselves. A life centered in God is at the heart of this total transformation.

B. Heaven in the Final Vision of Revelation
Rev. 19:5-9; 21:9-26

An angelic guide invited John to come with him to see the Bride, the wife of the Lamb (Rev. 21:9). In the Spirit, John was carried away to a great and lofty mountain from which he saw the Bride, the holy city Jerusalem, coming down out of heaven from God (Rev. 21:10). The holy city is the place of God's people from all tribes, peoples, nations, and languages. All parts of the city are equally beautiful, and no part is reserved for "those who are not quite as 'spiritual' as we are." The twelve gates of the city are of pearl, on which are names of the twelve tribes of Israel (Rev. 21:12-13). The twelve foundations, exposed so that their beauty can be seen, are made of various gems (Rev. 21:19-21), and the names of the twelve apostles of the Lamb (Rev. 21:14) are written on them.

The apocalyptic language about a bride represents the togetherness of God's people in the heavenly city. The invitation to the marriage supper of the Lamb is issued in Rev. 19:7, but the actual event is described in Revelation 21. In this metaphor of marriage, the Bride (God's people) and the groom (the Lamb, God's Son) celebrate their union in a setting of total dedication and complete harmony. There is no temple because the Almighty and the Lamb are the temple.

If we look carefully at the numbers used in describing the city, it readily becomes apparent that these are apocalyptic numbers, not literal measurements. For example, the city is said to be a cube of at least twelve thousand stadia. (It is interesting that the Most Holy Place in Solomon's temple also had the dimensions of a cube—twenty cubits long, wide, and high [1 Kings 6:20].) The holy city John describes is a cube at least 1500 miles wide, long, and high. Although the city is said to be at least 1500 miles high, the height of its wall is said to be only 144 cubits—or 216 feet.

Note that all the numbers used in describing the city are twelve, or multiples of twelve. The number twelve in Revelation seems to symbolize God's true covenant people—Jews and Gentiles who acknowledge Jesus as the Messiah. The one covenant people of God, glorified and triumphant, is the goal of the Old and New Testaments.

C. Pictures of Final Harmony
Rev. 22:1-5

Chapter two of Genesis portrays a garden in which a river divides into four rivers and in which the tree of life grows. A garden, a river, and a tree of life also appear in Revelation 22 in the picture of final harmony. In Revelation, however, the river flows from the throne of God and the Lamb. The tree of life here is not a single tree but a forest of many trees lining both sides of the river. These trees produce twelve kinds of fruit, one crop each month, for the healing of the nations. But why should healing be needed when the curse of sin and moral evil is forever gone? The healing is mentioned just before the statement "there shall no more be anything accursed" which may indicate that this fruit is part of God's healing from the after effects of moral evil. The curse mentioned in Genesis 3 is gone, and now all consequences of the battle with moral evil will be healed.

God's servants will worship and serve Him. They will see God's face just as Jesus promised: "Blessed are the pure in heart for they shall see God" (Matt. 5:8). They will forever belong to God; His name will be stamped upon their foreheads. There will be no more night and no more sun or artificial light. The Lord God will be their light, and they will rule over God's new creation forever and ever.

Summary

How much does God really want us to know about the end of history? Our answer will influence how we study prophecy. If we believe God has revealed blueprints for the future, we will read our ideas into the text. If we believe God has revealed little, perhaps we will be less open to what He wants us to know today.

How, then, do we study Daniel and Revelation? The words of Christ in Acts 1:7 must be held firmly in our minds. God has disclosed some things in these books, but with their rich apocalyptic symbols, we must not let our imaginations fill in what God has left ambiguous. These books are given to tell us how to live in the present, not to satisfy our curiosity about the future.

Daniel and Revelation speak in more apocalyptic than scientific language. Although both languages refer to physical realities, they function in different ways. Scientific language records what happens and seeks to explain the why and the how of the event. Apocalyptic language shows that God will use heavenly bodies and earthly phenomena to bring judgment but provides little insight into the circumstances surrounding these events.

Time measurements in Daniel and Revelation use both "common" and "apocalyptic" arithmetic; both literal and figurative ordinary time expressions appear. Apocalyptic time expressions are often connected with the future. Terms like "the end" or "the end of the age" point to severe crises in the future.

Revelation depicts the persistent conflict between moral evil and moral good, and it narrates how this conflict sharpens as moral evil gains dominance and history moves toward its close. Yet Satan's domain is always subject to God's control. When evil forces pursue their course, God uses not only the forces of righteousness but also the forces of wickedness to reveal the destructiveness of sin.

The term Antichrist appears only in 1 and 2 John, not in Revelation or Daniel. The term, however, is a synonym for one who is against the covenant God of Israel. The descriptions in Daniel seem to fit both known and unknown rulers who opposed God. Revelation speaks not of Antichrist but of a beast who seems to fill the same function.

God's judgments in history illustrate His conflict with moral evil, which has both immediate and recurring effects. How and why we employ force—military or otherwise—are moral issues. The wrong use of force eventually brings desolation to the user.

God's final judgment emphasizes the accountability of people to God. Although any word picture of final judgment is inadequate, both Daniel and Revelation use the language of thrones to describe it. Pictures of final punishment are no more complete, but all of them describe the utter tragedy of rejecting God.

The second coming of Christ inaugurates the visible worldwide kingdom of God with Christ's universal rule over all earthly kingdoms. The return of Christ, like His incarnation, will be an unparalleled event in human history, demonstrating the reality of heaven and the eternal realm.

Believers are told to prepare for the return of Christ, keeping themselves free from the defilements of moral evil. Upon His return, the saints who are living will be transformed and join Christ and those who come with Him.

Tribulation is the experience of all Christians until Christ comes. The "great tribulation" occurs whenever Christians are put to death for their faith in Christ. This has happened in every generation since the time of the martrydom of Stephen (Acts 6—7). But just as there will be a final Antichrist, so there will be a final great tribulation.

When Christ returns, the way to and from heaven will be opened and stay open. Those who go in either direction are fully under Christ's control. With their new bodies, the saints of Christ can function wherever Christ assigns them—in heaven or on earth. When moral evil has been forever banished, all God's people can move freely between the eternal heavenly realm and the material earthly realm.

John's apocalyptic imagery of the new heaven and new earth is largely beyond our understanding. There will be a new heaven, a new earth, and new things (Rev. 21:1, 5). The "holy city" belongs to both the new heaven and the new earth and links together the realms. It is the place of all God's people, who come from all tribes, peoples, nations, and languages. The Lord God will be their light, and they will be partners with God in ruling His creation forever.

Notes for Chapter 7

[1]Bauer, *gé*, p. 157. 1. soil, 2. ground, 3. bottom (of the sea), 4. land (as opposed to sea), region, country, 5. earth, a. in contrast to heaven, b. as the inhabited globe.

[2]*Ibid.*, p. 561.

[3]*Ibid.*, p. 350.

[4]Henry B. Swete, *The Apocalypse of St. John* (Grand Rapids, Mich.: Wm. B. Eerdmans Publishing Co., 1951), p. 212.

[5]Joachim Jeremias, *pollai*, TDNT, VI:536-545, especially pp. 536-537.

[6]Brown, Driver, and Briggs, pp. 988-989.

[7]*Ibid.*, p. 358.

Chapter 8

Fitting Our Short Lives Into God's Big Plan

This study has sought to affirm God's greatness and His plans as revealed in the books of Daniel and Revelation. The plan of God is described as His secret or mystery (Rev. 10:7), small portions of which He announced to His servants the prophets. He has appointed Christ to be the central administrator (Rev. 1:16-17; 5:1-14). The hymn, "How Great Thou Art," captures our proper response to God's grandeur. Yet our short sinful lives stand in such contrast to the eternal Being of God that we sometimes have trouble sensing any connection between ourselves and our Father. Our lives seem like one long series of puzzling predicaments, and our plans are often decimated without any way of recovering our agendas. Can Daniel and Revelation help us see how our brief lives fit into God's plan and the onrushing course of history?

I. God Must Be a Reality—Not an Idea

God must be a reality that we experience, not an idea that we embrace. But as we experience God, we must beware of putting more stress on the "experience" than on God. Neither can we know God by adding together a series of intellectual propositions and declaring, "Here is my idea of God!"

We experience God when we pray, worship, meditate, or cry out to Him in life's crises. We also come to know God through learning about His servants who lived before us (especially as recorded in the Bible), interacting with each other, and listening to what God's Spirit says to us as individuals and as churches. Because God is so great, our perceptions of Him will differ. But there is a sense of unity among those who fellowship with God as we recognize that we all are only beginning to know and to love our limitless God. We are to love Him from our whole heart and with our entire soul, our full strength, and our total mind (Mark 12:30; Luke 10:27). To know God is no mere intellectual experience; it is an experience of the total person.

Perhaps that is why the truths of God often came to His servants in times of crises. When God revealed Nebuchadnezzar's dream to Daniel, Daniel's life and the lives of his three friends and the other wise men (counselors) were at stake. What Daniel said about God and Nebuchadnezzar came out of this intense crisis (Dan. 2). The Christ who appeared to John was the one for whom he was imprisoned on the island of Patmos. Most of us cultivate an illusion of independence for ourselves that is shattered when crisis confronts us. Only God "in whose hand is our breath and whose are all our ways" (Dan. 5:23) is independent; we are all dependent upon Him.

God's plan emphasizes the one who is planning, not the events to come. Daniel and Revelation consistently remind us that God *has* acted, He *is* acting, and He *will* act. Creation and redemption were powerful acts of God, and Daniel and Revelation celebrate God as Creator and Redeemer. We who know God are the products of these actions. Our life and breath are in His hands, and in God's great plan we follow the Lamb wherever He goes (Rev. 14:4).

II. Believers Must Recognize Moral Evil for What It Is

Apocalyptic literature, which constitutes much of Daniel and Revelation, describes many forms of moral evil and points to its eventual defeat. In our own brief lives, we must recognize moral evil as early as possible if we are not to be destroyed by it. For example, tragic numbers of people are being killed by various drugs. Usually they are deceived into thinking that the drugs will give them some new kinds of good experiences, not lethal ones. We must recognize moral evil for what it is and realize that we do not have the power within ourselves to conquer it. God's power is granted to us when we repent (renounce loyalty to moral evil) and turn to Him, trusting His power to give us strength to be overcoming.

Moral evil often produces an unwarranted sense of superiority in individuals. Some persons think they can violate the laws of God and suffer no consequences. Or else they think there are no "laws of God." Moral evil emphasizes self-serving in several ways: "You deserve to get all you want of whatever you want. The more money or power you have, the more important you are. Look at our popular public heroes. They are famous for some skill, ability, or family name. They are paid well. They get everything they want." But behind this facade may be lives that are largely empty and purposeless. Moral evil glamorizes the broad gate and the spacious way that lead to destruction (Matt. 7:13). Daniel and Revelation show the nature of moral evil and the tragedies that it brings; both call for moral alertness. The verb "to watch" really means to be morally alert (Rev. 3:2-3; 16:15). If we respond to this call, our short lives will be victorious.

The Book of Revelation is a call to the one who is victorious (Rev. 2:7, 11, 17, 26; 3:5, 12, 21; 12:11; 17:14; 21:7). Part of life's purpose is to recognize the struggle against moral evil and to resolve to win that struggle with the help of God's power.

III. God's People Must Be Faithful to God and His Covenant

Both Daniel and Revelation stress that we are covenant people. Persons from every tribe, language, people, and nation are redeemed for God by the blood of the Lamb who was slain (Rev. 5:9-10), the one who inaugurated the new and final covenant. Consequently, faithfulness to God and His covenant is of paramount importance. Moral evil involves loyalty to sin, self, and satanic power. God's faithful people are to be loyal to righteousness, God, and His power. The adjective translated "faithful" (*pistos*) appears eight times in the Book of Revelation. Three times it is used of Christ who is faithful (Rev. 1:5; 3:14; 19:11); three times of believers (Rev. 2:10, 13; 17:14); and twice of the words that God reveals (Rev. 21:5; 22:6). Christ's faithfulness and our faithfulness complement each other. Daniel says the same thing: "Now I beseech thee, O Lord, the great God, the one inspiring reverence, the one keeping covenant and steadfast love to those loving Him and keeping His commandments" (Dan. 9:4).

We place our short lives into God's big plan (the small part that we experience) by being faithful to God and to our struggle in the contest with moral evil. This demands endurance in all pressures and forces that would move us away from God and loyalty to Him. When John wrote to his seven churches from prison on Patmos, he described himself as "your brother and fellow sharer in the tribulation and kingdom and *endurance* which is in Jesus" (Rev. 1:9). Because Christ is faithful, we will be faithful.

IV. Believers Should Glory in God, Not in Human Schemes of What God May Do

What does God really want us to know about the end of history? Daniel, Revelation, and Acts 1:7 all confirm that God does not intend us to know "times and seasons."

God has revealed some high points in His plan. For example, we know that God has used and will use nature to judge sin. We know that Satan's kingdom is organized but ultimately subject to God's control. We know there have been many earlier Antichrists and there will be a final Antichrist. We know that when believers are put to death for their faith, they have experienced "the great tribulation." In every generation, then, some believers have died for their faith. Because we share together in suffering and crises, including that of giving one's life for Christ, all Christians are coming out of the great tribulation (see chart on pages 242-243).

We know that God will come and make His kingdom both universal and visible in the world, which is probably what Dan. 2:35 means by stating: "The stone that struck the image [of earthly kingdoms] will become a great mountain and fill the whole earth." When Christ comes, heaven will open and stay open. Instead of our present two-realm universe (heaven and earth) whose boundaries cannot be crossed, there will be a one-realm universe with two parts: (1) the material earthly realm (our expanding Einsteinian universe) and (2) the eternal heavenly realm. Christ and God's people will rule for a long time, and then all moral evil will be removed. There will be a final judgment and a final separation from God for those persons in rebellion against Him. Finally, there will be a new heaven and new earth that encompass the Holy City. All of these comprise the eternal realm that Christ opened at His return.

This summary is my interpretation of God's plan as revealed in Daniel and Revelation. It has few details and is not based on any classical eschatological system of how history will end. Since my understanding of God's plan includes an earthly reign of Christ and His people, I would be classified as a premillennialist (one who believes that Christ's coming will precede His earthly reign and that of His people).

I believe that "the first resurrection" of Rev. 20:5 refers to a resurrection such as Christ experienced on the third day after His crucifixion. Those who are resurrected receive what Paul called "a spiritual body" (1 Cor. 15:42-44). My views differ from many forms of premillennialism in my conviction that the permanent opening of heaven when Christ returns refers to the removal of the present barriers to movement between the earthly and heavenly realms (see chart in Appendix, pp. 242-243). People with "spiritual bodies" will be able to function in either realm under Christ's orders. His return will certainly inaugurate a new epoch between God and His creation.

It seems to me that those who go much beyond these few details are going beyond what God has told us and what He intends for us to know. God has not chosen to give us a detailed picture of how He will wind up the world. Our faith and confidence are to be in Him, not in any secret or special knowledge of what will occur in the future. We all still "see through a glass darkly" (1 Cor. 13:12).

In our generation, as well as in past generations, certain people have been certain they know the exact day or month or year that Christ will return. Such people have always attracted followers, and we have seen the sad spectacle of people quitting their jobs, selling their belongings, and idly awaiting that day. When Christ does not come at the designated time, their pain and disillusionment are heartrending. God did not intend for His people to suffer that way.

All of us will no doubt be greatly surprised when Christ returns or when we meet Him beyond this life. God's plan is far more immense than our finite minds could ever comprehend. We have only small bits and pieces of the total plan, but He has communicated enough so that we see our responsibilities to stand true to Him and to depend on His leadership.

It is sad that so much time and energy have been used by Christians to build elaborate schemes of what will take place in the future and to refute other elaborate schemes. We have all been exposed to one or more such schemes, and some have become so popular that many Christians assume that they are taken directly from the Bible.

My own mother told me years ago that when she was a young woman, she attended classes in an evening Bible school where such detailed schemes of the future were taught. She came home to share with her carpenter father the exciting news of what was going to happen in the coming history of the world. He listened carefully to all she had to say, then studied the same passages in the Bible. After days of study, he finally said to her, "I'm sorry, Annie, but I just don't find that in my Bible."

We all need to read Daniel and Revelation and other parts of the Bible without trying to fit the inspired contents into some structure we have already established in our minds or one that has been handed to us. Such structures and schemes tend to separate us from each other instead of building the unity of the body of Christ. In the face of the greatness of God and of His future, debate and controversy should be replaced by reverence and awe.

We face this future without any confidence that we have arranged things well or that we have a particular gift to unfold the future. Our confidence is in God and in His ability and power to do what He has promised. Our confidence is in Christ, God's administrator: "The Lamb on the center of the throne will shepherd them [lead to pasture, protect, care for, nurture], and He will guide them to fountains of living waters. And God will wipe away every tear from their eyes" (Rev. 7:17).

The right kind of confidence and conviction is focused upon the Shepherd who is our guide for this life and the unending ages of His eternal kingdom. Consequently, with each day that God gives us, we are to seek to do justice, to practice righteousness, and to be consecrated to our Shepherd (Rev. 22:11). Only in this way can we be winning victory over the moral evil that seeks to destroy us. God's universal victory in the future must be seen in the individual, daily lives of his saints.

Appendix

Appendix I

Explanation of chart on pp. 240-241.

Title. From Incarnation to Eternal Illumination (22:5). The Book of Revelation covers an extremely long period: from the foundation of the world (Rev. 13:8) to eternal illumination and everlasting harmony. This chart, however, concentrates on a shorter period. It begins with the incarnation of Christ (Rev. 12:2, 5) and ends with the period of eternal illumination free from any possibility of moral evil.

Two realms. The chart shows the two realms of heaven and earth. The term *heaven* can refer to the atmospheric heavens and the astronomical heavens, but here it means the eternal realm. Likewise the term *earth* can mean particles of dirt, land in contrast to sea, particular places or nations on this one land mass or, as we define it here, the material earthly realm. All parts of God's physical creation with a similar chemical, atomic structure would be included in the material earthly realm. For example, the moon does not have any water or atmosphere, but it is part of the material earthly realm. This applies also to the other planets in our solar system.

One horizontal line. This line separates the material earthly realm from the eternal or heavenly realm. Note that this one horizontal line disappears at the time of Christ's second coming.

Left vertical line, arrow pointing down. This line shows the importance of the incarnation of Christ. The chart includes verses to study on *logos* ("word, message, communication"). Scripture passages are noted on His birth, death, and resurrection. What Jesus taught, did, and experienced and what God did with Him and through Him gave us an unparalleled breakthrough in our knowledge of God.

Second vertical line, arrow pointing upward. This emphasizes the ascension of Christ that is announced in Rev. 12:5b. A fuller sketch is given in Acts 1:9-11, and Luke 24:50-53. Only in Rev. 12:7-12 do we learn that when Christ ascended to heaven, Satan was removed from heaven and no longer had access to God's presence as he had before, for example, in the Book of Job (Job 1:6-12; 2:1-7).

Third vertical line, arrow pointing downward. This line represents the second coming of Christ. If the Incarnation (Christ's first coming) had importance for humankind, the second coming of Christ

239

has even greater importance. What will happen at His second coming is based upon what He accomplished at His first coming. The whole plan of God for humankind centers around these two comings.

Fourth vertical line, arrow pointing in both directions. The messianic reign is pictured by some as very earthly and by others as very heavenly. We see it as earthly and heavenly in the first part of the reign and also in the unending second part of the reign. These two periods involve (1) a process by which moral evil is completely eliminated from the totality of God's creation, and (2) unending growth and development of people in the new heavens and the new earth completely freed from the presence and possibility of moral evil.

Period between the ascension of Christ and His second coming. The chart indicates only three known events or situations: (1) Pentecost and its meaning for the churches; (2) affliction and tribulation—the situation of Christians in a world hostile to Christ and His gospel that desperately needs the remedy that flows from Christ and His gospel; and (3) messianic judgments just prior to Christ's second coming. In these judgments God will further unbalance nature to remind sinners that He is in full control of every aspect of nature and that these judgments come as a consequence of moral evil.

Key events at the Second Coming. Three events are listed. (1) Heaven is opened and stays open. The solid line separating the heavenly realm from the earthly realm is gone. What had appeared to be a two-realm universe becomes a one-realm universe. (2) Christ's coming will mean the defeat of Christ's enemies, those who are destroying the earth. (3) Christ's coming will mean the first resurrection for the saints. In this earthly realm the saints will stand up to celebrate their triumph over sin, death, and the gates of Hades (Matt. 16:18).

What is involved in the messianic reign. There are two periods in the messianic reign but only one messianic reign. Revelation teaches about God's rule, His kingdom, and the rule of His people. The one messianic reign is not only the reign of Jesus as the Messiah but also the reign of the Lord Jesus and His people. The Lord God will shine upon His people with a brilliance they have never known, and they will reign forever and ever (Rev. 22:5).

Immensity of the one-realm universe. The bottom of the chart indicates that the only way to know the immensity of this one-realm universe is by the experience that lies ahead for all who are Christ's people. In science today we can get a hint of the immensity of the physical creation of God. By revelation we can get a hint of the immensity of the eternal realm of God. In continued firsthand experience of both, we will be learning about God forever and ever.

Two-Realm Universe of the Heavenly and the Earthly

Heavenly, Eternal Realm			
	Logos John 1:1-18 1 John 1:1-4 Rev. 19:13		War In Heaven (Satan excluded) Rev. 12:7-12

Earthly Material Realm

Incarnation John 1:14

Ascension Rev. 12:5b

Pentecost 2:7, 11, 17, 29 3:6, 13, 22 5:6; 22:17

Affliction/Tribulation (*thlipsis*): whenever and wherever people suffer for Christ's sake (Rev. 1:9; 6:9-11; 7:9-14).
Antichrist: present in every age, the final one destroyed by Christ at His coming (1 John 2:18, 22; 4:3; 2 John 9; Rev. 19:19-20).

Birth
12:5a

[Events in Revelation]

Death
1:18; 5:9
Resurrection
2:8

Messianic Judgments Prior to Christ's Second Coming: Seven Seals-6:1-17; 8:1 Seven Trumpets-8:2-9, 21; 11:15-19 Seven Bowls of Wrath-15:1—16; 21

Expanding knowledge of the immensity of God's creation.

TO ETERNAL ILLUMINATION

One-Realm Universe of United Heaven and Earth

Messianic Reign

Heaven opened
and stays opened
(Rev. 19:11)

A thousand years (20:1-6, 11-15).
A transition period when moral
evil is banished by God and His
people; Final Judgment ends
this period.

Second
Coming
of
Christ

Eternal
Light
(Rev. 22:5)

Communication
and movement
between heaven
and earth

New Heavens and New Earth
(21:1—22:5)
An unending period of
unbreakable fellowship with
and constant learning about
God; the New Jerusalem, the
capital.

Defeat of destroyers
of the Earth
(11:18; 19:11-21)
Resurrection of the
Saints (20:5-6).

Separate realm for those banished
to the Lake of Fire (21:14-15).

First-hand knowledge of one-realm universe.

Appendix II

Some Apocalyptic Time Expressons Referring to Severe Crises and the Final Crisis in the Future

Daniel		Revelation	
2:28	what will be in the end of the days	1:1	soon, in a short time, without delay
7:12	until the appointed time and the epoch of time (duration)	1:3	because the time is near
		3:11	quickly, at once, soon
		6:11	rest still for a short time
7:25	until a time, and times, and half a time (time as duration)	11:2	for forty-two months
		11:3	for 1260 days
		12:6	for 1260 days
		12:14	time and times and half of a time
		13:5	allowed to exercise authority for forty-two months
8:14 26	two thousand, three hundred evenings and mornings		
8:17	the vision is for the time of the end	17:12	they will receive authority as kings for one hour
8:19	in the end or latter part of the indignation	18:8	in one day her plagues will come
8:23	in the afterpart or end of their kingdom	18:10	in one hour your judgment came
8:26	for many days (distant)	18:19	in one hour she is desolated
10:14	in the end, afterpart of the days, because the vision is for the days	20:2	and he bound him (Satan) for a thousand years
11:27	because the end is yet to be at the appointed time	20:3	until the thousand years were finished
11:29	at an (or the) appointed time	20:4	they came to life and reigned with

			Christ a thousand years
11:35	until the time of the end because it is for the appointed time	20:5	until the thousand years were finished
11:40	at the time of the end	20:6	and they shall reign with Him a thousand years
12:1	at that time		
12:4	until the time of the end	20:7	and when the thousand years are finished
12:6	how long until the end of these wonders?	22:6	soon, quickly, in a short time
12:7	(answer) for a time, two times, and half a time	22:7	quickly, at once, soon
12:8	what is the ultimate issue, end, of these things?	22:10	the time is near
12:9	shut up and keep close these words until the time of the end	22:12	soon, quickly, at once
12:11	there shall be 1290 days		
12:12	blessed is the one who waits and comes to 1335 days		

Bible Reference Index

Subject Index

Abednego; 75-76, 104, 161

Aegean sea; 163,164

Ahasuerus; 16

Alexander the Great: 14, 36, 83, 195, 207

Altar of Incense; 173

Alpha and Omega (see names of Christ)

Amen (see names of Christ)

Angels, seven; 61, 107, 143, 172, 187-190, 203-204, 221

Anthropomorphism; 41

Anthropopathism; 41

Anti-Christ
  climax of age, 61
  in Book of Daniel, 65, 209
  beast as anti-Christ, 118, 139, 143
  earlier versions, final version, 123-124, 132, 135-136, 148-149, 153, 195, 208, 234
  other terms for, 127
  supporters, 138
  army of, 155, 188,
  clash with saints, 178

rulers aligned with, 192
term only in John's epistle, 207
in Revelation, 209-212
victory over, 224

Antipas; 25, 60, 165, 177

Antiochus III; 13, 145

Antiochus Epiphanes IV
  description of, 3, 145-146
  abolished burnt offering, 10
  military exploits, 12-14
  Book of Daniel not composed
    in time of, 17, 18
  little horn of Daniel 8; 36, 195
  identified with fourth empire, 65
  information about, in Daniel
    and in I, II Maccabees, 83-84
  earlier version of final
    anti-Christ, 121-123, 127, 135, 207-209
  hatred of holy covenant, 169
  profaning of temple in Dan.
    9:27; 197, 202
  God's judgment upon, 212

Apocalyptic language and
    symbols
  use of similes and metaphors,
    24-25

257

makes God personal and
unique, 30-31
different from philosophical
language, 39-40
uses concrete terms, 71, 138-139
referring to physical changes,
86
not scientific statements, 112,
185-195
describes judgment and
conversion, 155, 156
describes purifying and
refining, 160
clouds, 219
harlot and beasts, 136
harvests, 220
horses, locusts, time periods,
places, 203-206
darkness, lake of fire, throne,
scrolls, 214-216
facts, not how or why, 189
heavenly city, 226
four metals, 132-133
heavenly and earthly armies,
138-140
describes moral evil, 232
new heaven and new earth, 225
temple and lamb, 40, 70

Apocalyptic numbers; 178, 226,
228

Apocalyptic time; 96, 190-196,
198-202, 228

Apocalypse; 22, 24-25, 27, 91

Apollo; 165

Apollyon; 203

Apostles, twelve; 5, 153, 226

Aramaic; 16, 121, 158

Armageddon; 139, 205, 213

Artaxerxes I; 199

Artemis; 164, 166

Asklepios; 165

Athene; 165

Attalia; 163

Augustus; 135

Ahaziah; 207

Babylon
capital city, 11, 79, 92, 104,
122, 142
province, 11, 75, 102
history of new Babylonia
(empire), 15
city where exiled Jews lived,
29, 141
empire, 76, 92, 121, 135, 144,
161, 195, 214
represented by gold, 133
refers to Rome, 190

Beast
wars upon saints, 23
government and ruler, 25, 110,
136, 210-212
two beasts, 61
use of militarism, 61, 118-119
other descriptive terms, 123-124
wrong use of power, 127
allies of, 139
final version of anti-Christ,
139, 146, 155
capital city, 143
mark of, 189
part of evil trinity, 218

Beasts, four; 36, 65, 83, 133-136,
209-210

Belshazzar; 12-15, 77, 93-94,
98-99, 106-107, 121, 131

Belteshazzar; 161

Boanthropy; 82

Bowls of wrath
as messianic judgments, 22,
61-62
as seven last plagues, 96
meaning of third bowl, 96, 112